The European Union and Border Conflicts

The Power of Integration and Association

Edited by

Thomas Diez,

Mathias Albert

and

Stephan Stetter

CAMBRIDGE
UNIVERSITY PRESS

CAMBRIDGE UNIVERSITY PRESS
Cambridge, New York, Melbourne, Madrid, Cape Town, Singapore, São Paulo,
Delhi

Cambridge University Press
The Edinburgh Building, Cambridge CB2 8RU, UK

Published in the United States of America by Cambridge University Press,
New York

www.cambridge.org
Information on this title: www.cambridge.org/9780521709491

First published 2008

Printed in the United Kingdom at the University Press, Cambridge

A catalogue record for this publication is available from the British Library

ISBN 978-0-521-88296-5 hardback
ISBN 978-0-521-70949-1 paperback

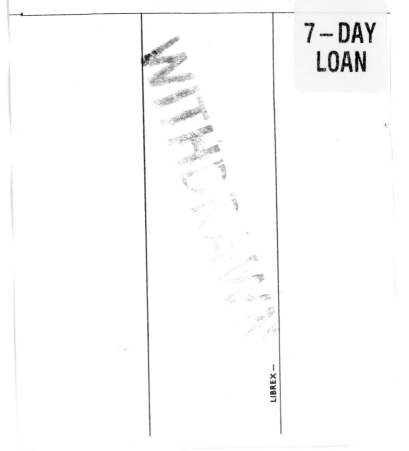
MATHIAS ALBERT is Professor of Political Science in the Faculty of
Sociology at Bielefeld University, Germany and a co-director of the
Institute for World Society Studies.

STEPHAN STETTER is Associate Professor in Political Science in the
Faculty of Sociology at Bielefeld University, Germany.

Contents

Tables

Notes on contributors

MATHIAS ALBERT is Professor of Political Science at the Faculty of Sociology of Bielefeld University. Current research interests focus on theories of international and world society, global law-formation, critical geopolitics, peace and conflict studies, and youth studies. His latest book publications include *Weltstaat und Weltstaatlichkeit. Beobachtungen globaler politischer Strukturbildung* (2007; ed. with Rudolf Stichweh) and *Jugend 2006. 15. Shell Jugendstudie* (2006; conceptualisation with K. Hurrelmann and TNS Infratest Sozialforschung).

OLGA DEMETRIOU is a researcher at PRIO Cyprus Centre. She has previously held fellowships at Cambridge and Oxford Universities and holds a Ph.D. in Social Anthropology from the London School of Economics. Her work focuses on issues of identity and nationalism, political subjectivity and the construction of borders. Her recent publications include articles in *Identities, Cultural Anthropology, New Perspectives on Turkey, Ethnic and Racial Studies* and *History and Anthropology.*

THOMAS DIEZ is Professor of International Relations at the University of Birmingham. He has previously held research positions at the Copenhagen Peace Research Institute and the Mannheim Centre for European Social Research. Among his publications are *Neues Europa, altes Modell* (1995) and *Die EU lesen* (1999). He is the editor of *The European Union and the Cyprus Conflict* (2002) and co-editor of *European Integration Theory* (2003).

KATY HAYWARD is Government of Ireland (IRCHSS) post-doctoral research fellow at the Institute for British–Irish Studies, University College Dublin. She has previously held a research fellowship at Queen's University Belfast and a visiting fellowship at the University of Wales, Aberystwyth. She has published in the fields of Irish politics, EU studies and nationalism and her current research is on the role of multilevel partnership in conflict transformation.

PERTTI JOENNIEMI is senior research fellow at the Danish Institute for International Studies (DIIS) and previously the Copenhagen Peace Research Institute (COPRI). His research covers themes such as the concept of the West, the changing understandings of war and the figure of Europe. He has recently edited a book on *The Changing Face of European Conscription* (2006) and edited *Wider Europe: Nordic and Baltic Lessons to Post-Enlargement Europe* (with Fabrizio Tassinari and Uffe Jakobsen, DIIS 2006). He is co-editor of *The NEBI Yearbook on North European and Baltic Sea Integration*.

DAVID NEWMAN is Professor of Political Geography in the Department of Politics and Government at Ben Gurion University in Israel. He was previously a faculty member in the Geography Department. Newman is editor of the journal *Geopolitics*. During 2006–7 he was the Leverhulme Visiting Professor of Geopolitics at Bristol University, UK. Newman also serves as the Chairperson of the Steering Committee of the Centre for the Study of European Politics and Society at Ben Gurion University. His BA is from the University of London and his Ph.D. from the University of Durham (UK). Newman specialises in the study of territorial conflict and the contemporary functions and roles of borders. He has published widely on the territorial dimensions of the Israel–Palestine conflict.

MICHELLE PACE is Research Councils UK fellow at the European Research Institute (ERI), University of Birmingham. She has previously taught at the School of Oriental and African Studies, University of London, European Business School, Regent's College London and the University of Malta. Among her publications are *The Politics of Regional Identity: Meddling with the Mediterranean* (2006) and 'The Construction of EU Normative Power', *Journal of Common Market Studies* (2007). She is convenor of the British International Studies Association (BISA) working group on International Mediterranean Studies and member of the editorial board of *Mediterranean Politics*.

BAHAR RUMELILI is Assistant Professor in the Department of International Relations, Koc University, Istanbul. She received her Ph.D. from the Political Science Department of the University of Minnesota (2002). Her research focuses on international relations theory, processes of European identity construction, EU impact on Turkish domestic reform and Greek–Turkish relations. Her articles have been published in the *European Journal of International Relations*, *Review of International Studies* and *Journal of Common Market Studies*.

STEPHAN STETTER is Associate Professor in Political Science at the University of Bielefeld. He holds a Ph.D. from the London School of Economics and Political Science. He is the author of *EU Foreign and Interior Policies: Cross-Pillar Politics and the Social Construction of Sovereignty* (2007) and the editor of *Territorial Conflicts in World Society* (2007). His articles have been published in *International Organization*, *Mediterranean Politics*, *Journal of European Public Policy* and the *Working Paper Series of the Robert Schuman Centre for Advanced Studies at the European University Institute*.

ANTJE WIENER is a Professor of Politics at the University of Bath. She holds a Ph.D. from Carleton University Canada and an MA from the Free University of Berlin, and has taught at FU Berlin, Stanford, Carleton, Sussex, Hanover and Queen's University Belfast. She is member of executive committees of various international associations including the ECPR and the ISA, and co-edits the new *European Political Science Review* (*EPSR*) as well as *ConWEB Papers on Constitutionalism and Governance Beyond the State*. Her research interests lie in international relations theory, democratic constitutionalism, international public law, comparative politics, citizenship and European integration theory.

HAIM YACOBI is lecturer at the Department of Politics and Government at Ben Gurion University. His academic work focuses on the geopolitics of cities, in particular the production of urban space, social justice, the politics of identity, migration, globalisation and urban planning. He is the editor of *Constructing a Sense of Place: Architecture and the Zionist Discourse* (2004), the co-editor of *The Israeli City or Cities in Israel?* (in Hebrew, Hakibutz Hameuchad and Van Leer Institute Jerusalem, 2006) and the co-editor of *Separation – the Politics of Israeli Space* (in Hebrew, 2007).

Acknowledgements

This book is the result of an international research project, which the project team has presented and discussed in many different locations. It is impossible to list all the many friends and colleagues here who have, at various stages, made important contributions to the development of this project. However, we do want to take the opportunity to thank the members of the international advisory board for their support and constructive comments: Tarja Cronberg, Yosef Lapid, Hugh Miall, Martin Pratt and William Wallace. The research presented here would have not been possible without the support of the European Union's Fifth Research Framework Programme and the additional funds provided by the British Academy. Our particular thanks go to Angela Liberatore, who as the responsible officer in the European Commission has provided crucial support throughout the various stages of this project.

Editors' note

No attempt has been made to standardise the transliteration in chapters 3 and 4 of this volume.

Abbreviations

AEGEE	Association des états généraux des étudiants de l'Europe
BIC	British–Irish Council
BIIC	British–Irish Intergovernmental Conference
ÇABP	Solution and EU Party [Cyprus]
CAIN	Conflict Archive on the Internet [Ireland]
CFSP	Common Foreign and Security Policy [EU]
DFM	Deputy First Minister [Northern Ireland]
DG	Directorate-General [European Commission]
DIKKI	Democratic and Social Movement [party, Greece]
DISY	Democratic Rally [party, Cyprus]
DUP	Democratic Unionist Party [Northern Ireland]
EC	European Community
ECJ	European Court of Justice
ECSC	European Coal and Steel Community
EEA	European Economic Area
EEC	European Economic Community
EFC	External Frontiers Convention [EU]
EMP	Euro-Mediterranean Partnership
EMU	Economic and Monetary Union [EU]
ENP	European Neighbourhood Policy [EU]
EOKA	Ethnikí Orgánosis Kypríon Agonistón [Cyprus]
EP	European Parliament
EU	European Union
EUSR	European Union Special Representative
FTD	Facilitated Transit Document [Kaliningrad]
FYROM	Former Yugoslav Republic of Macedonia
ICAHD	Israeli Committee Against House Demolitions
ICJ	International Court of Justice
Interreg	Interregional Cooperation Programme [EU]
IR	International Relations

IRA	Irish Republican Army
LVF	Loyal Volunteer Force
MEP	Member of European Parliament
MEPP	Middle East Peace Process
NATO	North Atlantic Treaty Organization
NGO	Non-Governmental Organisation
NSMC	North–South Ministerial Council [Ireland]
NWRCBG	North West Region Cross Border Group [Ireland]
OFM	Office of the First Minister [Northern Ireland]
PA	Palestinian Authority
PASOK	Pan-Hellenic Socialist Movement
PCA	Partnership and Cooperation Agreement [EU–Russia]
PEACE	Special Support Programme for Peace and Reconciliation [Ireland]
PHARE	Poland and Hungary: Assistance for Restructuring their Economies [EU]
PLC	Palestinian Legislative Council
PLO	Palestine Liberation Organisation
QC	Queen's Counsel [UK]
REDWG	Regional Economic Development Working Group [Israel/Palestine]
RoC	Republic of Cyprus
SDLP	Social Democratic and Labour Party
SEUPB	Special EU Programmes Body [Ireland]
TACIS	Technical Aid to the Commonwealth of Independent States [EU]
TD	Teachta Dála: member of Dáil Éireann, the lower chamber of the Irish Parliament
TGNA	Turkish Grand National Assembly
TMT	Türk Mukavemet Teşkilat [Cyprus]
TRNC	Turkish Republic of Northern Cyprus
UDA	Ulster Defence Association
UFF	Ulster Freedom Fighters
UK	United Kingdom
UN	United Nations
UNCLOS	United Nations Convention on the Law of the Sea
UNDP	United Nations Development Programme
UNFICYP	United Nations Peacekeeping Force in Cyprus
UNOPS	United Nations Office for Project Services
UNSCOP	United Nations Special Committee on Palestine

US(A)	United States
USAID	United States Agency for International Development
USSR	Union of Soviet Socialist Republics
UUP	Ulster Unionist Party
UVF	Ulster Volunteer Force

Introduction

Thomas Diez, Stephan Stetter and Mathias Albert

Integration and peace

At the start of the twenty-first century, European integration is generally seen as not being in the best of shapes.[1] Budgetary quarrels and the persistence of national differences in various policy domains, including foreign policy, dominate the headlines; the majority of voters reject the proposed European Constitution in referenda in two founding member states; the Euro is derided as having made life more expensive after its introduction as a common currency in many member states. Perhaps most importantly, many European Union (EU) citizens (but also academics) believe that this organisation is by its very nature characterised by a democratic deficit (for a discussion of whether there is a democratic deficit or not see Decker 2002; Moravcsik 2002; Schmidt 2004). Put bluntly, against the background of its widespread negative image, why should we bother about this seemingly undemocratic, expensive, wasteful and illegitimate organisation?

Leaving aside the problematic assumptions on which the populist calls for a downscaling of or even withdrawal from the European integration process are based, even those critical of the EU in its current shape usually find at least one core argument that speaks in favour of integration: its contribution to peace. Indeed, all the grand speeches on European integration, past and present, tend to stress that a return to a Europe of nation states without an integration framework would mean a return to the seemingly eternally violent and war-torn centuries before 1945, culminating in the horrors of the Second World War and the Holocaust (see Welch 1999). Thus, when EU political leaders justified the 2004 enlargement, they, too, invoked the horrors of nationalism and the benefits of integration for peace to make their case for taking up the new member states in central and eastern Europe (Higashino 2004).

---

[1] The authors gratefully acknowledge research assistance from Lea Moubayed.

But what is the underlying logic of this often-assumed link between integration and peace? Most of the political arguments and academic discussions resort to high-level, abstract reasoning when addressing this question. They tend to follow the classical approach of liberalism in international politics in their focus on the dependencies generated by integrated economies that make war too costly (see Doyle 1997), and the long-term reorientation of identities and interests towards a common whole (Ernst Haas's 'shift of allegiances'; Haas 1968: 5) that makes war increasingly unthinkable.

When on 9 May 1950 French Foreign Minister Robert Schuman proposed the pooling of European coal and steel production in what then became the European Coal and Steel Community (ECSC), the first supranational institution from which today's EU has developed, he started from the assumption that '[w]orld peace cannot be safeguarded without the making of creative efforts proportionate to the dangers which threaten it'; and that '[t]he coming together of the nations of Europe requires the elimination of the age-old opposition of France and Germany'. He continued to make his case through the arguments of the changing material structure and the change of minds triggered by supranational integration: 'The pooling of coal and steel production should immediately provide for the setting up of common foundations for economic development as a first step in the federation of Europe ... The solidarity in production thus established will make it plain that any war between France and Germany becomes not merely unthinkable, but materially impossible ... that fusion of interest ... may be the leaven from which may grow a wider and deeper community between countries long opposed to one another by sanguinary divisions.'[2]

Schuman and one of his civil servants (and later High Commissioner of the ECSC), Jean Monnet, who was largely responsible for the so-called 'Schuman Plan', picked up the functionalist arguments of David Mitrany and others (cf. Mitrany 1965) and transferred them to the regional level. They enriched Mitrany's functionalism by emphasising the central role of a supranational body (today's European Commission) to guard and promote the integration process. Schuman's and Monnet's 'method' thus became known as neofunctionalism. Yet their basic ideas were widespread among liberal thinking in the interwar years (see de Wilde 1991), and variations can be found in many writings of the 1950s and 1960s, from John Burton's cobweb model (Burton 1972) to Deutsch's transactionalism and security community concept (Deutsch *et al.* 1957).

---

[2] Robert Schuman, Declaration of 9 May 1950, text version on http://europa.eu.int/abc/symbols/9-may/decl_en.htm.

In each, placing nation states in an international network curbs their power, and people are brought together in various forms of cooperation and societal exchange. As a consequence, states can no longer easily resort to violent unilateralism, and their citizens see the value of cooperation and develop or 'discover' common interests and identities.

While these arguments are also at the heart of our analyses, taking them on their own throws up at least two problems that we will address in both our theorisation of the relationship between integration and the transformation of border conflicts and our empirical studies. Firstly, since Deutsch's work, analysts have lost interest in the link between integration and peace, with the idea of security communities only finding its way back into the mainstream International Relations literature in the late 1990s (Adler and Barnett 1998), and so its empirical validity remains largely unexplored. Secondly, this link cannot be studied properly on the level of nation states and the reorientation of national identities alone, as it involves the changing social practices of border communities and the transformations of entire regions *across* national borders. Thus, our analyses need to focus on the transformation of border conflicts in their concrete social and political settings across several layers. Have they changed to become less conflictive on the regional and national levels? Has the meaning and significance of borders changed for those who live in the border region or for the political elites in these countries at large? If so, what has been the contribution of the integration process to such developments? Does association as a weaker form of 'membership', when compared to integration, also make a difference? What role do specific actors – local, regional, national, European – play in this process? Or is the context of integration alone sufficient to do the trick? In this volume, we address these questions on the basis of a comparative study of five cases of border conflicts within the EU, at its borders and between associated members. Our comparison will show that integration does have a positive effect on border conflict transformation, but that this effect is far from automatic. As our cases will demonstrate, there are circumstances in which the impact of integration is to hinder cross-border cooperation and to introduce new conflicts to a border region. Even if integration has helped to transform a border conflict towards a more peaceful situation, its success is often dependent on events outside the EU's control and on local actors making use of the integration process in ways that are conflict-diminishing (what we will call 'desecuritising') and not conflict-enhancing (or 'securitising') (see Buzan *et al.* 1998).

It is this emphasis on both the positive and the negative effects of integration (and association) which distinguishes our study from those approaches in the field of 'regional studies' that assume a more direct and automatic linkage between integration and peace (see Tavares 2004). We share the assumption of these studies that higher levels of 'regionness' (Tavares 2004: 29), such as the European integration project, are characterised by a mushrooming of different peace agents and peace instruments as well as a fundamental transformation of the very concept of peace in line with Galtung's (1969) notion of a positive peace. Thus, 'regional communities', such as the EU, are indeed often characterised by an 'empirical association between regionalism and the *possibility* to achieve peace' (Tavares 2004: 43; our emphasis). However, we maintain that the impact of integration and association also always leaves open another possibility, namely to nurture or breed conflict. As Noutcheva *et al.* (2004: 25) have argued in their study on the role of the EU in the resolution of secessionist conflicts at the EU's periphery, the EU's attempts in conflict resolution can have both intended and unintended consequences, not all of them beneficial. The subsequent chapters of this book will accordingly specify these conditions of positive *and* negative EU impact on border conflict transformation from an empirical and theoretical perspective.

The Franco-German example

The one example of border conflict transformation that dominates the historical literature in particular, but is also a common reference point in political speeches, is the Franco-German border, and in particular the border region of Alsace. Alsace changed hands four times in the nineteenth and twentieth centuries, during or as a consequence of the Franco-German war of 1870/1 and the First and Second World Wars. From a French perspective, the Rhine constituted a 'natural' border in the East, while Germans made reference to the local culture and language (van Dijk 1999: 27–32 cited in Walters 2002: 566). Until the Second World War, France and Germany were often constructed as 'hereditary enemies' who would never escape the security dilemma of two competing, neighbouring great powers. The Rhine border was a core prize to be won in that struggle for power in the centre of the Western half of the continent (cf. Schulze 1991).

Yet today's situation could hardly be more different. While the border still exists, it mainly serves administrative purposes. People are free to travel across (and many do so on a near-daily basis living on one side and working on the other side of the border); the EuroAirport in Mulhouse serves three countries with a common French/German exit (the third country is Switzerland, a non-EU member who at the time of writing had signed but not yet implemented the Schengen Treaty); and in

October 2003, French President Jacques Chirac famously represented Germany in the European Council. This is not to say that the border has disappeared, and the different administrative systems on both sides still make cooperation difficult at times (Pletsch 2003). Yet observed from a longer-term historical perspective, the changes that have taken place are astonishing. Who, just about a hundred years ago, would have thought that people would easily cross the Rhine for lunch?

Explanations for these changes vary, although their emphasis until the 1990s was on political rather than on the social and economic factors. Some authors have focused on the impact of particular personalities after the war who pushed both the integration process and Franco-German reconciliation (e.g. Simonian 1985: 378; Treacher 2002). But even though, as the findings in this book will also show, concrete actors driving the peace process are crucial in border conflict transformation, these actors are themselves to a considerable extent a product of their environment and engage in broader societal discourses to which they contribute but which also shape them – the example of the Rhinelander Adenauer is an illustration (Schwarz 1986). They also need a context that is favourable to their policies, and the European integration process, once set up, proved to be such a setting (Simonian 1985: 377). One of the aspects often commented upon in this respect, especially since the 1990s, is the social interaction across the border, following Karl Deutsch's notion of transactionalism (Deutsch *et al.* 1957). The interaction of 'ordinary' people in exchange programmes, twinning of cities and towns, common cultural projects or simply economic transactions, according to this view, is at least as important in reconciliation processes, transformations of identities and redefinition of borders as the high politics of individual states(wo)men (see e.g. Moreau 1993; Bock 1998; Defrance 2001; Krotz 2004). In all of this, one has to keep in mind that the former enmity has not been replaced by a single identity, and misunderstandings persist (Noll 2004). Yet the point of border conflict transformation is not that a single new identity is forged; it is rather that identities and borders are reconstructed in such a way that the border at a minimum is no longer the site of violence, and beyond that the identities constructed around it are no longer conceptualised in antagonistic terms.

The Franco-German history provides us with some initial clues about the relevance of European integration in the process of border conflict transformation (Miard-Delacroix and Hudemann 2005). Yet its discussion remains marooned in a single case. To proceed further, we need to first step back and define in general terms the core concepts at the heart of this volume, laying the groundwork for our theoretical approach and the case studies explored in the following chapters.

Border conflicts and European integration

Political discourse often tends to refer to a conflict in international politics as a relationship dominated by physical violence – and so does academic discourse on this subject matter. Consequently, common conceptualisations of conflict resolution are focused on the removal of such violence (see Elwert 2001). Yet the disputes about the meaning of peace alert us to the problems of such a narrow definition (Richmond 2005). Peace may be defined as the absence of war, but if this is the only criterion, systematic social and economic exclusion, political division and a war of words if not arms may still affect people within such a peace. It is like a volcano after an eruption: it may lie dormant now, but underneath the magma is still boiling, and is likely to erupt one day. Real peace therefore is not simply achieved by a signature underneath a treaty; it requires long-term political, social and economic transformation of conflict societies.

Similarly, violence is merely one way of dealing with conflict; it marks the eruption of long-standing disputes that define the conflict. Conflict is therefore a much more fundamental category of social and political life, as social sciences other than International Relations are much more ready to acknowledge (see contributions from Sociology or Social Psychology as well as Peace and Conflict Studies, e.g. Coser 1964; Azar 1990; Deutsch 1991). As chapter 2 will elaborate, we therefore take conflict to be the incompatibility of subject positions (Efinger *et al.* 1988). Subject positions are characterised by identities and interests that define a particular subject. If those identities are mutually exclusive, or if the interests contradict each other and cannot be reconciled without a transformation of the subject position itself, there is an incompatibility of subject positions and therefore a conflict.

Some have used this conflict definition to infer the existence of a conflict from material structures underlying a society (see Efinger *et al.* 1988). A conflict is therefore taken to exist if, for instance, the distribution of water or oil benefits one country over a neighbouring one, thus following classical balance of power assumptions. As neither water nor oil are easily substituted, and as there are natural limits to their exploitation while both are vital to the national economy in both countries, a situation of high vulnerability in a zero-sum game ensues, which makes the positions of the two sides incompatible with each other. Yet such a focus on material structures makes the rather heroic assumption that such structures lead automatically to particular claims and actions that follow from these claims. This, we argue, cannot be sustained, as any such material structure – often referred to as the 'root causes' of conflict – will first have to be translated into claims of one subject over another in order to become an incompatibility. The distributional problem is therefore insufficient to cause conflict in itself; it requires an act of communication to do so.

We thus follow a discursive understanding of conflict in this book. A conflict exists if actors articulate mutual incompatibilities. Whether these have their base in material structures does not interest us in our conflict diagnosis; indeed, insofar as material structures are themselves discursively constructed, the differentiation between such structures and discourse makes little sense. As we will spell out in more detail in chapter 1, securitisation – the representation of an Other as an existential threat against which the Self has to be defended (Buzan *et al.* 1998: 23–4) – is the main practice through which subject positions and their incompatibilities are constructed. We also argue that conflicts are characterised by different levels of intensity, and violence only comes into the picture in conflicts at their most intense degree of securitisation (see also Messmer 2003).

If integration or association are to have any effect on conflicts, they have to make a contribution to the transformation of the very communication that constructs a conflict in the first place. Such a contribution either will move the conflict towards a less intense stage; or it will change the self-definitions in such a way that the subject positions are no longer seen as incompatible. In the latter case, the conflict is truly resolved in the sense that it ceases to exist; in the former case, the conflict is merely transformed towards a less tense situation but remains, at best, what is often referred to as a 'fragile peace'. It would be wrong however to assume that integration always has a conflict-diminishing effect. Instead, our study has to be open to the possibility of integration leading to intensified securitisation, or bringing about new subject positions that are constructed as incompatible.

What then makes a conflict a border conflict? Our definition of 'border' initially links up with a traditional understanding of borders as the geographical lines that divide states or entities aspiring to statehood. Thus, the subject positions involved in such conflicts are likely to be those of 'nations', following the definition of a nation as a self-defined modern political community seeking its own political organisation as a state within its own territory (Gellner 1983; Weber 1988; Anderson 1991; Breuilly 1993). Because of such nations' search for a match between the nation and a clearly defined, contiguous territory on which to build their states, incompatibilities tend to be articulated in relation to the borders of this territory. A core characteristic of the modern state system therefore is the construction of a distinction between the peaceful and domesticated sphere 'inside' and the dangerous and anarchic sphere 'outside' these borders (Ashley 1988; Walker 1993). In this construction, the 'outside' is dangerous because it is populated by equals that accept no higher authority. As long as no incompatibilities are articulated, this is of no great bother to the nation state, but once they are, incompatibilities crystallise around the border that 'shields' the inside from the outside.

As the Schuman Plan made clear, European integration is a political project that seeks to overcome the inside/outside divisions. Whether or not it would replace these divisions with a new federal polity, as Schuman and others envisaged, and what exactly such a federation would look like need not interest us at the moment (see Padgen 2002 for a history of European federal ideas). Suffice it to say that integration was supposed to bring the incompatibilities between the European nations to an end, and transform their borders so that they were no longer markers of a division between a peaceful and secure inside and a dangerous and anarchic outside. It therefore makes sense to start from a traditional concept of borders. Yet we do not stop here. Instead, we follow developments in the study of borders, among others by critical geographers since the 1990s, in which the border is no longer merely a line on a map or indeed in the proverbial sand (e.g. Paasi 1999; Albert *et al.* 2001; Newman 2003). There is a shift in this work from the border as a geographical feature towards a focus on the political and cultural practices that construct, sustain, transform or multiply the border; the bordering, debordering and rebordering practices that define social and cultural identities, delineate economic spaces and sustain political orders. This move is consistent with our discursive definition of conflict: the articulation of an incompatibility always implies the inscription of a border between two subjects. While this applies in principle to all sorts of social groups and how they set themselves apart from each other, our cases of border conflicts have a 'traditional anchor' in that they are related to, but not necessarily confined to, disputes about a border between states or state aspirants.

The case studies in this book therefore start from the aim of Adenauer, De Gasperi, Monnet, Schuman and their contemporaries to make Europe a peaceful place by transforming the borders between and identities and interests of its nation states through a process of political integration. We argue that if this project is successful, it indeed transforms the border practices in such a way that they no longer articulate incompatibilities. This can take different forms: the border might disappear as a marker of any social significance; debordering practices might establish societal links across the border without the latter vanishing; the border might become a focal point for common identification; or rebordering practice might shift the border to a new place or move it from the realm of territorial nation states to social interest groups, in which case old incompatibilities might simply be replaced with new ones.

In order to trace this change of practices and the impact of integration or association upon them, chapter 1 offers not only an elaboration of the different conflict stages and how to assess them, but also develops four 'pathways' of the impact of the EU and of the European integration process itself on border conflict discourses. The two dimensions along which we develop these pathways are firstly, whether EU actors are directly involved, or whether the integration process as such interferes with an existing conflict; and secondly, whether the impact is targeted at specific policies or the population at large. We call the resulting pathways *compulsory* (involvement of EU actors and aimed at concrete policies); *enabling* (on the basis of the integration process but also aimed at changing specific policies); *connective* (focused on EU actors, but aimed at society at large); and *constructive* (a change of subject positions induced, or aided, by the integration process). Each pathway is one avenue for the EU or for the integration process to contribute to a change in the way conflicts are being articulated and managed, or to change the way in which the border at the heart of the conflict is represented and how identities and interests are constructed.

Our focus on these four pathways bears some similarities with the study by Noutcheva *et al.* (2004), who analyse the impact of Europeanisation on the resolution of secessionist conflicts at the EU's external borders. They argue that the EU can have a positive impact on such conflicts 'by linking the final outcome of the conflict to a certain degree of integration of the parties involved in it into European structures' (*ibid.*: 7). Noutcheva *et al.* argue in particular that it is the impact of conditionality and socialisation that might have a positive effect on conflict transformation, thus emphasising both the direct and the indirect forms of EU impact. However, their study is limited to conflicts external to the EU, since they maintain that the 'dynamics of the Europeanization process are different' at the EU's periphery in comparison to the EU core (*ibid.*: 7). While we do not dispute that this is the case, we insist that in principle, as we have argued above, association should at least have the potential to bring about some of the effects that integration does. We therefore need empirical studies that compare the impact of association to that of integration, and analyse the conditions of positive and negative effects of EU involvement.

Our five case studies

In order to assess the impact of European integration and association on border conflicts, we apply our framework in chapters 2–6 to five cases: Northern Ireland, Cyprus, Greece/Turkey, Russia/Europe's North and

Israel/Palestine. Each of these cases stands in a different relationship to the present EU and the integration process: Northern Ireland is a conflict that has been fully within the integration framework for more than three decades at the time of writing. Cyprus is a case where an internationally not recognised border runs through a new member state that joined the EU on 1 May 2004. Besides the particular challenge of a conflict about a non-recognised border, this case allows us to trace the impact of accession negotiations, as does, at least in part, the case of Russia and Europe's North. The latter case consists of three sub-cases: the long-standing border disputes of Karelia (between Finland, an EU member since 1995, and Russia); Pskov (at the Estonian–Russian border – Estonia joined the EU with Cyprus in 2004); and Kaliningrad (a Russian enclave surrounded by EU territory since the 2004 enlargement with Poland and Lithuania). The Greek–Turkish conflict involves a member state since 1981 (Greece) and a country that was made an EU membership candidate at the Helsinki European Council in 1999. Finally, the Israeli–Palestinian conflict involves two actors associated with the EU without being full member states or indeed seeking, or planning to seek, full membership at the time of writing.

Given the diversity of the cases, the point of comparison is not to identify the variables that determine the impact of integration or association across similar cases of EU involvement. There is not a sufficient number of cases to do this, and if we want to say something useful for future EU involvements in border conflicts, we need to address the variety of engagements in an integration context that we are confronted with. The purpose of our comparison is therefore to look for commonalities across our cases with different degrees of EU involvement, but all affected by integration or association in one way or another, and to trace the impact of the different ways in which the EU is involved on these border conflicts.

It is also important to note that we are not investigating the impact of the EU on border conflicts outside the framework of integration and association. Our focus is not on the EU as a third party in border conflicts, but rather on the impact of the integration process as such. EU-level actors such as the Commission, Council or Parliament come into the picture in this context only as part of the integration process. The closest we come to the EU as a third party is in the case of Israel/Palestine. We have included this case because association, while falling short of full integration, does have integration elements and obliges the associate members to implement parts of the *acquis communautaire*, the established set of EU rules and norms. The concrete specification of the rules applicable differs from association agreement to association agreement. In the case of Israel/Palestine, they include for instance the integration of Israel into European frameworks for research and development and public procurement, while Palestine has since the mid-1990s become closely linked to the EU through massive financial assistance for the Palestinian Authority. Moreover, the new generation of European Neighbourhood Agreements, in particular the Action Plans, explicitly refers to the extension of the internal market *acquis* to associated states and territories. The impact of association is also of particular interest insofar as association has become a popular tool for the EU to pursue as a stabilisation instrument in cases where membership is not (yet) on the cards, assuming that at least some of the principal benefits of integration will also result from a lower form of integration (Stetter 2005).

Each of our case study chapters starts with an overview of the border conflict it analyses, its development and EU involvement, before assessing the relevance and effectiveness of each of the four pathways, including a specification of the facilitating conditions that allowed EU action or integration to have an impact. On this basis, the concluding chapter of this book draws out in a systematic and comparative manner the commonalities of our cases in terms of the impact of European integration on border conflict transformation, both in terms of the effectiveness of the different paths; whether they have a positive or a negative impact on border conflicts; and the conditions under which they are more likely to have one or the other. One of our main arguments throughout this book will be that the impact of integration and the EU is neither guaranteed nor automatic but depends on a mix of different conditions, which are to a large extent outside the EU's direct control. Thus, the subsequent chapters of this book provide comparative empirical evidence that EU impact depends on a complex interplay between domestic and EU-level conditions. While the EU has some leverage on determining the structural conditions for border conflict transformation (e.g. by linking a credible membership offer with desecuritisation policies by those conflict parties which want to join the EU), the actual use made of integration and association ultimately depends on how these (dis-)incentives by the EU play out in the domestic context, which is beyond the direct reach of the EU.

As our case studies indicate, in most cases, the key contribution of the EU therefore is to provide a reference point that can be used by local actors to make a change and also to sustain continuous border conflict transformation. This is by no means a negligible role; indeed, our case studies show that integration or association has played a major role in each of them. They also however demonstrate that this role is not positive throughout. In each case, there are some aspects where EU impact has led to a reproduction of existing conflict communication, and in some cases, notably in Russia/Europe's North and to some extent in Cyprus, existing securitisations were given new force, and new securitisations emerged as a consequence of EU involvement.

Before we proceed to our conclusion, chapter 7 takes a look at how EU actors themselves conceptualise their role in border conflict transformation. This allows us to come to a more reflective assessment of the impetus and formation of EU policy. Following recent work about the EU as a 'normative power' (Manners 2002; Diez 2005; Bicchi 2006; Scheipers and Sicurelli 2007), our main argument in this chapter is that EU actors often see themselves, and are seen by conflict parties, as a 'force for good'. This reinforces the power of integration to some extent, and it does give individual actors more clout at times, but it also allows some conflict parties to use the EU's self-construction as a normative power to push the EU towards policies that privilege one party over another and therefore limit the possibilities of positive EU impact.

As our case studies demonstrate, integration and association provide the EU with potentially powerful means to influence border conflicts. However, these means can neither be applied irrespective of the specific circumstances of the border conflict in question, nor do they present themselves as a ready-made 'toolbox' which would relieve the European Union of the necessity to constantly readjust its policies in relation to the conflict dynamics in each particular case. Needless to say that the same holds true for the *analysis* of the influence which the EU can wield on border conflicts through integration and association. And it is in this sense that the present volume not only addresses a substantial issue. It also demonstrates the need for devising and adjusting research tools which not only lie at the interstices of conflict and integration studies, but also require to draw on and combine approaches from various disciplinary backgrounds. Thus, although the present volume and most of its authors are firmly grounded in the fields of political science and international relations, the theoretical framework required to draw on sociological approaches to conflict as much as the empirical analysis of changing identity scripts led to an in-depth analysis of conflict settings normally encountered more in ethnographic studies than in political science writings. Although this book is primarily about the possible EU impact on border conflicts through integration and association we thus also hope that it will stimulate methodological and cross-disciplinary debate on how to conduct further such comparative studies in the future.

1 The transformative power of integration: conceptualising border conflicts

Mathias Albert, Thomas Diez and Stephan Stetter

The puzzle of integration and peace

As we discussed in the Introduction, there has always been a close link between European integration and peace.[1] Reference to the war-torn Europe of the past has become the most consistent, most frequently cited legitimisation of integration. It has provided the EU and its predecessors with a form of identity (Wæver 1998b: 90; see also Wallace 1999 and Diez 2004). It is against this background that the European Union is, therefore, often regarded as a successful example of (border) conflict transformation.[2] The very process of integration is seen as having led to the evolution of a 'security community' among former long-time foes. Cross-border cooperation has flourished not only between nation states, but also between local and regional bodies in the context of the Interreg programme, and not only across internal EU boundaries, but also across its external borders.[3]

This largely uncontested success story notwithstanding, the theoretical account of the link between integration and peace marks, at best, a dormant issue within the academic fields of European studies and International Relations, with only a very limited number of exceptions (Noutcheva *et al.* 2004; Tavares 2004; Tocci 2005a; 2005b). However,

---

[1] Previous and different versions of this chapter have been presented on many occasions within and outside of the EUBorderConf project, making it impossible to individually thank all those who provided valuable comments in the course of its evolution. In its current form it strongly builds on Diez *et al.* (2006); however, it substantially expands this article's theoretical agenda while leaving out empirical references, left here to the more in-depth case studies of the following chapters.

[2] Wallensteen thus argues that integration studies are (or have been) conflict analyses. They are triggered by an interest in 'the simultaneous and surprising experience of the integration of two former enemies, Germany and France, [which] illustrated the potential of reversing dynamics' (2002: 33).

[3] See for a discussion on the construction of such regions and identity Pace (2006). See also the discussion in Albert and Brock (1996); Diez (1997); Ribhegge (1996). The transformation of border identities is the subject of another EU-funded research project, see Armbruster *et al.* (2003).

13

such a theoretical account is not only of academic, but also of a highly practical, interest in that it enables the systematic comparison of empirical cases, and allows drawing conclusions for EU policy towards border conflicts within the scope of integration and association, as is the purpose of this volume.

This chapter develops a theoretical model involving four pathways through which the EU can have an impact on border conflicts, not only through integration within its territory, but also through association agreements beyond its borders. In contrast to overly optimistic approaches, the model presented here is open to the possibility that the EU's impact can, and sometimes does, also lead to the intensification of existing conflicts, or to the creation of new ones, especially at the EU's own external borders. In what follows, we deduce a set of general hypotheses about how the *successful* link between integration (and association) and peace might work in concrete cases, which are then subjected to empirical investigation in the case studies of this volume. In the next section, we develop a discursive understanding of border conflicts, as well as the idea of the EU as a 'perturbator' to such conflicts. At the heart of our model we then suggest four pathways through which the EU can contribute to the desecuritisation, and eventually the successful transformation of a border conflict.

To avoid misunderstandings, it is necessary to reiterate that the main concern of the present undertaking is with the impact of integration and association, not with the EU as a more traditional third party intervening in conflict resolution.[4] The question of the EU as a foreign policy actor in conflict resolution is different from the question of the impact of integration and association, and requires further reflections on the literature on Common Foreign and Security Policy (CFSP) as well as on third party intervention. This does however not mean that the conceptual framework cannot be applied to conflicts with EU involvement beyond integration and association (see Loisel 2004), but it would almost certainly have to be adapted for this purpose.

The discursive nature of border conflicts

Conflicts as the articulation of incompatibilities

As we argued in the Introduction, conflict is often associated with violence. The European Union would, therefore, be seen as having

---

[4] Although chapter 5 necessarily forms somewhat of an exception to this rule.

influenced a conflict successfully if it helped to stem the violence. Not all conflicts, however, involve physical violence. Most international regimes, for instance, are set up in order to deal with conflicts in a peaceful way without actually resolving them. Consequently, conflict resolution very often does not lead to the disappearance of a conflict, but, at least as a first step, to its regulation through non-violent means. A comprehensive understanding of conflict, therefore, emphasises the incompatibility of subject positions (see Efinger *et al.* 1988; cf. Galtung 1975: 78). These 'subject positions' include the specific interests and identity of a subject (possibly, but not necessarily a state). According to this definition, a conflict only disappears if the subject positions involved are altered to such an extent that they are no longer incompatible. The European Union would therefore be seen as having successfully influenced the conflict only if it helped to fundamentally change these subject positions, as is generally claimed for the impact of European integration on the transformation of the previously antagonistic interests and identities of Germany and France.

One possible way to understand the notion of an incompatibility of subject positions is as a material underpinning of conflicts. In this view, conflicts can be manifest as well as latent (Dahrendorf 1957 and 1961; Galtung 1975; see Efinger *et al.* 1988: 46–7). In latent conflicts, actors show no conflictual behaviour although their 'objective' situation (e.g. ethnicity, geography) should lead them to do so. Often conflicts are kept in a latent state in situations of conflict overlay, for instance during the Cold War (see Buzan and Wæver 2003). With the end of the overlaying conflict, the incompatibility of subject positions is expected to come to the fore again, and the latent conflict turns into a manifest one. The unravelling of former Yugoslavia is conventionally told within such a framework, where ethnic conflicts were 'kept under the lid' during the Communist era.

Yet the example of ex-Yugoslavia also exposes the limits of such a narrative. It relies on an 'ontopological' Balkanisation of the break-up of the republic: it assumes the primordial existence of ethnic groups, and that the peaceful coexistence of these groups within the same territorial space is impossible (see Campbell 1998a). Similar narratives can be found in relation to many other so-called ethnic conflicts, including some of those the EU is now confronted with, such as Cyprus (see Polat 2002). However, these assumptions are largely untenable from a constructivist point of view, and are indeed highly contested in the literature on nationalism. Instead of being given, group identities – ethnic, national or otherwise – rely on their continuous discursive reproduction and are set in historically contingent contexts (see Anderson

1991; Hobsbawm 1991). Furthermore, a standard practice of their reproduction is the representation of an Other as a threat to an in-group, whose
existence is assumed but really only asserted through such a rhetorical
move (Ashley 1988; Campbell 1998b; Connolly 1991; Walker 1993;
Wilmer 2002). Conflicts are therefore not the natural outcome of incompatible subject positions; they are part of the *(re-)production* of subject
positions, the articulation of which in turn reproduces the conflict.

Conflicts are, therefore, brought into being through discourse. The
distinction between objectively latent and manifest conflicts recognises
that communicative interaction is required in order to turn a latent into a
manifest conflict. The problem with the very notion of a latent conflict,
however, is that we cannot know about the existence of the conflict unless
an incompatibility is uttered. Whatever its ontological status, for our
purposes it is therefore not useful as an analytical concept.[5]

Stages of conflict

This discursive definition of conflict as the articulation of an incompatibility of subject positions bears striking similarity to the one provided by
Niklas Luhmann in his conceptualisation of society as a communicative
system. According to Luhmann (1984: 530), a conflict comes into being
in 'all those cases in which there is a disaccord to a communication. One
could also say: if a disaccord is communicated.'[6] Social processes are
usually based on the expectation that the continuation of communication
is ensured by the acceptance of prior communication (accord). This is not
the case with conflicts. Being based on the communication of disaccord,
conflicts not only point to the constant possibility of a 'no' inherent in all
communication, but through their specific discursive framework they
facilitate the actual, repeated communication of the 'no'. Hence, the
stabilisation of conflict dynamics and the repeated non-acceptance of

---

[5] A weaker, more subjective notion of latent conflicts does not refer to objective characteristics but to subjective preferences the incompatibility of which is not apparent to the
actors involved (Efinger *et al.* 1988: 52). Such a concept of latency offers a more fruitful
conceptualisation and characterises a state that we will later call 'conflict episode', where
incompatibilities surface only as isolated incidences.

It should be emphasised that our understanding of 'discourse' here is a broad one (see also
the next section in the main text) in which 'discourse' is used to describe the many facets of a
social world constituted communicatively. This broad understanding of discourse does not
position discourse in opposition to, for example, institutional or material, 'non-discursive'
'facts' conditioning social life, but we see those in discursive terms as well insofar as they
need to become discursive in order to become meaningful for the social world.

[6] Our translation.

communication become expected, much more than the termination of the conflict.

Moreover, conflicts have a tendency to escalate. The more a conflict develops, the more all communication between conflicting parties tends to relate all action to the incompatibility. Hence, conflicts not only exist in parallel to other societal communication but also have the tendency to dominate and overarch previously unrelated communication in society. In this context, Heinz Messmer (2003) has suggested a process model of social conflicts, in which he proposes four different stages of a conflict.[7] Drawing on Messmer's work, we distinguish between conflict episodes, issue conflicts, identity conflicts and subordination conflicts. These different stages are characterised by different kinds of subject incompatibilities, and by different ways in which these incompatibilities are articulated. As we move from conflict episodes to subordination conflicts, conflicts become both more securitised and wider in their societal reach: the Other of the conflict is increasingly constructed as an existential threat against which measures outside normal, regulated political interaction, and ultimately physical violence, become legitimate (i.e. in relation to which practices of 'securitisation' occur; see Wæver 1995; Buzan et al. 1998). In addition to this, particular incompatibilities increasingly tend to be linked to all forms of societal interaction so that seemingly innocent daily practices cannot be performed outside the discursive framework of the conflict.

Conflict episodes are isolated instances of the articulation of the incompatibility related to a particular issue. They do not necessarily result in stable conflicts. Often, conflict parties regard the mere voicing of mutual disaccord as sufficient, and there is no follow-up. In the European context, such (border) conflict episodes occurred during the early 1990s when, for example, the government of Hungary repeatedly claimed that the treatment of Hungarian minorities in neighbouring states such as Slovakia or Romania was discriminatory. However, unlike in former Yugoslavia, these conflicts remained rather isolated events, and were quickly settled by the conclusion of Basic Treaties between Hungary, on the one hand, and Slovakia and Romania, on the other. It can be argued that the perspective of integration and association in the framework of the enlargement process contained these conflicts at an early stage and thus prevented them from further intensification, not least

---

[7] Messmer is not alone in suggesting such a process model, although he does so from a constructivist position, which provides sufficient connection points to our theoretical framework. Other process models of conflict can be found in Dahrendorf (1957), Azar (1990), Giegel (1998) and Thiel (2003).

because the EU required all applicant countries to sign and live up to international conventions on the protection of national minorities (European Commission 2003a).

This contained status of conflicts, however, changes at the stage of *issue conflicts*, when both parties attempt to convince the other of the truth of their respective position. Issue conflicts are limited to argumentation about the issue as such. Identities themselves are not yet thematised, although they are reinscribed into discourse by the very opposition between self and other articulated in relation to the issue incompatibility. In issue conflicts, the conflict starts to develop structurally more stable notions of 'opposition', which facilitates collective groups to relate communications to the other party. A prominent example of a border conflict that got 'stuck' at the stage of an issue conflict is the struggle between the governments of Spain and the United Kingdom on the territorial status of Gibraltar in the context of the negotiations on the External Frontiers Convention (EFC) of the EU. Both parties base their contradictory claims on legal arguments and – rather unsuccessfully – attempt to convince the other side of the validity of their respective claims. In spite of continuous disagreement – the conflict dates back to the Treaty of Utrecht of 1713 – current conflict communication between the two governments reveals no signs of change to more intense forms of conflict, for example a spill-over to other issues or a move towards accusation or threat. Although the conflict has not yet been resolved, and the adoption at the EU level of the EFC is blocked until today, it can nevertheless be argued that the context of integration within the EU framework has at least provided a framework for the stabilisation of the Gibraltar-struggle on the level of an issue conflict, at least as far as the governments of both countries are concerned (cf. Müller 2004).

In *identity conflicts*, disaccord becomes explicitly personalised and moves of the other side are increasingly interpreted on the basis of hostile motives. One party now rejects an utterance by the Other merely because it comes from the Other. Such conflicts are characterised by diametrically opposed ways in which both sides experience the conflict in the context of an increasingly self-referential perception of it. Responsibility for the conflict is seen to rest with the other side, and both Alter and Ego become 'blind' to the perceptions and motives of the other side. The border conflict between Greece and Macedonia is a telling example of such an identity conflict. Both sides observe each other with great suspicion and attribute inimical motives to the claims of the other side. In this example, Greece even objected to the name of its new neighbour, insisting that 'Macedonia' implied a Macedonian territorial claim on the Greek province of Macedonia. Of course, it can only be speculated as to what extent the integration of Greece into the EU framework prevented this identity conflict from further intensification, but there is some indication that the EU framework allowed Greece to channel its opposition into Europeanised fora. Notwithstanding this stabilisation of the conflict, the ongoing suspicion and attribution of hostile motives by Greece is exemplified by its successful attempt to convince other EU countries to formally refer to Macedonia as FYROM (Former Yugoslav Republic of Macedonia; Ioakimidis 2000). The aforementioned Gibraltar conflict, too, appears in a different light when we move from an issue conflict between the two national governments, to the conflict communication predominant in British and Spanish mass media, and among the population of Gibraltar. In this context, the conflict reveals characteristic features of an identity conflict. This example points to the need in empirical research to carefully specify the interrelationship between different conflict stages in order to identify, at specific historical moments and on different levels of the conflict, the dominant forms of conflict communication.

In a final stage, conflicts can turn into *subordination conflicts*. The primary function of the communication of disaccord now is no longer the demarcation from the Other, but the subordination, and possibly the extinction of the Other. Systematic physical force becomes an acceptable means of dealing with and 'convincing' the other side. This projection of 'superiority', enforced through the use of physical means, radically interferes into a previously accepted autonomy of identities and *inter alia* legitimises the systematic use of violence. In the European context, the Yugoslav Wars serve as the prime recent example of border conflicts that took the form of subordination conflicts.[8] The impact of the EU on these conflicts remained small, and integration and association were not an option until the conflicts ceased to be (violent) subordination conflicts. It was only after this change that the Stability Pact put integration on the (long-term) horizon of relations between the EU and the states of the former Yugoslavia, thereby providing a framework for durable conflict transformation (see Bendiek 2004).

The distinction of these four stages of conflict identifies an increase in the frequency, intensity and acceptance of both securitisation practices and the overall reach of such securitised discourses in society as the prime early warning signal for the occurrence of violence. It is only when conflicts turn into subordination conflicts, and the securitisation of the Other pervades most spheres of societal discourse, that physical violence against

---

[8] The only exception was Slovenia which managed already in the early 1990s to 'escape' from the dynamics of a subordination conflict.

the Other is seen as legitimate. Cases of physical violence can occur during the stage of identity conflicts, but the lack of general legitimacy will ensure that these cases remain isolated. In any case, the distinctions between the different stages should be seen as fluid and highly dynamic. While they do serve as useful analytical devices, it will be difficult to identify a given conflict to clearly exhibit the features of only one stage at any given time.[9] However, the purpose of the model of stages of conflict is not to be able to unambiguously classify a conflict as being at one or the other stage, but rather to identify the mix of securitisations at a specific moment in history and to observe movements along this continuum over time. Integration or association are seen to have had a positive impact if we can observe that they have contributed to the movement of a conflict from stages of higher conflict intensity to stages of lower conflict intensity. Conversely, integration and association are seen to have had a negative impact if a conflict intensifies and moves, for instance, from an issue conflict to an identity conflict.

It follows from this logic that any attempt to *resolve* a conflict is an attempt to transform discursive behaviour into less securitised stages within fewer social domains. Conflict resolution as a step towards the regulation of conflict through peaceful means will have to move a conflict from being about subordination at least to being about identity, and ideally then about issues (see also Pearson 2001). As long as identity conflicts prevail, the danger of sliding back into subordination is too big to guarantee permanency, as Northern Ireland, but in particular the Israel/Palestine conflict, has demonstrated repeatedly. In contrast to conflict devolution according to this model, *conflict resolution* as a step towards the disappearance of the conflict has a much grander agenda: it is about the rearticulation of subject positions so that they are no longer seen as incompatible in most respects, and conflict does not move beyond conflict episodes. Indeed, the former foes might no longer be recognisable as completely distinct subjects. This is, ultimately, what visions of European integration as a motor for peace have been and are about.

Conflicts, borders and identities

Since conflicts are about subject positions, and in their last two stages explicitly about identities, they involve the (re-)drawing of borders.

---

[9] The general model of social conflicts presented here thus does of course not include an empirical claim that conflicts would necessarily proceed through these steps slowly; conflicts can escalate in the sense of moving through the stages of conflict very quickly, possibly generating the impression of 'starting' with a subordination conflict right away.

Traditionally, borders have been seen as physical lines, and border conflicts were, therefore, conflicts of subordination where rules were to be
extended beyond the existing geographical borderline. This characterises
a good deal of border conflicts, but it is nonetheless an impoverished
understanding. It focuses on states as actors in international politics, and
neglects both the impact of borders on the daily life of those living in
border regions and beyond, and the very construction of borders through
day-to-day social practices. It does not pay sufficient attention to the
border as a symbol of and means towards demarcation, and to the multi-
plication of borders in towns and cities beyond the contested border, such
as in the Northern Ireland case. Moreover, such a perspective neglects the
poly-contextual nature of different kinds of social borders, such as religious, economic, ethnic or legal borders, which do not necessarily corre-
late with geographically represented ethnic or national borderlines.
Borders provide specific mechanisms for inclusion and exclusion into
different social realms, with citizenship as 'membership' in the political
community of a nation state being the most visible one (Nassehi 2003).

Borders are hence more than just physical lines. New approaches in
Political Geography and International Relations have instead proposed to
study borders as socially constructed institutions (see Newman 2003;
also Kolossov 2005). A significant body of literature has since the early
1990s emphasised that borders need to be seen as social structures that
are constantly communicatively reproduced.[10] Yet geographically represented border conflicts are a particularly stable form of conflict because
they provide a clear-cut physical distinction between two easily identifi-
able sides (Forsberg 1996; Houtum and Naerssen 2002). In such conflicts, borders have a 'double function' in that they provide a means of
both territorial inclusion and exclusion, but in parallel also for 'functional' inclusion or exclusion. There are reinforcing tendencies between
borders, identities and particular social orders (Albert *et al.* 2001). They
are hence a means of both territorial *and* functional inclusion and exclusion (Flint 2003). Being 'excluded' by a border frequently implies not
only being locked out in a physical–geographical sense, but also in an
economic or legal sense. The exclusion of ethnic minorities from participation in certain national organisations is an interesting example in that
respect. For example, for security reasons, Israeli citizens with Palestinian
ethnicity are not allowed to serve in the Israeli army. While probably
many Israeli Palestinians would themselves oppose being conscripted to

---

[10] Anderson (1996: 4) has eloquently termed borders and the construction of border
   identities as the prime 'mythomoteur of a whole society'. See also Wilson and Donnan
   (1998).

serve in the Israeli army, the problem with this form of exclusion is that it stretches beyond the question of who participates in a military organisation. As empirical studies have shown, not only does military exclusion 'reproduce' the very identity-assumptions which originally constituted this specific form of exclusion, but also fosters exclusion within other social domains, such as spatial exclusion, exclusion from equal access to the labour market and, ultimately, the emergence of 'qualified rights to citizenship' (Smooha and Hanf 1992). Identity and subordination conflicts are, therefore, never about identity alone, but also about access to social goods and in that sense incorporate issue conflicts, and they constitute vested interests in their prolongation.

At the same time, however, the discursive nature of borders as well as conflicts makes change an always existing possibility. Albert and Brock (2000; 2001), for instance, observe processes of 'de-bordering' pointing to possible changes not only in relation to the location of specific borders, but also regarding the very function(s) borders serve, most radically from lines of conflict to lines of identification at which the utterance of non-conflictual discourses replaces the prior utterance of disaccords. Conflict resolution in the sense of peaceful regulation will often leave the physical borders intact, but change their discursive construction and their symbolic place in the public debate, as well as the very appearance and symbolism of the border itself. Conflict resolution as the transformation of subject positions however will have to change the very nature of the border.[11] If the subjects are no longer who they used to be, the borders between them will no longer be the same either. Again, this is the promise that European integration as a motor for peace holds out: to do away with the former physical borders separating the member states, as happening in the context of the abolishment of internal border controls in the Schengen framework, or at least to radically transform their nature and function.

The EU as a perturbator of conflicts

Despite their tendency to become locked-in, conflicts are not structurally given, and there is no historical determinacy. Conflicts are reliant on the continuous communication of incompatibilities, which are themselves no ontological givens but dependent on discursive 'processes of constructing a shared understanding of what is to be considered and collectively responded to' as a social phenomenon (Wæver 2003: 10). Hence,

---

[11] See also the discussion on generic conflict transformation in Miall *et al.* (1999).

conflicts remain highly contingent, and there is always the potential of conflict transformation, through moving into a less belligerent mode of communicating the incompatibility (and therefore regulating conflict management), or through a transformation of the construction of subject positions.

We have already referred to both of these options in the context of European integration at the end of each of the two preceding subsections. Establishing organisations dealing with specific functional tasks such as the internal market does not make conflict among EU member states disappear, but it civilises the way in which comparative advantages are pursued by putting in place a new institutional and discursive framework, and thereby ensuring a predisposition towards accepting communication. Over time, this may also lead to a change of national identities through socialisation, or even to a convergence of national identities with an emerging European identity, in which the very subject positions are redefined.[12]

The central function performed by the EU in these cases is that it unsettles conflicts by confronting the reiterated communication of disaccord. Although for member states, the EU is not really a 'third party', the very discourse of integration is external to previously existing discourses of conflict. This should not lead to the conclusion that the new frameworks offered by the EU are immune against conflict. Indeed, they very often introduce new conflicts, which sometimes even take the form of an identity conflict, as in the reconstruction of national identities versus 'Europe' for instance during the Danish referendum on the Euro or, less so, the French referendum on the Constitution. Integration, therefore, has the capacity to unsettle conflicts as a 'perturbator', a worrying disturbance for the conflict. The crucial task, therefore, becomes to identify the mechanisms through which the EU has acted and can act as a perturbator of conflicts. Three things are important to note in this respect.

Firstly, the EU is in itself no single, unified actor. It is at the same time a set of actors who may or may not agree, and an institutional and discursive frame, although even here the plural would be more appropriate as there are many constructions of this frame. The impact of integration and association can, therefore, be seen as the effect of a perturbance of a

---

[12] The empirical evidence regarding such a change of national identities is mixed. On the one hand, national identities seem to be particularly sticky, and are reflected in particular constructions of European governance (Jachtenfuchs *et al.* 1998; Wæver 1998a; Marcussen *et al.* 1999). On the other hand, Europe has now become an integral part of the construction of national identity in its member states (Wæver 1996).

conflict either by EU actors individually or collectively, or by the provision of a particular institutional and discursive frame.

Secondly, the EU's capacity as a perturbator of conflict extends beyond the limits of integration (see also Diez and Whitman 2002). Most obviously, it affects membership candidates, although these can be conceptualised as being part of integration. Beyond that, it may affect conflicts at the external borders of the EU itself (or of any future members). Furthermore, the EU has a number of association agreements, and not only is there a theoretical possibility that these will strengthen the perturbation, but this has been underlying concrete policy-making, as the example of the Stability Pact for the Balkans illustrates.

Thirdly, the degree of perturbation and its success in bringing about conflict transformation in the sense of the desecuritisation of conflicts outlined above will differ from case to case. Some of this variation will depend on the concrete form the perturbation takes, and the next section will outline both the main pathways and the main contextual factors through which the EU can act as a pertubator. But the effectiveness of any sort of influence on the conflict will also depend on the way in which the perturbation is reacted to. Communication can never be fully controlled, because it is always interpreted, used and therefore transformed in other discursive contexts, which are powerful in their own right (Ferguson 1990: 19–20; Foucault 1990: 95). We will return to these questions on the conditions under which conflict perturbation by the EU can be successful in the following section.

The impact of integration and association: forms of perturbation by the EU

Four paths of EU perturbation

Following the argument developed above, perturbation means that the EU destabilises the conflict by provoking a 'conflict with the conflict', i.e. the utterance of communications that are either challenging existing conflict discourses or opening windows for non-conflict related discourses. The actual forms of perturbation, however, vary. We suggest that there are four paths through which the EU, in the context of integration and association, can perturbate a conflict. These paths can be categorised alongside two dimensions.

Firstly, the perturbation can be driven by concrete interventions of EU actors, such as in membership negotiations, Commission reports or Council Presidency conclusions; or it takes place through the discursive, legal and institutional framework offered by the integration or association process. The latter impact is usually less powerful in cases of association (such as Israel/Palestine) than in cases where both conflict parties are EU members, and are therefore directly subject to the *acquis communautaire*. The more structural impact of the integration or association process and the agency of specific EU actors are not independent from each other, and actor-driven approaches reproduce or reconstruct the EU framework, in which they are situated. Indeed, some EU activities, such as the Euro-Mediterranean Partnership, which is linked to association, can be seen as attempts to facilitate the perturbation through the EU framework. Furthermore, the structure of this framework is by no means fixed. It is internally contested, and it relies on the reproduction of EU actors. Yet, actor-driven and structural influences nonetheless follow two different logics. Actor-driven approaches are direct, and often interpersonal and short-term. The impact of integration or association may or may not be intended, is indirect in that it relies on being taken up by actors from within the conflict, and is often long-term. They should therefore be kept analytically separate, although at the same time it is the interplay between these two approaches that is of particular importance.

Secondly, the perturbation can be directed at a particular policy or address the broader societal change. Association or membership, for instance, demands the implementation of the concrete policies in line with the *acquis*, and the latter can also be used by political actors to legitimise specific policies (see below). Yet the neofunctionalist logic of a reorientation of daily practices towards a new centre through the integration process affects not a specific policy, but societal actors as such. Likewise, the support for bicommunal activities in Cyprus or through the PEACE programme in Northern Ireland is not so much about changing policies but about bringing people together and therefore transforming their daily lives and worldviews.

Of course, integration or association is always only one among several factors that influence the development of a border conflict, and it is difficult to empirically clearly distinguish between these various factors. Thus, the transformation of border conflicts might also be related to the role of other actors (e.g. the USA or the UN; see Tocci 2005c). Moreover, European integration typically goes along with other forms of international cooperation (e.g. in NATO). Finally, democratisation processes (e.g. in Greece or Turkey) stand in an often mutually reinforcing relationship with integration, and both democracy as well as integration can be the cause of border conflict transformation. The demonstration of the impact of integration and association therefore has to rest on a number of indicators that amount to a plausible story across cases. In this respect, the impact of integration is similar to the

Table 1.1: *Paths of EU impact (Diez et al. 2006: 572)*

		Approach by EU	
Target of impact		**Actor-driven**	**Integration process**
	Policy	(1) *compulsory impact*	(2) *enabling impact*
	Society	(3) *connective impact*	(4) *constructive impact*

impact of ideas (Yee 1996). In order to tell such a story, we rely on a variety of social science approaches, which, rather than being incompatible, alert us to the different dimensions of EU impact on border conflicts.

We propose to distinguish four different possible pathways of EU impact in the transformation of border conflicts. These four pathways relate to the two dimensions outlined. In conceptualising these pathways, we also used the work of Michael Barnett and Raymond Duvall (2003; 2005) on different categories of power in international politics. Barnett and Duvall distinguish between direct and diffuse power, on the one hand (close to our second dimension), and power through the actions of specific actors or through social relations, on the other hand (close to our first dimension). It makes sense to use Barnett and Duvall as a starting point, since 'impact' signifies an effect of power, and since we agree that rather than setting different forms of power against each other, we need to think of them in a complementary way, and observe their interplay. We have also borrowed from Barnett and Duvall one of their categories of power ('compulsory power'), but have otherwise varied the labels for our different forms of impact to provide a better fit with the specific question that we are addressing (Table 1.1).

Path 1 (compulsory impact) works through carrots and sticks, compelling actors through the mechanisms of integration and association to change their policies vis-à-vis the other party towards conciliatory moves, rather than deepening securitisation (Dorussen 2001). The main carrot that the EU has at its disposal is membership (Wallace 2003). In membership negotiations, as well as by setting conditions for the opening of membership negotiations, the EU insists on the implementation of its legal and normative framework, the *acquis communautaire*, including the resolution of border disputes (Schimmelfennig and Sedelmeier 2004). This path is obviously dependent on the conflict party wishing to become an EU member: if it does not, it will not regard membership as an incentive to change its policies. If it does follow the EU carrot, this does not mean that it has altered its views of the other party, or its beliefs about the conflict – the change might simply reflect strategic behaviour. In that sense, the compulsory impact is short-term and very effective in membership negotiations, but it may also be superficial. Yet, as Thomas Risse *et al.* (1999) have shown in their analysis of human rights and domestic reform, such strategic moves can, in the long run, and provided the right context, lead to deeper reforms through continued pressure and socialisation. In our case, EU membership can be considered a framework in which both pressure and socialisation are likely, thus linking compulsory impact with what we will below call constructive impact.

In comparison with membership, other EU incentives can be regarded as relatively minor in weight and importance. Association agreements do not entail all the benefits of full membership, in particular not the symbolic importance of being an EU member. Financial or other forms of aid or free trade agreements, part of the traditional set of diplomatic instruments to influence third parties, can be important carrots especially outside the geographical neighbourhood of the EU, but they are unlikely to be as sweet a carrot as membership. Likewise, the EU is short on sticks (Smith 1998; Hill 2001). While it can impose sanctions, its most important stick is in the withholding of carrots, in particular the threat of declining membership.

Path 2 (enabling impact) relies on specific actors within conflict parties to link their political agendas with the EU and, through reference to integration, justify desecuritising moves that may otherwise have not been considered legitimate (Buzan *et al.* 1998: 41–2). In conflict situations, civil society actors in favour of a peaceful resolution are often marginalised and ridiculed, or accused as traitors. Alternatively, governmental and other political leaders may be pushed towards further securitising moves by the public in the heated atmosphere that characterises identity and particularly subordination conflicts, in which rally-around-the-flag effects drive policies.[13] In both cases, if EU membership or association is widely seen as an overarching goal, actors can use the legal and normative framework of the EU to substantiate their claims and delegitimise previously dominant positions. Perhaps ironically, if utilised by governments, this path relies on what is otherwise seen as a problematic feature of EU governance, its democratic deficit, in that political leaders use the EU framework to push through policies against the preferences of their electorate.[14]

---

[13] Adamson (2002) for the case of Cyprus in 1974.
[14] Newman (1996: 189); but see Moravcsik (2002: 612), for the view that decision-making at EU level is much more tightly scrutinised.

Path 3 (connective impact) supports contact between conflict parties, mainly through direct financial support of common activities. Such contact is in itself of course not a step towards desecuritisation. Sustained contact within the context of common projects may however lead to a broader societal effect in the form of social networks across conflict parties, which in turn should facilitate identity change as foreseen within the constructive impact below. Outside the EU, support for such activities largely takes the form of traditional grants. At the EU's borders, as well as at member states borders, the Interreg programme provides funding for such cross-border cooperation. Within the EU, the PEACE programme in Northern Ireland is also an example of how structural funds, which are not part of the Interreg programme, can be used to support specifically cross-border and cross-communal projects (see Anderson and O'Dowd 1999).

Path 4 (constructive impact) is the most indirect but – if successful – also most persuasive mode of transformation, since it 'aims' at changing the underlying identity-scripts of conflicts, thus supporting a (re-)construction of identities that permanently sustains peaceful relations between conflict parties. This pathway is based on the assumption that EU impact can put in place completely new discursive frameworks, in which novel ways of constructing and expressing identities are created within conflict regions, as the peaceful transformation of Western Europe since the end of the Second World War illustrates. These new identity-scripts will foster desecuritisation in a virtuous circle. Ultimately, this may lead to the eventual resolution of the conflict, i.e. the disappearance of articulations of the incompatibility of subject positions. This is clearly a long-term process, but its applicability is corroborated by the claim that while there may not (yet) be a single European identity, 'Europe' has become an integral part of the identity/-ies in each of the EU's member states (Wæver 1996).

There are two often-discussed influences of integration on conflicts that do not seem to fit easily into the four paths as outlined above. The first of these is the essentially neofunctionalist logic that conflicts can be overcome by bringing actors to cooperate on functional matters, this process leading to a change in preferences and ultimately in individual 'allegiances' (Haas 1968; 2001). Yet, there are in fact two mechanisms that this logic rests upon: the facilitation of cooperation by focusing on seemingly technical matters, and the long-term shift of subject positions that this might bring with it. Both mechanisms are contained in the connective and the constructive impact, respectively.

The second possible gap in our scheme is the argument that integration leads to increased wealth and employment, and that this will take people off the streets and alter their preference structures so that violent conflict is no longer a desirable option – an argument often found in the early discussions on Northern Ireland in the European Parliament (Pace 2005). This possible influence can however be seen as an economic version of the constructive impact because it ultimately leads to a change of subject positions that is caused by the incentive structures within a European framework, the effect of which cannot be controlled through direct EU policies.

While we have presented all paths as possibly leading to a reduction of securitisation, and therefore to a successful impact of integration on border conflict transformation, their influence can also be negative. Regarding the compulsory impact, this is for instance the case if new member states are required to implement policies to satisfy the *acquis*, which are seen as securitising moves by the neighbouring states: the implementation of visa regimes on the border of Russia and the EU is an example. Likewise, integration can enable actors to pursue policies that have the effect of intensifying conflict discourse, such as in the case of Cyprus, where Greek-Cypriots after membership have adopted the discourse of a 'European solution' to insist on the four freedoms, which would have been compromised under the UN-sponsored Annan Plan for a solution in Cyprus, which had the backing of most other EU actors. EU policies can have a disconnective rather than a connective impact if new visa regimes make contact across the border more difficult, as is the case not only in Russia and Europe's North, but also between Greece and Turkey. In particular in cases of conflicts between EU member and non-member states, integration can foster a European identity that is constructed against the neighbouring conflict party outside the EU. Whether or not integration does have an impact on border conflicts, and whether or not such an impact is positive or negative, can therefore not be determined in the abstract, but is a matter of empirical investigation. Finally, we argue that the different paths do not occur in isolation from each other. Instead, we need to observe their interplay, including reinforcing effects between them.

Contexts of perturbation

The perturbation of border conflicts does not happen in a vacuum. A number of factors need to be considered that influence both the form and the success of the perturbation. Two bundles of factors are of particular importance: the relationship between the EU and other perturbators, as well as structural changes in the environment of the conflict; and the relationship between the EU and actors within the conflict setting.

Firstly, the EU is not the only perturbator to border conflicts. Other international actors, such as states, international organisations, NGOs or international networks, might attempt to impact conflicts in parallel to the EU.[15] Furthermore, there may be changes within the discourse of the conflict parties independent of international involvement, and such 'internal' perturbation will change the way integration and association are perceived, and which access points for change there are. Finally, long-term structural developments in world society, and in particular the political, economic and cultural effects of globalisation, as well as specific events, must be accounted for in how they relate to the impact of the EU in conflict transformation (see also Richmond 2001b: 337–8).

While every conflict is thus embedded in a wider international setting, the specification of EU impact also requires a focus on *constellations of perturbation* between the EU, on the one hand, and the conflict parties, on the other. As has been mentioned above, the EU is not a homogeneous actor but rather a complex political organisation that includes a diverse set of collective actors, which in turn often have diverse perceptions both on specific border conflicts and on the conflict parties. These actors are, just to mention a few, the Council and individual member states, the Commission, the European Parliament or the High Representative (Gehring 2002; Stetter 2007; see also Pace in this volume, chapter 7). Against this background of intra-organisational fragmentation, perturbation by the EU must, therefore, be put in relation to how key institutional mechanisms and perceptions shape both the EU's relation with the conflict parties and its policies vis-à-vis the conflict. Having emphasised the relevance of EU internal characteristics, the significance of institutional and perceptional characteristics of the conflict parties in their relations with the EU should also not be underestimated, as the following chapters will illustrate. Institutional fragmentation and perceptional diversity are not unique to the EU but shape the relations of the conflict parties with the EU as well. Therefore, the focus on the constellations of perturbation requires the assessment of how these mutual constellations relate to each other and, thereby, shape the way in which the EU can impact a conflict.

Conclusion

European integration was designed to bring peace to a continent of war. It has been more successful in this project than the initiators of integration could have wished for. Today, whatever the problems of European

---

[15] The case studies in the next chapters occasionally consider other actors in addition to the EU in their analyses of the specific conflict settings. However, a systematic comparison between the EU's and other actors' influence would have been far beyond the scope of the present book.

governance, the European Union has become a model for regional integration in other areas of conflict, and since 1973, the Union has itself continuously attracted new members by the prosperity and peace that it promises. In popular parlance, the EU might not have a lot of military power, but in relative terms at least, it looks like paradise (Kagan 2003).

While there is considerable evidence that the European Union can make use of its institutional and discursive structures in order to project notions of peaceful coexistence into previously conflict-ridden territories within and beyond its borders, traditional accounts of the link between integration and peace are restricted in their conceptualisation of the changes they predict, and in their application to new conflicts within, at the borders and in the near abroad of the EU. In this chapter, we have developed a model of how the EU, through integration and association, can make a difference to border conflicts. We have understood such conflicts discursively, and the EU's role as a perturbator to the prevailing conflict communication. If successful, this perturbation leads to a desecuritisation of conflict communication, and a transformation of identity and subordination conflicts into issue conflicts, and ultimately to a change in the way identities are constructed vis-à-vis each other, removing the discursively constructed incompatibilities of subject positions, and changing the way in which borders are constructed, and their function for the constitution of identities. Eventually, the story of integration is a story about the partial domestication of politics, and the question at hand is how such a partial domestication is brought about in a variety of contexts.

We have suggested that there are four paths that may contribute to such a transformation, and have identified contexts that have an impact on how, and how successfully, these paths operate. These arguments can be summarised as follows:

- Perturbation is an effect both of communications by EU actors and of structural qualities of the integration or association framework.
- Perturbation can follow a bottom-up or top-down logic.
- Perturbation can relate to actors within the conflict setting both affirmatively and negatively.
- Perturbation sometimes addresses the incompatibility directly, sometimes only indirectly.
- The impact of perturbation is dependent on the existing relationships between various EU actors internally and relations with the conflict parties, which are themselves no homogeneous actors. Moreover, the impact of perturbation also depends on the constructions of the conflict by the EU and the conflict parties as well as the constructions by the conflict parties of the EU.

- The EU's impact must be located within a broader framework, involving other state and non-state actors, as well as the general constellation of international society, all of which may also act as perturbators, and may enhance or constrain the EU's impact.

Each of these arguments presents factors that influence the way in which perturbation takes place, and whether it is successful or not. Consequently, the success of integration after the Second World War was not only an effect of the neofunctionalist logic, but also of the perspectives on integration in the aftermath of the war and the international context of the Cold War. A different context as well as the realisation of different paths of perturbation has different effects, and sometimes they may well take the opposite effect to what we have described here as successful conflict transformation. We cannot, in the abstract, generalise about the impact of each of the factors identified. Instead, we have provided plenty of examples for the different forms of perturbation throughout this chapter, and it is now the task of the following chapters' empirical research on individual conflicts to see how our model plays out in detail.

2 The influence of the EU towards conflict transformation on the island of Ireland

Katy Hayward and Antje Wiener

Overview of the conflict

Although relatively recently drawn (1920) in comparison to other European state borders, the Irish border has been the focus of the most enduring and explicitly violent conflict situation within the European Union. The Good Friday (Belfast) Agreement of 1998 brought together the two governments and the main parties in Northern Ireland to construct an agreement for peace built on new institutional and constitutional dynamics within Northern Ireland, within the island of Ireland, and between Britain and Ireland. The Irish case study is unique in that the EU membership of both states concerned has enabled the EU to both directly intervene in the peace process (such as in the provision of funds for cross-community and cross-border projects) and indirectly affect the context for peace-building. This chapter charts the multifarious nature of the EU's influence in transforming the Irish border from a line of conflict to a line of cooperation.

The Irish border and the conflict

This research is based on the fundamental premise that the conflict in Ireland is a border conflict. This is not to disregard the significance of religious,[1] cultural,[2] socio-economic[3] or any other interpretation of the cause of the conflict. Neither are these explanations simply subjugated within an analysis of the conflict as a disagreement over the partition of the island. Nonetheless, it is notable that the 1998 Agreement itself is founded on a definition of the conflict in terms of a binary opposition

---

[1] Analyses of the conflict in Northern Ireland in terms of a religious or theological divide include Fulton (2002) and Mitchell (2005).

[2] Nic Craith's (2003) work emphasises the importance of linguistic and cultural signifiers in Northern Ireland politics and society.

[3] For examples of literature which emphasises the centrality of socio-economic disparity to the Northern Ireland conflict, see Probert (1978) and Smith and Chambers (1991).

between British/unionist and Irish/nationalist, with their contrasting interpretations of the legitimacy of the border. As will be elaborated, the notion of the conflict as one between British and Irish identities has also informed the EU's approach to the situation in Northern Ireland since the early 1980s. This chapter begins, therefore, with an examination of the development of the Irish border as the embodiment of historical difference between British and Irish nationalisms, i.e. more than a dividing line between the jurisdictions of the Republic of Ireland and the United Kingdom.

The first fifty years of partition Partition of the island of Ireland was, in effect, a product of the politicisation of differences between north and south in the late nineteenth century.[4] The drawing of the border was considered by the British government as a temporary solution to the problem of stark unionist and nationalist opposition regarding British sovereignty in Ireland. For this reason, the Government of Ireland Act 1920 (which established Northern Ireland in the six north-east counties of the island) had allowed for the formation of a Council of Ireland to link the parliaments in Dublin and Belfast and facilitate the negotiation of an all-Ireland settlement. However, by the time the Free State was consti-tuted in the twenty-six southern counties in 1922, the all-island Council was suspended and with it went formal and official means of contact between the two administrations. Outside the surreptitious cooperation between governmental officials on specific matters of mutual benefit (see Kennedy 2000), the border was left as it was, to steadily take a more concrete form as a customs barrier,[5] political separation,[6] cultural divi-sion[7] and security frontier.[8] The general pattern of relations at all levels

---

[4] For more information on developments at this period relating to north–south difference, see Bardon (1995) and Coakley (1999).

[5] The customs land boundary was drawn in April 1923.

[6] There were no meetings between the two Prime Ministers of Northern Ireland and the Free State respectively after December 1925. The concern of both governments to consolidate their internal position and independence meant that political difference between north and south became increasingly entrenched. This was solidified with the declaration of the Republic of Ireland in the twenty-six counties in 1948.

[7] In a study of a border region in the 1950s, Harris (1986: 19–20) identifies the border as a 'definite influence on the pattern of social relationships in the area' since partition. This she attributes to the different view that Catholics and Protestants hold of the border, the former viewing it as 'invalid', the latter as 'vital to freedom' (Harris 1986: 20). Heslinga (1971) goes so far as to view these different visions of the border as relating to contrasting identities that predate the border.

[8] The securitisation of the border increased in response to the activity of the IRA, for example during its border campaign of December 1956–February 1962, when security forces of north and south cooperated to combat the threat posed by the paramilitary force.

between north and south, unionist and nationalist after partition, therefore, was one of growing polarisation (Kennedy 1988).

For the first fifty years of its existence, then, the border was essentially the subject of an *issue conflict* between the British and Irish
governments. Attempts at engagement between political leaders in
Northern Ireland, Britain and the Republic of Ireland in the 1960s
consequently sought to overcome the detrimental effects of this divide
without tackling the ideological gulf. In 1965, the Anglo-Irish Free
Trade Agreement was signed between the two close and yet uncom-
municative trading partners and saw the removal of some north–south
tariff barriers within the island. During the same year, the Irish
Taoiseach (Prime Minister) Seán Lemass met his counterpart of the
devolved Stormont Assembly in Northern Ireland, Terence O'Neill,
twice, first in Belfast and then in Dublin. Negotiations proceeded with
caution, as each government was conscious of the highly sensitive
nature of any cross-border relationship. O'Neill, as leader of the largest
unionist party, was in a particularly vulnerable position and events
within Northern Ireland were soon to force him out of office and the
province into civil chaos.

As communal dissent took to the streets of Northern Ireland (originally in the form of civil rights marches for Catholics), distrust of the
government spread throughout the province, galvanising support for
more hardline nationalism/republicanism and unionism/loyalism. As
levels of violence increased, so the subject of the border was projected
into the centre of north–south and British–Irish antagonism. This was
epitomised in the explosive effects of the Irish government's decision to
deploy the Irish army to the southern side of the border in August
1969.[9] Within a week, British troops were sent to Northern Ireland to
help the security forces cope with the mounting violence in the province. The presence of the army and the effects of this on daily life
signalled that the situation had rapidly reached the stage of a *subordination conflict*. The period of the so-called 'Troubles' in Northern Ireland
was characterised by paramilitary activity, securitisation of daily life as
well as of the border and increasing polarisation between unionist and
nationalist identities.

---

[9] This troop deployment took the form of setting up field hospitals to treat 'those injured in
the disturbances in the Six Counties who did not wish to be treated there' (Government of
Ireland press release, quoted in Kennedy 2000: 341). Despite the Irish government's
explicit commitment to unification by exclusively peaceful means, let alone the fact that
the army was not equipped for invasion, speculation that the Irish army was preparing to
invade the Catholic Bogside area of Derry was rife at the time.

The border and 'the Troubles' The arrival of British troops plus the reintroduction of internment without trial for terrorist suspects showed that the Northern Ireland administration had effectively lost both autonomy and control. The subsequent imposition of direct rule from Westminster in April 1972 was seen by all concerned as a disappointing and temporary step. At this point, both governments conceived the problem as being one of opposing conceptions of the legitimacy of the border. This is evident in the holding of a 1973 poll on Northern Ireland remaining part of the UK or integrating with the Republic (see Lawrence and Elliott 1975), archive material showing both governments' serious consideration of the option of repartition[10] and in the short-lived Sunningdale Agreement's provision for an all-island Council of Ireland. This period of the early 1970s was one of the most extremely violent during the 'Troubles' (Fay *et al.* 1998). The reinstatement of direct rule after the collapse of Sunningdale in 1974 signalled the British government's belief (similar to that in 1920) that the nationalist and unionist parties were too polarised and the situation too securitised to find an internal solution.

The Irish border at this time went from being 'not only psychological but physical ... strongly maintained by the army'.[11] The securitisation of the border came as a result of increased republican paramilitary activity in border areas and perception on the British side that the Republic was a 'haven' for republicans. This had been made worse by the trial of two Irish cabinet ministers and an Irish Army Intelligence Officer in 1970 (all of whom were acquitted) on accusations of using government money to import arms to be smuggled across the border to the IRA (O'Brien 2000). On the other hand, the southern government suspected collusion by British security forces in the loyalist bombing of Monaghan and Dublin in 1974.[12] Army checkpoints and roadblocks along the border meant that, even in Donegal, 'where people can look across the river and see the North ... people would have avoided going to Derry [in Northern Ireland] unless they had to during the conflict'.[13] This vision of Northern Ireland as a 'no-go area' for those outside the border is understandable

---

[10] Even British government documents published at the time reflect its willingness to consider radical changes to the Irish border. The Green Paper on 'The Future of Northern Ireland' (October 1972: Art.42), for example, suggested that the British government could 'provide specific machinery' or 'lay out a theoretical path towards closer integration, and possible ultimate unity in Ireland'.

[11] Interviewee 6, Cross-community youth worker in north-east Co. Donegal. Interviewed by the author in St Johnston, 6 May 2004.

[12] See the Report of the Independent Commission of Inquiry (the 'Barron Report') into the Dublin and Monaghan bombings of 1974, 10 December 2003.

[13] Interviewee 6.

Table 2.1: *The three strands of the 1998 'Good Friday' Agreement*

Strand one: Northern Ireland	Strand two: north–south	Strand three: British–Irish
Executive	North–South Ministerial Council	British–Irish Council
Devolved Assembly	Implementation bodies	British–Irish Intergovernmental Conference

given that the vast majority of the deaths and injuries arising from thirty years of the 'Troubles' occurred within the province.[14] Just as the border became more firmly entrenched as a physical and ideological barrier between north and south during the Troubles, so the division it represented became replicated *within* Northern Ireland. As Boal *et al.* (1976) noted in the case of Belfast, the security situation meant that the 'national conflict' led to the creation of more barriers between the communities in Northern Ireland. Analysis of the census results of 1971, 1981 and 1991 from Northern Ireland shows that the violent conflict of subordination at this time was accompanied by a deepening physical segregation of society.

The Irish border and the peace process

The 1998 Agreement In the 1990s, the British and Irish governments began to draw together two previously separate strategies for conflict resolution – politically 'bolstering moderates' (as in the 1985 Anglo-Irish Agreement) and militarily tackling paramilitarism – in a joint initiative to 'incorporate extremists' in a political settlement (Cunningham 2001: 160). The all-party negotiations centred upon a three-stranded approach formally introduced in 1991 and institutionalised in the 1998 Good Friday Agreement (Table 2.1).

The success of this Agreement was due to the fact that it drew together both desecuritisation and increasing politicisation of the conflict, i.e. the forum for the expression of disaccord became the democratic

---

[14] Malcolm Sutton's (1994) study of deaths from the conflict is updated by the author up to October 2002 on a website (http://cain.ulst.ac.uk/sutton/). Cross-tabulation through this site shows that, of the 3,523 deaths related to the Troubles between July 1969 and December 2001, 113 were in the Republic of Ireland, 125 in Britain and 18 in Europe. Republican paramilitary groups were responsible for 2,055 deaths, loyalist paramilitaries for 1,020 deaths, and British security forces for 363 deaths during this period.

political sphere. Institutions for devolution, north–south cooperation and east–west communication were to alter the means by which nationalist and unionist identities are articulated in the three strands. Framing these institutions were constitutional adjustments in the two states to include Ireland's acceptance of the continuation of the status quo and British acceptance of the possibility of change in Northern Ireland's constitutional status (Coakley 2003).[15] Yet, although the British and Irish governments have taken a step back from a zero-sum approach to the border, the Agreement institutionalises a binary that keeps the border central to the identity of the groups concerned: unionist/north/British versus nationalist/south/Irish.

Core actors

The Good Friday Agreement is geared more to the recognition and accommodation of different national and cultural identities than normatively promoting their transformation. (Cunningham 2001: 163)

The origins of the binary in the Agreement lie in the coordination of pan-nationalist and (to a significantly lesser degree) pan-unionist approaches to negotiations in the early 1990s. The basic structure for these blocs involved three levels of actors. Firstly, and underpinning the agreement, were the two governments and government officials from Britain, Northern Ireland and the Republic. Secondly, driving the negotiations were the two moderate parties, which dominated the political scene in Northern Ireland at the time, the nationalist Social Democratic and Labour Party (SDLP) and the Ulster Unionist Party (UUP). Finally, there were the hardline parties, such as Sinn Féin and the small loyalist parties,[16] whose participation in the peace process was considered essential to securing ceasefires by paramilitary organisations (namely the IRA[17]

---

[15] The constitutional amendments accompanying the 1998 Agreement embody an attempt to show both governments' willingness to move away from exclusivist solutions to the border conflict. The Government of Ireland Act of 1920 was repealed by Westminster and the irredentist claim over the territory of Northern Ireland was removed from Articles 2 and 3 of *Bunreacht na hÉireann* (the Constitution of Ireland).

[16] Unionism/loyalism is a lot more diverse than nationalism/republicanism in Northern Ireland when it comes to political representation. The two largest parties by far are the UUP and Democratic Unionist Party (DUP), but there exist on the margins a range of less well-established parties such as those affiliated with loyalist paramilitary groups (e.g. the Progressive Unionist Party and Ulster Democratic Party) and those anti-Agreement, abstentionist parties such as the UK Unionist Party.

[17] The IRA is not the only significant republican paramilitary group in Northern Ireland, yet it is the most significant, and its dominant position was reinforced through its intervention in intra-republican feuds, for example the Irish People's Liberation Organisation disbanded in 1982 following the involvement of the IRA (CAIN).

and the Combined Loyalist Military Command).[18] The implicit assumption of fundamental unity within the British/unionist/loyalist and Irish/nationalist/republican blocs facilitated progress from a conflict of subordination to an identity conflict through negotiations.

Institutionalising a binary This binary is replicated in the institutions of 1998. For example, the Agreement requires Assembly members to be designated as either unionist or nationalist in order to receive full voting rights. This was a means of ensuring 'bread and butter' issues could be dealt with by the Assembly on a demonstrably cross-party, and thereby cross-community, basis (Hayes and McAllister 1999: 39; Morgan 2000: 186). However, as chapter 1 outlines, the expression of difference in an identity conflict is still accusatory and hostile, albeit non-violent. The suspension of the devolved Assembly and Executive in 2001, within two years of their establishment, and in 2002 replicates the logic employed thirty years previously to reinstate direct rule, namely that the parties within Northern Ireland are too polarised to come to an agreed compromise. Yet, although again considered a temporary solution, direct rule has failed to stifle even further polarisation. This time, however, polarisation is within as well as between nationalist and unionist parties in Northern Ireland.

Problems in implementing the Agreement As elite actors have moved to the boundaries of their ideological position in order to reach the Agreement, so sensitivity has been heightened around issues viewed as symbolically significant for community identities. The recurrent problems in Northern Ireland since the Agreement concern just such issues, specifically decommissioning of weapons and policing. Despite the intervention of external actors in relation to the most controversial sticking points (such as the Independent International Commission on Decommissioning chaired by General John de Chastelain), political progress relies on local political leaders having the ability to lead their communities along an enduringly rocky path. A problem for the enactment of the Agreement is that the institutionalisation of the binary has led individuals to question who best represents the interests of their community, and the majority on both sides have turned to parties and leaders who are associated less with compromise and more with confidence in a staunch unionist/nationalist position.

[18] The Combined Loyalist Military Command acted as spokesbody for the main loyalist paramilitary groups, including the Ulster Volunteer Force (UVF), Loyal Volunteer Force (LVF), Ulster Freedom Fighters (UFF) and Ulster Defence Association (UDA).

For this reason, parties that have sought to construct an alternative approach to politics in Northern Ireland (such as the Northern Ireland Women's Coalition) have lost out to the gains of the hard-line parties on all sides since the Agreement.[19] Five years after the Agreement, Sinn Féin and the Democratic Unionist Party replaced the SDLP and the UUP as the largest parties in the province in the elections to the (suspended) devolved Assembly in November 2003. The dominance of the 'hard-line' parties was confirmed in the 2005 Westminster and local elections, leaving the two central architects of the Agreement very much on the political margins. Whereas Sinn Féin gained by stepping into the SDLP's shoes as a pro-Agreement yet strong voice for nationalism, the then anti-Agreement DUP gained from unionist concern that the UUP had been irredeemably weakened by the compromise.

The erosion of the middle ground within and between the parties was mirrored in growing physical segregation in Northern Ireland. Research suggests that segregation continued to worsen after the 1998 Agreement (Shirlow 2002). The number of 'peace walls' separating troublesome 'interface' residential areas tripled in the ten years after the 1994 para-military ceasefires.[20] The experience of Northern Ireland since the Agreement may suggest that as state borders become less a focus of distrust and disaccord, so internal boundaries can increase in potency and significance. The next section of the chapter examines the relevance of the European Union to the three strands of the Agreement.

The EU context for the three strands of agreement

British–Irish relations: Strand Three

Foundation for intergovernmental relationship
The process of European integration ... permitted the Northern Ireland problem to be redefined as an exceptionally intractable transfrontier problem. (Coakley 2001: 22)

The conflict emerged in Northern Ireland at the same time as Ireland and Britain prepared for accession to the European Economic Community. Although the EEC was not seen at the time by either government as a

---

[19] This was dramatically illustrated by the results of the November 2003 election to the Northern Ireland Assembly in which the Women's Coalition and the small Northern Ireland Unionist Party, United Unionist Assembly Party and Independent Unionists lost all the seats that they had held since the 1998 Assembly elections.

[20] Robin Wilson, 'Next Steps'. Paper delivered to ESRC Conference, 'Devolution in Northern Ireland: Record and Prospects', Belfast, March 2003.

possible 'third party' in the conflict, the Irish government did see the European forum as an opportunity to place pressure on Britain to internationalise the search for a solution. The equal status that the Irish state was given with the United Kingdom in the European Council and Council of Ministers was a substantial boost to this end. On occasion, tense British–Irish relations had repercussions at a European level, for example when Ireland refused to endorse EEC trade sanctions against Argentina during the Falklands War (Arthur 1983: 172). Yet for the most part, the EEC – specifically the Council – was a forum around which a positive and cooperative intergovernmental relationship was built (O'Dowd *et al.* 1995; Arthur 2000; Meehan 2000). Prime Minister James Callaghan and Taoiseach Jack Lynch's meeting on the sidelines of the European Council summit in Copenhagen in 1978 was the first between the leaders of the two governments in this neutral context. Regular meetings on the fringes of EU Council summits created a context for a bilateral approach to the conflict, leading to the Anglo-Irish Agreement in November 1985. This Agreement created formal structures for a consultative role for the Irish government in certain areas, including cross-border cooperation, and expressed the 'determination of both governments to develop close cooperation as partners in the European Community'. The repetition of this phrase in the 1993 Downing Street Declaration and the 1995 Framework Documents[21] and the intergovernmental agreement incorporated in the Good Friday Agreement of 1998 – 'wishing to develop still further ... the close cooperation between their countries ... as partners in the European Union' – embodies the position of the EU as primarily a framework for British–Irish cooperation at the heart of the peace process.

The informality, secrecy and regularity of meetings between government ministers at the European level proved to be invaluable in the development of an 'agreed approach' to Northern Ireland. Albert Reynolds pins the strength of the peace process on the 'great personal relationship' he first built with John Major when they were both Finance Ministers in the Council of Ministers (Reynolds 2003). This strong

---

[21] Article 3 of the Downing Street Declaration reads: '[The Governments] also consider that the development of Europe will, of itself, require new approaches to serve interests common to both parts of the island of Ireland, and to Ireland and the United Kingdom as partners in the European Union.' The Framework Documents noted that 'an agreed approach for the whole island in respect of the challenges and opportunities of the European Union' would need to be found (Article 26 of 'A New Framework for Agreement') and Article 2 of 'A Framework for Accountable Government' urged the establishment of new institutions taking into account 'newly forged links with the rest of Europe'.

British–Irish relationship continued through to the 1998 Good Friday Agreement and is frequently credited by both governments to the EU context:

the relationship between the two Governments has been, and very much continues to be, the bedrock on which the peace process has been built. Without our shared engagement in Europe, it is difficult to see how this would have come about.[22]

... from a political point of view, the European project has actually brought together the Irish and British Governments in a very special way that has considerably helped the peace process. I think we owe the European Union a great deal in Northern Ireland.[23]

New approach to cooperation The process of European integration has also impacted on the working-out of the British–Irish relationship at a practical level, increasing the plausibility of a bilateral approach to matters of mutual interest (Ruane and Todd 1996: 281; Guelke 2001: 259). The Strand Three institutions provide 'a framework for enhanced practical cooperation across these islands'.[24] Common policies may be developed through the British–Irish Intergovernmental Conference (BIIC) on areas of mutual interest in the EU as well as on cross-border matters that are beyond the powers of the devolved institutions. The broader British–Irish Council (BIC) includes the executives of Northern Ireland, Scotland and Wales and the administrations of the Isle of Man and the Channel Islands, as well as the two governments. Its most significant function is symbolic: the British and Irish nations are internally diverse, they share common interests, their territorial borders are causes for cooperation rather than conflict. Yet the Strand Three institutions, according to government leaders involved, serve not merely to 'reflect and explore' opportunities for new relationships between Ireland and the United Kingdom but also to enable their 'cooperation to be wider and more fundamental still – above all in Europe'.[25]

---

[22] Brian Cowen, 11 October 2002. Remarks by the Irish Minister for Foreign Affairs, Conference on the Future of Europe after Enlargement, Derry.

[23] Paul Murphy, 21 June 2004. Interview with the Secretary of State for Northern Ireland, Radio Ulster, www.nio.gov.uk/press/040621b.htm.

[24] John Reid, 21 February 2001. Speech by the Secretary of State for Northern Ireland to business leaders in Dublin, www.nio.gov.uk/press/010221a-nio.htm.

[25] Tony Blair, 26 November 1998. Speech by the British Prime Minister to the Houses of the Oireachtas, Dublin.

North–south relations: Strand Two

Cross-border cooperation The European dimension is also central to Strand Two of the Agreement. The remits of the six all-island Implementation Bodies include areas tightly linked into EU competences (e.g. EU Programmes, fisheries) as well as those specific to the island (e.g. languages, tourism). The North–South Ministerial Council (when in operation; NSMC) is charged with ensuring the representation of all-island interests at the EU level, both informally and through the inclusion of NSMC members in Irish delegations to the Council of Ministers and its working groups. The importance of the EU for Strand Two relates both to specific Community Initiatives for interregional cooperation and to the general process of integration between member states. Firstly, 'dynamic cross-border development and cooperation' was to become an integral element of strategies for economic and social cohesion between EU regions, particularly those lagging behind in development, as the island of Ireland was (McAlinden quoted in McCall 1998: 394). Several pre-existing cross-border structures between Northern Ireland and the Republic were thus consolidated and strengthened in the 1994–9 round of EU Structural Funds (ADM/CPA 1999: 12). Furthermore, the number and effectiveness of cross-border networks of cooperation across the island substantially increased with the Interreg Community Initiative, particularly in its third phase (Interreg IIIA) (Laffan and Payne 2001). Moreover, the dual purpose of programmes such as Interreg – 'to help integrate the economic space of the Community as a whole and to address the negative legacy of border areas' – demonstrates the way in which wider EU ambitions held direct relevance for the situation in Ireland (European Commission 1991: 169).

Cross-border integration

The European Union is now a single market and, as I say, if you look at the border in Ireland now, if you drive across the border there's no stopping, so in that sense, physical borders all over Europe have gone, not just in Ireland.[26]

Although trade between Britain and the Republic of Ireland historically represented a virtual common labour, trade and agricultural market for most of the twentieth century, this was not replicated in trade between

---

[26] Interviewee 9, John Hume, Nobel Peace Prize winner, former MP, MEP, Member of Legislative Assembly (MLA) and leader of the Social Democratic and Labour Party. Interviewed by the author in Belfast, 1 June 2004.

north and south on the island (Hederman O'Brien 2000: 11).[27] The
introduction of EEC regulations on customs declarations in 1987 had
an immediate effect on the ease with which goods could be transported
across the border (MacEvoy 1988: 11; McCracken 2003: 22). Many
further obstacles to cross-border trade and economic development were
eroded with the creation of the Single European Market in 1992. Their
shared boundary lines meant that Ireland had to join Britain in staying
outside the Schengen Agreement, yet Ireland's participation in the
Eurozone without Britain had the potential to have an even greater effect
on the border. While the pro-European SDLP views it as 'imperative that
Northern Ireland accepts the Euro', given its 'peripheral location within
the European Union and [its] geographic border with the Republic',[28]
others consider the area around the border to have effectively become a
'dual currency region' (Bridle 2002). In an amusing twist, among the
clearest physical indicators of having crossed the border into the Republic
(since the dismantling of the army checkpoints) are the prominent signs
displaying the EU flag in acknowledgement of EU funding for road
improvements. In the conditions of the peace process, the ease of crossing
borders in the EU is an experience now shared in Ireland.

Within Northern Ireland: Strand One

Direct EU involvement in Strand One In addition to the support
contributed through its Community-wide programmes, the European
Commission directly responded to the specific needs of the province
with the Special Support Programme for Peace and Reconciliation
(PEACE)[29] (established in response to the ceasefires in 1994) and
its donations to the International Fund for Ireland. Altogether, the
Commission's contributions have been significant not only in terms of
the necessary boost they have given to the infrastructure of the province
but also because they have been a means of bypassing central government
(Loughlin *et al.* 1999: 316). It was anticipated that the decentralisation of
decision-making processes in the 1998 Agreement would enable the
Northern Ireland Assembly to play 'an increasingly significant part in

---

[27] 9 per cent of manufacturing sales in Northern Ireland in 2001 were with the Republic of
Ireland, compared to 12 per cent to EU countries. These figures are still substantially less
than the 35 per cent share held by Great Britain (see Bridle 2002).

[28] John Hume, 10 November 2001. Speech by the SDLP leader, Annual SDLP
Conference, Slieve Donard Hotel, Co. Down.

[29] The aims of this Special Support Programme are to: 'combat social exclusion, promote
reconciliation and cross-border development, and contribute to the social and economic
regeneration of Northern Ireland and the six adjacent border counties' (Logue 1999).

determining how Northern Ireland can get the most out of UK membership of the EU' (European Commission n/d: 1). However, apart from some consultation conducted by Westminster with devolved assemblies (to a degree decided at a national level), the most impact Northern Ireland politicians can have in relation to the practice of subsidiarity in the EU is through participation in relevant committees in the House of Commons (Phinnemore 2003). Strand One of the Agreement does give the Northern Ireland civil service and the departments of the Executive (coordinated by the Office of the First Minister and Deputy First Minister (OFM/DFM)) new responsibility for EU-related matters and in developing a united approach to the EU. While these have limited power in the absence of devolution, the Strategy document on the EU produced by OFM/DFM in 2004 reflects recognition of the need to promote Northern Ireland's regional interests in the EU.

How local actors view the EU Any analysis of the EU's role in Northern Ireland has to acknowledge that it is not a neutral player by virtue of the contrasting opinions held by nationalists and unionists regarding the involvement of external actors. The difference in nationalist and unionist support for EU involvement lies not only in their traditionally opposing conceptualisations of the Irish border but also in their affiliation to governments with different approaches to the EU (Brennan 1995: 75). Indeed, the different approach taken by nationalists and unionists to the EU reflects the centrality of national ideology in the delineation of identity in relation to Europe (Bew and Meehan 1994). The SDLP has shared the Irish government's generally pro-integrationist vision of the EU and, under the leadership of John Hume MEP, disseminated a vision of the EU as a crucial context for redefining Irish nationalism and national identity. From an originally eurosceptic stance, Sinn Féin's move into mainstream politics in Northern Ireland has been accompanied by recognition of the value of the EU in internationalisation of the conflict and cross-border cooperation. This was reflected in the effort Sinn Féin put into elections to the European Parliament in 2004, in which it took the seat vacated by Hume's resignation. In contrast, unionists have generally opposed an active role for the EU in Northern Ireland, mirroring the British government's concern to maintain a clear distinction between national and European realms of competence. Given that, as Ruane and Todd (1996) note, interested international observers tended to be more 'in tune with' nationalist than unionist interpretations of the conflict, there are certain grounds for unionist wariness towards external involvement in Northern Ireland. Nonetheless, the involvement of the European Union in the three 'strands' noted above has meant that the EU has become increasingly seen as less of an external actor than as a context enabling previously inconceivable developments for the purpose of practical gain. While the DUP is overtly eurosceptic and the UUP is suspicious of European integration in a way similar to that of the British Conservative Party, both acknowledge the benefits of EU membership for Northern Ireland.[30]

EU Representation in Northern Ireland The Representation of the European Commission in Northern Ireland has become increasingly important as the EU has grown in significance for policy and development at local, regional and national levels. The Commission first established a Representation Office in Northern Ireland in 1981, reflecting its recognition of regional differences within its member states. The Office sees its role as twofold, acting as a 'shop window' for public information on the Commission and as the 'eyes and ears' of the Commission in Northern Ireland.[31] In the first of these roles, the Office is subject to lobbying from local interests to access decision-making in Brussels, provides briefings on European issues to politicians, businesses etc. and organises public information events etc. In the second, the Office regularly updates the Commission on developments (particularly in relation to the peace process) in the region, provides briefings for EU institutions prior to EU decisions/press releases on Northern Ireland matters, and works very closely with the Directorate-General for Regional Policy as the overseer of Structural Funds and the PEACE Programme. The profile of the Commission Representation is largely dependent on coverage in the local press, not least because its proactive role in publicising the work of the EU in Northern Ireland is delimited by the Commission's caution regarding interfering in domestic UK politics. The location of the Commission's Representation in Northern Ireland within the UK Representation means that there is little overlap with the work of the Commission Representation in the Republic, although at times information is shared between the two offices. The main area in which the Commission Representation Office is involved in cross-border activity is through the Special EU Programmes Body, with whom it has to ensure it is 'singing off the same hymn sheet'.[32] Thus, the role of the Commission Representation in Northern Ireland has developed in

---

[30] For instance, in their manifestos for the 2004 elections to the European Parliament, both the DUP and the UUP acknowledge the growing influence of the EU and the need to secure further EU funding, most specifically an extension of the PEACE II funds.

[31] Interviewee 21, Head of Office of the European Commission Representation in Northern Ireland. Interviewed by the author in Belfast, 11 May 2004.

[32] Interviewee 21.

parallel with the growing relevance of the EU for funding and policy but there is little room for innovation when it comes to developing its role and profile, given that it is essentially restricted to working within the structures set by local and national political conditions. This is similar to the general experience of the EU pathways of influence in the conflict as a whole.

Four pathways of EU influence

Compulsory impact: not evident

The EU is a major context for policy development in its member states, but the direct 'compulsory' impact of the EU on elite actors has been virtually non-existent in the case of Northern Ireland. The EU's direct compulsory influence on the political leaders had to be exercised towards the two governments. One example of an attempt by the EU to force a core actor to engage in desecuritising moves in Northern Ireland is that of the European Parliament vote (October 1984) in favour of a motion calling on the British government to ban the use of plastic bullets. However, the lack of 'compulsory' power behind this action was aggravated by the fact that, within days of the EP passing this motion, the European Commission on Human Rights (which had been the focus of international intervention in the conflict) found that the use of plastic bullets in a rioting situation is justified. More common has been the use of special EU funds as a 'carrot' to encourage cooperation between parties to the peace process, exemplified in the announcement by the Commission following the IRA ceasefire in 1994 that it was increasing its contribution to the International Fund for Ireland by a third (CAIN). Yet, the 'carrot' of EU funding is yielded rather than wielded: the more it is used, the more it is taken for granted. Moreover, the ones who are most affected by this 'carrot' are neither political leaders nor paramilitaries, but community-level actors, as discussed below. Ultimately, the influence of the EU on political leaders in relation to the conflict in Northern Ireland has been most significant and effective in indirect, structural forms.

Enabling impact: crucial for peace process

Model of multilevel cooperation A far more significant impact of the EU, particularly for the peace process in Ireland, has been its indirect structural influence on the political leaders involved. This has occurred through the EU's provision of a new context, model and inspiration for British–Irish and cross-border relations. As Hume notes, 'the framework on which the Union was created has been mirrored in our own local political institutions'.[33]

The application of the EU model of multilevel cooperation is embodied in the three-stranded institutions of the Good Friday Agreement.[34] The Strand Three institutions in particular, with their mix of supranational cooperation, intergovernmental agreement and sub-national coordination, reflect the model of cross-border partnership at work in the EU (Kearney 1998). The relevance of the EU's model is heightened by the fact that, at a broader structural level, the process of European integration has significantly altered the policy context in Ireland, north and south. This is notably recognised by regional-level actors supporting cross-border cooperation:

European policies are all about addressing the negative impact of borders and creating parity for border regions. The EU is therefore totally relevant to our role and to the actions we take. It provides a bigger framework and support. There is no point in a development policy that doesn't tie in with European as well as national policy.[35]

Indeed, the significance of the EU for cross-border cooperation in Ireland is epitomised in the European dimensions of the new institutions. This was laid out by the speech given by the then Secretary of State to the European Parliament on the Agreement:[36]

One of the roles of this [North–South Ministerial] Council will be to consider the EU dimension of relevant matters, including the implementation of EU policies and programmes and proposals under consideration in the EU framework. There will also be a new body bringing together the British and Irish governments with new devolved institutions in Northern Ireland, Scotland and Wales to consider matters of mutual interest, including approaches to EU issues.[37]

---

[33] John Hume, 4 July 2000. 'Moving into a New Europe', Speech by the SDLP leader, www.sdlp.ie/media/speeches/humeaneweuropejuly2000.htm.

[34] Hume views the institutions established by the Agreement as embodying the application of the three principles behind European integration: respect for difference, institutions that respect difference, a healing process in working together for common interests (Interviewee 9).

[35] Interviewee 12, Development officer, North West Region Cross Border Group. Interviewed by the author in Derry city, 14 July 2004.

[36] Mo Mowlam, 29 April 1998. Speech given by the Secretary of State for Northern Ireland to the European Parliament.

[37] Whereas Mowlam views the institutions of Strand Two and Three as important for monitoring the impact of the EU, John Hume sees them playing a more proactive role for the region in Europe: '[they] will have a vital role in ensuring that the voice of the island as a whole is heard at the highest levels of the European Union' (Hume, 18 November 2000. 'Building the Peace – Making a Difference', Speech by SDLP leader at the 30th Annual SDLP Conference, Slieve Donard Hotel, Co. Down).

The 'win-win' model of the EU has helped to legitimise cross-border cooperation in Ireland, facilitating acceptance of the cross-border institutions across the political spectrum. As Quinlivan (1999: 14) notes:

Cooperation across the border, previously either impossible, impractical or stereotyped as an activity of the nationalist tradition within Northern Ireland, can now be viewed as a 'normal' and beneficial activity ... and one which is supported by the policies of both governments and the EU.

The EU has been an inspiration to leading players in the peace process in Ireland, as a model both of cross-border cooperation and conflict resolution.

Inspiration of the EU

Drawing on the inspiration of Monnet and Schuman, the two Governments, in partnership with the European Union, must respond with boldness, imagination and generosity to the full implementation of the Good Friday Agreement.[38]

The motivating example of the European Union in the peace process is acknowledged by political actors from across the spectrum, albeit with very different emphases. The most explicit proponents of the EU's role in this regard have been the Irish government and the SDLP. Membership and the model of the European Union have always fitted well with moderate Irish nationalists' aim to internationalise the issue of Northern Ireland and to build meaningful north–south relations.[39] Even at the time of accession to the European Economic Community, the Irish government and politicians viewed membership as changing the context for cross-border relations on the island:[40]

Apart from the economic reasons for entry, we have a national incentive in believing that entry into Europe will do away with the Border and make the artificial line between north and south of our country meaningless.[41]

---

[38] Brian Cowen, 20 July 2003. 'Clarity; Courage; Change', Annual John Hume lecture delivered by the Minister for Foreign Affairs, MacGill Summer School.

[39] Interviewee 14, Former government minister and leader of Fine Gael. Interviewed by the author in Dublin, 9 September 2004.

[40] Information pamphlets published by the Department of Foreign Affairs prior to the 1972 Irish referendum on EEC membership demonstrate this. See, for example, *Ireland North and South in the EEC* (Department of Foreign Affairs 1972, Dublin: EEC Information Service).

[41] T. J. Fitzpatrick, 9 December 1971. Contribution by the Fine Gael TD to Dáil Debate, quoted in J. A. Foley and S. Lalor (1995) *Gill and Macmillan Annotated Constitution of Ireland (with commentary)*. Dublin: Gill and Macmillan, p. 195.

As Cunningham (1997) contends, a neofunctionalist vision of the EU's impact on cross-border relations in Ireland could be interpreted as a restatement of basic nationalist principles:

> The EU commits all its members to an 'ever-closer union' among the peoples of Europe. That includes an ever-closer union between the people of Ireland, North and South, and between Ireland and Britain. Borders are gone all over Europe, including in fact the Irish border. (Hume 1996: 46–7)

The SDLP is quite explicit in its vision of the north–south institutions as progress towards the development of more elaborate representational all-island institutions in the future, i.e. towards Irish unity:[42]

> Our politics does not grind to a halt at the border, it never has, it never will. There is much work to be done within the North/South Ministerial Council. There is also an agenda for future work: for example the creation of an all-Ireland parliamentary forum and an all-Ireland consultative council.[43]

Moreover, the meaning of 'Irish unity' itself has changed over the course of thirty years, and the Irish government no longer anticipates 'an end to partition'[44] through EU membership but simply 'greater North–South cooperation' (see Hayward 2004).[45] The fact that this language of 'overcoming barriers' is not confined to nationalist discourse, as the speech by Secretary of State Mo Mowlam shows below, reflects the EU's capacity to depoliticise cross-border cooperation and identities:

> And we look to the European Union for inspiration too. To a situation where old enmities have been put aside. Where boundaries and divisions are overcome

---

[42] See also the following statements by SDLP leader, Mark Durkan: 'we need to reassure people that a vote for unity is not a vote against the Agreement' (16 November 2003, Speech by the SDLP leader at the launch of the SDLP strategy document on a United Ireland (www.sdlp.ie/prdurkanunitedireland.shtm)). Also: 'We must now get ready for the job of persuading the people of Ireland that this vision is the best way forward for us all, that the united Ireland we believe in holds out the guarantee of permanent peace, economic growth and an inclusive and fair society.' (26 April 2003, 'The Future of Northern Nationalism', Speech by the SDLP leader to the Irish Association, http://cain.ulst.ac.uk/issues/politics/docs/sdlp/md260403.htm). It is important to note that both these speeches were given in a context of increasing competition between the SDLP and Sinn Féin.

[43] Bríd Rodgers, 22 March 2002. 'Is the "New Ireland" Now a Real Possibility?', Speech to the Irish Association by the Minister for Agriculture and Rural Development and SDLP deputy leader, Mansion House, Dublin.

[44] Seán Lemass, 30 October 1962. Response by An Taoiseach to Questions on EEC application. Dáil Éireann, vol. CXXXVII, 18.

[45] Dick Roche, 8 September 2003. 'The North–South Dimension in Ireland's Future Relationship with Europe', Speech by the Irish Minister of State with responsibility for European Affairs, Armagh City Hotel.

recognising that we achieve more much more – when we work together. Most of all where a sense of belonging exists beyond national boundaries.[46]

Legitimisation of cross-border cooperation Aside from the inspirational role of the EU, its context has certainly supported the primary justification for cross-border cooperation in Ireland, namely that of economic benefit. Irish nationalists have been keen to emphasise the 'common ground' of 'economics'[47] and the immediate goal of 'integrated development' in cross-border cooperation.[48] Teague argues that multi-level, multi-sectoral cross-border cooperation for economic gain, as seen in the EU, should result in 'a growing trust that relaxes unionists' attitudes to the island-wide imagined community' leading to 'positive political spill-overs for the legitimacy of the [north–south] institutions' (quoted in Kennedy and Lynch 2003: 9). This analysis appears to have been borne out in the words of the UUP leader, who presents the new institutions as a reason to trust that cross-border cooperation 'is no longer a strategy for creeping unification'[49] but rather a pragmatic development that 'threatens no-one and benefits everyone'.[50] Similarly, the DUP's Ian Paisley Jr's description of a cross-border cooperative established by farmers to save a chip factory in Ballymoney as 'a fine example of genuine economic cooperation' illustrates the importance of material benefit in legitimising what would previously have been seen as controversial ventures.[51]

Nevertheless, unionists are careful to play down the significance of the cross-border institutions, as UUP leader David Trimble clarifies: 'it would be misleading of me if I did not caution against unrealisable expectations with regard to North/South Implementation Bodies'.[52] Instead, they are careful to stress the enduring bonds between Northern Ireland and Britain by placing north–south cross-border cooperation

---

[46] Mowlam, 29 April 1998 (n. 36).
[47] John Hume, 14 March 1995. Lecture by the SDLP leader, Mount Holyoke College, USA.
[48] Bertie Ahern, 19 February 1999. 'Urban Ireland – Rural Ireland: Bridging the Gap or Deepening the Divide?', Address by An Taoiseach to the General Council of County Councils Conference, Malahide.
[49] David Trimble, 20 November 1998. 'Post-Agreement Ireland: North and South', Speech by the First Minister and Ulster Unionist Party leader to the Annual Conference of the Irish Association at The Glenview Hotel, Glen Of The Downs, Co. Wicklow.
[50] David Trimble, 17 December 1999. Comments by the First Minister at the Inaugural Meeting of the British–Irish Council. (Source: BBC News online.)
[51] Ian Paisley (Jr), 12 March 2004. Comments reported by BBC Northern Ireland online.
[52] Trimble, 20 November 1998 (n. 49).

alongside that of east–west cooperation, e.g. 'We look forward to continued valuable exchanges with the Republic on a wide range of issues bilaterally and in the British–Irish Council.'[53] The British government also places the Strand Two institutions very much in the context of Strand Three:

these institutions are designed to enhance practical cooperation for the benefit of all the people of these islands. That is why they bind our two governments and our diverse regions into a framework that allows us to share what we have in common and respect what makes us different.[54]

Although it served to stimulate positive intergovernmental relations in the first place, the ongoing importance of the EU context for cross-border cooperation lies increasingly at the non-elite level in Ireland.

Connective impact: increasingly apparent

Direct economic support The active direct role of the EU in Northern Ireland has been essentially conducted through its programmes for economic and regional development. Given that the most 'clout' the EU has is economic, it is not surprising that its most significant competence regarding societal conflict resolution lies in economic measures (Brown and Rosecrance 1999; Piening 1997). More dramatically, Bradley's (1995: 49) prediction that, '[j]ust as the Single European Market and EMU contain an internal logic of further integration, so too a process of North–South co-ordinated development is likely to lead inexorably to suggestions for further harmonisation and policy convergence', was borne out by the straightforward economic necessity for cooperation (Cook *et al.* 2000: 5; Goodman 2000; Tannam 1996).[55] The economic boom in the Republic of Ireland – linked at least in part to 'enthusiastic embracing of EU initiatives' – has encouraged individuals and organisations in Northern Ireland to be increasingly open to 'economic interaction with their island neighbours' (Bradley and Hamilton 1999: 37; D'Arcy and Dickson 1995: xv). Politicians from all sides of the spectrum have noticed that the Republic is not only a more attractive

---

[53] Trimble, 20 November 1998 (n. 49).

[54] Peter Mandelson, 2 December 1999. Address by the Secretary of State for Northern Ireland at the Exchange of Notifications Ceremony at Department of Foreign Affairs, Iveagh House, Dublin.

[55] FitzGerald *et al.*'s (1988: xiv) study of cross-border shopping in the late 1980s (submitted to the European Commission) highlighted the need for greater harmonisation between the Republic and Northern Ireland 'even without the requirements of the completion of the Single European Market'.

economic partner but also an example to follow in the context of EU membership.[56]

We see a changed Republic of Ireland today ... a country part of Europe's mainstream, having made the most of European structural funds but no longer reliant on them.[57]

The Commission has been generally seen as an external and beneficent player in relation to Northern Ireland as a region of the EU (Teague 1996). The funding given by the EU to community groups in Northern Ireland and the border counties is recognised as profoundly important due to its direct impact at the grass-roots level and its implications for peace-building.[58] A number of interviewees draw explicit connections between projects being funded by the EU and a decrease in the level of sectarian violence in those localities (Interviews 2, 4, 6, 7).[59] Others trace a more indirect route for the impact of PEACE funds: for example, in projects that develop skills in individuals enabling them to become social actors themselves, first as contributors to their local community and then as lobbyists for peace.[60] Certain claims are made of EU Community Initiatives (such as Interreg and LEADER) and the PEACE programme, distinguishing them from other funding available for peace work in the region. In facilitating 'innovative, risk-taking projects',[61] that 'come[ ] in at the bottom level',[62] the EU has not only helped to build a strong culture of partnership and peace-building at a community level, it has also 'changed the nature' of voluntary work itself.[63]

---

[56] 'The Republic today, after 30 years of membership of the European family of nations, is a different Ireland. On our side of the Border we are trying to make Northern Ireland anew.' (David Trimble, 28 March 2003. Address by the leader of the Ulster Unionist Party to The Irish Association for Cultural, Economic and Social Relations, Trinity College Dublin.)

[57] Blair, 26 November 1998 (n. 25).

[58] It is important to note, however, that this result is no doubt affected by the fact that all of the community-level interviewees were linked to projects that had received EU funding.

[59] For example, Interviewee 4 is a highly experienced project manager, interviewed by the author (Londonderry, 28 April 2004) in her capacity both as an employee of Derry City Council and as leader of a youth club in a Protestant 'enclave' in the city. She says that the club would not have existed without EU funding, 'There'd have been much more violence if we [the youth club] hadn't been there. We cut interface violence by 65 per cent in the two months of the summer scheme.'

[60] Interviewee 1, Cross-community and cross-border project coordinator, Derry city. Interviewed by the author in Derry, 27 April 2004.

[61] Interviewee 13, Development officer, Area Development Management Ltd/Combat Poverty Agency. Interviewed by the author in Monaghan, 24 August 2004.

[62] Interviewee 11, Director of Community initiatives, Special EU Programmes Body. Interviewed by the author in Monaghan, 14 July 2004.

[63] Interviewee 7, Community youth worker, south-east Co. Donegal. Interviewed by the author in Ballintra, 6 May 2004.

The European Parliament as a new forum for debate Since direct elections to the European Parliament in 1979, the Parliament has been used as a forum by MEPs from Northern Ireland to bring their concerns to a wider audience. Examples of this include John Hume's (SDLP MEP) proposal in March 1993 for EU support for conflict resolution in Northern Ireland and Ian Paisley's (DUP MEP) attempts to interrupt the speeches made by Taoiseach Jack Lynch, Prime Minister Margaret Thatcher and Pope John Paul II in plenary sessions. Yet, in an action signifying a new public profile for the European Parliament as well as the lack of outlets for democratic expression within Northern Ireland, the family of Robert McCartney (murdered by IRA members in January 2005) brought their campaign for justice to Strasbourg. The Parliament subsequently approved a motion condemning the murder and calling for EU financial support for any future civil proceedings brought by the McCartney family against the suspects. The fact that the two Sinn Féin MEPs abstained from the vote on the grounds that it 'politicised' the problem epitomises the move of the EU into new territory regarding the conflict in Northern Ireland, i.e. operating not on the level of governments or even parties, but at a community level. Notably, the two unionist MEPs welcomed the intervention of the European Parliament, with DUP MEP Jim Allister going so far as to name the IRA suspects during the plenary session. Comparison with the McCartney family's visit to the United States highlights a new and unique element in the European forum, namely that the pressure placed on local politicians (in this case Sinn Féin) was much more direct and immediate.

Constructive impact: latent potential

Cross-border cooperation The wider consequences of the EU context for societal change point to the more obtuse 'constructive' impact of the EU on the conflict. Most notably for this study, the context of the European Union has both facilitated and 'normalised' cross-border activity. Although some level of cross-border cooperation occurred prior to the EU initiatives in this area, it was not 'fashionable' and bodies such as the North West Region Cross Border Group (NWRCBG) did not formalise or announce their activities.[64] In line with the aims of the Special EU Programmes Body (SEUPB), 'north–south relationships have been made real and impacting, plus there is a greater degree of integration and north–southery', not least because local organisations recognise that

---

[64] Interviewee 12.

joint applications for EU funding are 'more likely to be favourably received' (O'Neill 1998: 8).[65] Increasing partnership is made all the more significant by the fact that the SEUPB has encouraged 'collaborative working across sectors ... as well as across borders'.[66] This has potential implications for the alignment of economic interests, territorial locality and political representation. For example, just as fishermen and farmers in Northern Ireland have been known to lobby the relevant Irish (rather than British) ministers to support their interests at the EU level, one TD (member of Parliament) from Donegal (in the north-west of Ireland) notes that she now receives almost as many representations from people across the border in Northern Ireland as from her own constituents on the big issues.[67] She attributes the way in which people now gravitate towards the politician who best represents their needs, regardless of the border, to the impact of the EU.[68] The Special EU Programmes Body sees the development of such cross-border links as the reinstatement of 'the normal physical, economic and emotional links between regions' previously hindered by partition.[69] It is not so much the actors or structures of the EU but the actual process of European integration itself that has served to transform factors that would previously have contributed to the conflict into bases for cooperation across ideological, political and territorial borders.[70]

Changing identity scripts? The EU has also helped to stimulate change within community groups, areas and subject positions. For instance, a corollary of EU funding for community development is the growth in confidence of 'previously silent section[s] of the population' such as the Protestant community in the southern border counties.[71] A different example of the indirect constructive impact of the EU is seen in the role played by the SDLP over the past thirty years. Even since the SDLP has been supplanted by Sinn Féin as the largest nationalist party in Northern Ireland, changes to Sinn Féin's own ideological and constitutional position in and around its engagement in the peace process point to the significant if indirect influence of Hume's decision to 'redefine[ ] the battlefield as Europe' (Todd 2001). Neither the individual member states nor other international actors were able to effect a 'change of scripts' in

---

[65] Interviewee 11.   [66] Interviewee 11.
[67] Interviewee 10, Fianna Fáil TD and former county councillor, north-east Donegal. Interviewed by the author in Dublin, 1 July 2004.
[68] Interviewee 10.   [69] Interviewee 11.
[70] This hypothesis is supported by Anderson (1998).
[71] Interviewee 8, Development officer, Protestant community group, north-east Donegal. Interviewed by the author in Raphoe, 20 May 2004.

Northern Ireland to the same degree that the EU has indirectly managed to achieve, in part through Hume's influence. Such ideological and constitutional change, however, does not necessarily entail a decreasing role for identity difference in contemporary Europe. It is clear that the 'reconstruction of identities' envisaged in this pathway is not occurring along the lines of what might be termed 'Europeanisation'.

Conditions of impact

The unique role of the EU

The subtle influence of the EU stands in contrast to the role of other external actors in relation to the conflict, most particularly the United States which is, first and foremost, a very different type of 'perturbator'. For a start, the Irish-American diaspora has been both a source of support for republicans in Ireland and a potential source of votes for US politicians. Secondly, the USA has provided key individual political figures to actively participate in the peace process, as in President Bill Clinton's policy of 'selective engagement', Senator George Mitchell's role in facilitating the 1998 Agreement, and the so-called 'Four Horsemen' (Briand 2002). As pointed out in chapter 1 of this volume, part of the difficulty faced by the EU in terms of gaining recognition as a perturbator arises from the fact that the EU is not a homogeneous actor, but that it rather must be seen as a complex political organisation which includes a diverse set of collective actors. The EU's identity is defined more by institutions than by individuals, thus lacking the media-friendly face of US politicians. The United States has also played a normative role in the peace process. Similarities between the Dayton Accords in the former Yugoslavia and the Good Friday Agreement point to the influence of the USA (as well as the EU) in the design of Strand One.[72] However, a significant difference between the two agreements is that the Good Friday Agreement was ratified by the popular vote. In relation to this, the European Union provides something that no other external actor can contribute: a democratic political context and a direct functional relevance for the institutions of the Agreement. Moreover, as noted by the Cross-Border Consortium (2003: 3), the European Convention sets out

---

[72] The Dayton Accords share the following features with the 1998 Agreement: power-sharing institutions with weighted voting (elections to which are conducted through the use of proportional representation), demilitarisation and formal provisions for human rights protection. (Nicholas Whyte, 'The Peace Process in Northern Ireland and the Former Yugoslavia', John Whyte memorial lecture, University College Dublin, November 1999.)

principles on 'rights, citizenship, equality, inclusion, culture, participation, difference and diversity' crucial for the resolution of conflict. The EU has changed the economic and policy context for local actors and institutions, yet the influence that it has on society is mediated through these multilevel actors and institutions. Its role may be summarised as being that of context rather than player, underlying rather than high-profile, continuous rather than circumstantial and (for the most part) circumspect rather than controversial. This is evident in closer examination of the conditions of the EU's impact.

The mediated role of the EU

The conceptual framework presented in chapter 1 acknowledges that the form and success of the EU's perturbation of a conflict is influenced by the structural environment of the conflict and the relationship between the EU and actors within the conflict setting. The research performed in this case study to date suggests that these local conditions do not merely 'influence' the impact of the EU but actually serve to determine it. The precedence of domestic over international conditions in this case is secured by the fact that the EU's involvement has always been a consequence of the EU membership of the two protagonist states. In order to gain any access, let alone to have an influence, in the conflict situation, the EU had to wait for an agreement between the governments and the coalescence of the conflict parties themselves. Hume goes so far as to say that, 'had the two governments been quarrelling about it, we wouldn't have got a united European Union approach'.[73] Hume sees this as the major limitation to the EU's role in conflict resolution:

> at the end of the day it is for the different sides of the conflict to reach agreement and the European Union can support them in creating the process for agreement and can support their agreement. But the European Union can't impose an agreement on them.[74]

Even with intergovernmental agreement, the EU's direct impact on political practice in Northern Ireland is delimited by the national structures of the United Kingdom. With regard to the cross-border impact of the EU in Ireland, cross-border initiatives from the EU are enacted differently between the two jurisdictions as a consequence of differing national legislation, regulations and civil service cultures north and south, although the Special EU Programmes Body is working to ensure a more even implementation of EU cross-border initiatives.[75]

---

[73] Interviewee 9.   [74] Interviewee 9.   [75] Interviewee 11 and Interviewee 13.

The lack of independence for the EU in relation to its role in the conflict is inseparable from the nature of the EU as an organisation and its relationship to the core elite actors in the conflict. The impact of the EU on the conflict is mediated in two regards: local political actors inform both (a) the EU's image of the conflict society and (b) the conflict society's image of the EU. Firstly, the official approach of the EU to the conflict is shaped by the opinions submitted to it by core elite actors in the conflict with access to the main EU institutions. John Hume, for example, explicitly acknowledges that his leading position in the largest political grouping in the European Parliament provided him with regular meetings with 'Prime Ministers and European Commissioners'.[76] As Hume enjoyed the attention of colleagues within the EU, so the discourse he was advocating gained a wider European audience.

the European Union conception of the conflict in Northern Ireland is the conception put to it by both governments and by representatives from Northern Ireland.[77]

Thus, even Hume, the most ardent advocate of the EU as the leading model and context for conflict resolution in Ireland, acknowledges that its position as a perturbator regarding the conflict is decided not so much by neutral, transcendent European ideals, but by physical proximity and personal relations between elite actors.[78] An upshot of this process is that local political actors are keen to gain recognition for their own role in relation to even the most direct interventions of the EU.[79]

Local political debate on 'Europe'

The debates that accompanied the 2004 elections to the European Parliament in Northern Ireland epitomise the secondary role conceived for the EU by local political actors, as seen in analytical comparison of the electioneering material of the candidates. The two largest parties cast the

---

[76] Interviewee 9.   [77] Interviewee 9.

[78] This points to the value of a reflexive approach in assessment of the processes of conflict transformation at every level. The creation of a context for meaningful interaction and engagement between key players (in this case Hume and Commission officials) enables the production of policies and strategies that resonate with actors in both the EU and the SDLP.

[79] See, for example, the way in which Ahern portrays the PEACE II programme as the outcome of lobbying by himself and Prime Minister Blair at the European Summit in Berlin, thus taking credit on behalf of the governments for the substantial EU funding (Bertie Ahern, 29 April 1999. Address by An Taoiseach at the Mainstreaming Gender Equality Conference, Co. Cavan).

election as a referendum on the Good Friday Agreement, with Sinn Féin seeking to 'defend the Agreement' and the DUP leader arguing:

This election, of course, is about *more than European issues*. It is also about re-affirming Ulster's determination to replace the failed Belfast Agreement with stable and democratic devolution.[80]

Both unionist parties approached the election as a crucial test for unionism for two reasons. Firstly, in relation to nationalism, the UUP was concerned to retain the third seat and thus allow 'Ulster's ... unionist majority [to be] reflected in Europe'.[81] The DUP's goal was greater, claiming that 'only the DUP stands in [the] way' of Sinn Féin's 'naked ambition to top the poll in this election' and thus end up 'strutting the world stage as the Voice of Ulster'.[82] Secondly, in relation to each other, the UUP candidate 'is dedicated to keeping Unionism at the political centre', whereas the DUP focuses on 'Keeping Unionism Ahead'.[83] Although less explicitly concerned with each other than their unionist counterparts, the election materials of the nationalist parties were even less informative with regard to their EU policy. Fighting under the slogan, 'An Ireland of Equals in a Europe of Equals', Sinn Féin's only exclusively European concern was to 'secure peace funding'.[84] The SDLP emphasised its record of achievement in the EU (e.g. 'fought for' PEACE and Structural Funds), but its only definitively 'European' agenda items were for promoting the Euro, increasing EU support for developing countries and extending PEACE funding.[85] The fact that the extension of PEACE funding was listed as a priority by all four main parties (and constituted the most specific 'European' policy agenda of them all) reflects the primary association of the EU with economic gain.

Limited capacity to effect change

The conditions of EU influence mean that the EU is not so much an independent force for conflict resolution but that its main role is to *build upon and facilitate further change* within the conflict society. Given the nature of the change that has occurred so far in Northern Ireland, what

---

[80] Ian Paisley, DUP leader, in Jim Allister's campaign leaflet, Election to the European Parliament, 10 June 2004, Democratic Unionist Party (emphasis added).

[81] Jim Nicholson, Election to the European Parliament, 10 June 2004, Ulster Unionist Party campaign leaflet.

[82] Allister, campaign leaflet (n. 80).   [83] Nicholson (n. 81) and Allister (n. 80).

[84] Bairbre de Brún, Election to the European Parliament, 10 June 2004, Sinn Féin campaign flyer.

[85] Martin Morgan, Election to the European Parliament, 10 June 2004, Social Democratic and Labour Party campaign flyer.

are the prospects for EU influence in the future? For one thing, it is clear that the EU cannot hope to forge reconciliation between nationalism and unionism, given that (despite claims made by some advocates of the Agreement)[86] the conditions of the Agreement were always unlikely to draw unionists and nationalists closer together. This complies with the European Union's own conception of the conflict as set out in the 1984 Haagerup Report to the European Parliament on the situation in Northern Ireland. Describing the situation as one of two 'conflicting national identities', Haagerup (1984: 7) recognised the limitations of the EU's capacity to effect change in this regard. The report therefore recommends a supportive role for the EU, endorsing the peaceful measures taken by the British government and (it urges) by the British and Irish governments together. In fact, the only unique and independent contribution the EU can make according to Haagerup (1984: 74) is to 'provide the inspiration for the people of Northern Ireland to oppose and reject violence as a political instrument and eventually to accept a formula of tolerance thus resolving their conflict'. Even in the area of economic and social development (the primary operative role of the EU according to Haagerup), the report recognises that improved cross-border trade depends on British–Irish relations and the states' own approach to the EU rather than EU innovation. Thus, the EU acknowledges that economic integration, political cooperation and legal harmonisation do not eradicate borders, not least because their symbolic power becomes even more important for nationalism in the context of Europeanisation (Anderson and Bort 2001).[87] Nevertheless, what the EU can normatively contribute is to defuse the *conflictual potential* of national difference because, it assumes, as common economic needs and political interests are met through cooperation, greater understanding and toleration emerge between the member states. Certainly, it would appear that this model of cooperation, development and understanding has been successfully applied in British–Irish relations and, thereby, to north–south relations in Ireland. However, the matter of whether this effect can 'filter through' to the regional and community level depends on political conditions within Northern Ireland. During the suspension of devolution, and with it the most likely

---

[86] Some welcomed in the 1998 Agreement the creation of 'a unionism compatible with nationalism' (Roy Porter, Contribution to British Irish Association and the Institute for British–Irish Studies conference, 'The Act of Union 200 years on', Dublin, May 2000) and nationalism's 'historic reconciliation with unionism' (Maginniss 2001).

[87] This is at least in part due to the fact that territorially defined identities spring from 'the same source that informed the concept of the nation-state and, ultimately, that of a united Europe' (Kockel 1991: 41).

means by which a growth in moderation within nationalism and unionism can occur, the type of cooperation that the EU could support was
not between unionist and nationalist politicians but at a micro-level,
between community groups and local councils. In this way, through
structures supported and facilitated by the conditions that the EU
determines in accord with its funding, the EU could bypass the political
stalemate and work to counteract worsening polarisation at the local
level.

Conclusions

From enabling to connective

The pathways of influence of the EU in the conflict in Northern Ireland
reflect the different roles of the EU institutions in relation to different
levels of conflict communication. Table 2.2 sets out the findings of this
research, highlighting the EU institution and addressee mainly but not
exclusively involved in aspects of the EU's influence on the resolution of
conflict in Northern Ireland.

The 'compulsory' influence of the EU has not been evident in this case.
This is largely because the EU does not wield effective instruments of
compulsory influence against its existing member states. The 'enabling
influence' of the EU has been crucial for the peace process, particularly
with regard to creating a context that facilitates, legitimates and even
necessitates cooperation across borders for mutual benefit. The 'connective influence' of the EU on the societal level of the conflict has been most
effective in economic terms, given the opportunities for direct impact in
this area. The 'constructive' pathway is most unique and most elusive, yet
if the EU's success in the realm of facilitating cross-border cooperation
could be repeated within Northern Ireland, this pathway holds great
potential for deep and long-term change.

The impact of the EU through these pathways reflects the fact that
the influence of the EU is largely determined at the level of the recip-
ient. It also reflects the nature of the conflict in Northern Ireland itself,
which is multilevel and has required a peace process that works at all
these levels to achieve common interests through political cooperation.
Ultimately, it appears that it is not so much the actors or structures of
the European Union but the actual process of European integration
itself that has served to transform factors that would previously have
contributed to the conflict into bases for cooperation across territorial
borders. The unique example of the EU shows that cooperation needs
to be multilevel, multi-sectoral, self-perpetuating and change-inducing.

Table 2.2: *Overview of EU influence on Northern Ireland*

Pathway	Impact	Main EU institution	Main addressee	Nature of influence	Facilitating conditions
Compulsory	Not evident	–	–	–	–
Enabling	Crucial for peace process	Council of Ministers; European Commission	Governments and officials; regional (N. Ireland) politicians	Legitimised cooperation for practical gain	Political willingness to engage and cooperate
Connective	Increasingly significant	European Commission; European Parliament	Local authorities; community-level actors	Structural Funding; forum for debate	Need for economic development; profile of EU
Constructive	Latent potential	(European Commission)	Border-corridor groups; quangos; NGOs	Support for multilevel networks	Formative channels for communication at sub-regional level

Potential for further transformation within Northern Ireland may rest with the extension of the multilevel networks supported directly through EU funding and legitimised by the EU context. These networks offer a unique opportunity for communication and cooperation across borders and, thereby, for progress to a lasting peace.

3 Catalysis, catachresis: the EU's impact on the Cyprus conflict

Olga Demetriou

> In Europe they don't understand and they want to know if Cypriots understand that Europe is built on reconciliation.
>
> (UN official, interviewed on the eve of the referendum, evaluating reactions in the EU Commission to the prospect of a Greek-Cypriot rejection of the reunification plan prior to the Republic's accession to the EU)

The (hazy) edge of Europe

In considering[1] the impact of the European Union on the Cyprus conflict, it is important to keep in mind that Cyprus has long been a favourite example in International Relations (IR) of an 'intractable conflict'[2] and as such has been viewed as a challenge for the capacity of the United Nations for conflict resolution (Manrod 1974; Richmond 1998; Aall *et al.* 2000: 30; Hannay 2005). This decades-long history of failed attempts at resolution has provided the context, since the 1990s, to argue that a change in the dynamics of the resolution structures could be the answer to breaking the stalemate. The island's entry to the EU could in these terms be considered the most radical change to these dynamics imaginable (save war). Indeed, it is in this capacity that the EU has come to be viewed as a new dimension in discussions of the conflict (Joseph 1997; Brewin 2000;

[1] For comments on earlier drafts of this work, produced as working papers within the EUBorderConf working paper series I would like to thank Stephan Stetter, Michelle Pace, Thomas Diez, Bahar Rumelili and Myria Vassiliadou. For comments on the presentation of this work at the Cyprus case study workshop in Nicosia, I thank Michael Attalides, Costas Costantinou and Ahmet Sözen. I would also like to thank people in Cyprus who made this research possible in many different ways: politicians, activists and informants who accepted to be interviewed, staff at the Milli Eğitim Bakanlığı for making copies of schoolbooks available to me for research, staff at the Parliament of the Republic of Cyprus and especially Ms Androulla Lakes, for helping in my work with archival documents, and a large group of friends in Cyprus who discussed with me the issues explored here, including Themos Demetriou, Tania Demetriou and Murat Erdal.
[2] A small selection of indicative examples spanning the past three decades where this claim is made includes Väyrynen (1985: 195), Rothman (1991: 95) and Crocker *et al.* (2003: 4).

Diez 2002; Christou 2004; Tocci 2005b). More often than not, the EU has been seen in these discussions as the ultimate answer to the solution of the Cyprus problem. In this sense, Cyprus tops the list of cases where the EU's impact has for this long and with such conviction (both for and against) been seen as critical to the prospects of solving the political problem. It is for this reason that its inclusion in a project that seeks to monitor the effects of the EU's processes of accession and association on border conflicts was obvious. But beyond that, Cyprus's inclusion in the specific project as a 'case in transition', with research carried out at a time when the conflict was fundamentally challenged, also lends further significance to the analysis, as it is in precisely this period that the process of accession was concluded and all predictions about the EU's possible impact on the conflict overturned.

This chapter seeks, in the aftermath of accession without conflict resolution, to assess what the EU's impact on the conflict was, at different points in time, what it was thought to be, what it was hoped to have been and what it is still hoped to be in the future. In the aftermath of the failure of the thesis that EU membership would work as a catalyst,[3] it is important to make explicit the historical context in which this analysis is undertaken,[4] which is after the rejection of a UN-proposed reunification plan by the Greek-Cypriot public, and amidst a growing distrust between the leaderships on the two sides of the island following a period of cooperation unprecedented in the past three decades,[5] and a growing normalisation of daily life away from any sense of bicommunal cooperation across the Green Line that divides the northern and southern sides of the island and which after 2004 marks the edge of Europe, albeit in a very hazy fashion. In this context, the chapter seeks to square the view that accession to the EU would help bring about ('catalyse') a final solution to the Cyprus conflict and the view that increasingly seems to be gaining ground, and that is reflected in the quote prefacing the chapter, that the

---

[3] This was the thesis that dominated academic literature and public discourse on the island prior to accession and held that entry to the EU would 'catalyse a solution to the problem'. Further discussion of this thesis follows in later sections.

[4] This is especially important in light of the fact that many political science analyses on Cyprus have been carried out in other historical contexts, without making them explicit, and have as a result appeared irrelevant, outdated or fallacious in the light of following events – this point has been elaborated elsewhere (Demetriou 2004c).

[5] This point is made in reference to the intense negotiations the two sides have been involved in since 2002, and particularly in mind of the set-up of committees that worked on the harmonisation of legislation in place on the two sides of the island in which this negotiation process culminated prior to the final drafting of the solution plan that has come to be known as the Annan Plan. The distrust that ensued makes for good comparison with the case of Israel/Palestine in this volume.

EU's institutional capacity for reconciliation and conflict resolution was in fact ill-used (catachresis-ed) by the Republic to gain accession without compromising on a solution. It is thus the distance (temporal, structural and political) between these catalysis and catachresis views that the present chapter seeks to explore.

It should be noted here that the choice of the word 'catachresis', which could rather simplistically be defined as 'misuse',[6] is not meant to introduce a moralistic slant to the debate where none existed before. Rather, while accepting that the word 'misuse' may have a moralistic connotation, the point here is to use this as a counterpart concept to the one of 'catalysis'. In this sense, one of the key points of the chapter is also to show that the term 'catalysis', which has been a key reference in the literature on Cyprus and the EU, is equally not a value-free concept. It implies, on the contrary, a view of the EU's impact that is generally benign and positive in terms of conflict resolution. What the Cyprus case study highlights instead is that such impact can be both positive and negative, depending on how opportunities are utilised. And in this sense, the point of using the word 'catachresis' or even 'misuse' is to emphasise that irrespective of the intentions of EU actors in using tools such as an accession process, these tools can be used to enable actors to make further securitising rather than desecuritising articulations.

The conflict retold

One of the legacies of the conflict in Cyprus is that it seems to have involved, right from the beginning, a number of actors, many of them international, and alongside whom the EU has been asked to take its place. This involvement has not been confined to only governments and intergovernmental institutions but also involved many analysts, academic and non-academic, whose 'descriptions' of historical events have more often than not also entailed a good deal of political evaluation about the causes and identification of perpetrators. As a result, all claims to 'objective' points of view have become blatantly untenable, if they were ever possible. It is within this context that the present section seeks to retell the history of the conflict, by placing emphasis on the particular concerns of the project and with regard to the particular theoretical framework

---

[6] According to the *Oxford English Dictionary* 'catachresis' denotes the 'improper use of words; application of a term to a thing which it does not properly denote; abuse or perversion of a trope or metaphor', whereas *The New Shorter Oxford English Dictionary* defines 'catachresis' as 'misuse'. I here use both of these definitions ('abuse' and 'misuse') to respectively denote more and less wilful instances of catachresis.

employed. What is important then, is to point out the underlying political conviction that the EU can impact on conflicts in ways that promote their resolution and that where that fails, questions need to be asked about these failures.

The case of Cyprus presents a difficulty in isolating 'conflict episodes', i.e. instances where before escalation into full-fledged violence the two sides were in disagreement about specific issues that might or might not have been solved. Instead, such *conflict episodes*, and indeed, *issue conflicts* as well, became embedded in wider discourses about the conflict, mostly developed following the eruption of intercommunal violence, as ways of rationalising the *identity* and *subordination* conflicts already in place. In this sense, instances of such rationalisation could be seen as a response to attempts by mediators to lower the level of conflict but only within a general environment of pervasive *identity* conflict, by which I mean a situation where the separation into 'self' and 'other' was the chief form of identification. For this reason, I will take identification shifts as the chief referents in the historical overview undertaken here.

In his introduction to a historical analysis of the development of nationalism on the island, Kızılyürek speaks of a time 'in the near past' when the words 'Turk' (*Türk*) and 'Hellene' (*Helen*, presumably referring to the Greek *Èllines* which encompasses the implications of both ancient and modern Greekness) 'were not used' and where villagers instead distinguished each other on the basis of 'Christian and Ottoman/ Muslim' (2002: 11).[7] With the formation of the guerrilla groups EOKA (*Ethnikí Orgánosis Kyprion Agonistón*), which sought the island's unification with 'motherland' Greece (*enosis*), and TMT (*Türk Mukavemet Teşkilatı*), which called for the island's partition in the interests of Turkish-Cypriots (*taksim*), Kızılyürek also recalls policies such as the 'compatriot speak Turkish' campaign of the 1950s that aimed to separate the two identities (2002: 13). However idealising of the conditions of coexistence prior to the eruption of nationalist violence this view might be, the gradual segregation of villages during the first half of the twentieth century, i.e. at the time when nationalist ideology began to take hold, has been recorded since the late 1970s (Attalides 1979), and as Bryant (2004) suggests, the introduction of nationalism through the educational system

---

[7] All translations in this text are mine. Where reference is made to key concepts, however, such as identification terms here, the original words are given in italics. To facilitate reading, terms in Greek have been transliterated into the Latin alphabet, while Turkish ones are left in their original (Latin-script) spelling (e.g. *Helen*). Differentiation between them is maintained by the addition of intonational diacritics for the Greek transliterated terms (e.g. *Èllines*).

at the beginning of the century did not instil hatred about the other as much as disinterest.

The gradual institutionalisation of communal separation marked the turning of the *identity conflict* (focused on the differentiation between self and other) into a *conflict of subordination*, where violence could be legitimised on the basis of a discourse of conflicting interests. These became manifest during the EOKA struggle, at which point the British colonial policy of hiring Turkish-Cypriots as auxiliary policemen brought communal identities to a clashing point and marked, in the discourse of many Greek-Cypriots, the point at which they saw 'the enemy' in the faces of Turkish-Cypriots tasked with policing pro-*enosis* demonstrations (see also Anderson 1993). The objections to the terms of the Constitution to which the Greek-Cypriot leadership had to agree upon the Republic's Independence in 1960 can thus be seen as a sign of the entrenchment of *subordination* as the main characteristic of the conflict. By then, ethnic identification had become a clear sign of differentiation, the Turkish-Cypriot community acquired the status of a 'minority' and the rights enshrined in the Constitution that exceeded its demographic strength became key issues of conflict.[8] Within this precarious governmental structure, conflict characterised the wider political environment: the 1960 Constitution provided the tools not only for the growth of enmity that was now given political expression, but also for 'ethnic un-mixing' through its clauses defining communal identity, prohibiting mixed marriage and separating between 'Greek' and 'Turkish' airtime in national broadcasting, etc. (Republic of Cyprus Constitution: art. 2.7.a; 87.1.a; 87.1.c; 87.1.d; 171.2; 171.3). And it is within this high-level conflictual environment that *issue conflicts* and *conflict episodes* abounded, always overshadowed by the underlying *identity conflict*, and culminating in the rejection of the proposals for constitutional amendments by Turkish-Cypriot parliamentarians (Stavrinides 1976), their vetoing of the annual budget proposals in 1963 and the killing of the first two Turkish-Cypriots on 21 December of the same year, which within the next week had escalated to unprecedented proportions, claiming the lives of around 200 Turkish-Cypriots in a series of atrocities that included murders of hospitalised individuals. This prompted UN intervention, through the

---

[8] According to the 1960 Constitution the Turkish-Cypriot community, counted as 18% of the population, was given a 30% representation in Parliament and 40% in the police and civil service sectors. Attalides makes the sociological point that this political arrangement perceived by Greek-Cypriot nationalists as the embodiment of 'injustice' in fact also perpetuated the (still rather nascent) structures of economic domination, since it left the entrepreneurial sector largely in the hands of Greek-Cypriots (1979).

set-up of the UN Force in Cyprus (UNFICYP), which is, forty years later, still stationed on the island.

Yet while this might be considered as having resulted in the scaling down of the conflict, the parallel set-up of enclaves where the vast majority of Turkish-Cypriots took refuge is perhaps the clearest image of the *subordination conflict* at its peak: the creation of highly guarded areas of autonomy, where people effectively without rights in the rest of the island lived in tents, were conscripted into the TMT fighting corps and waited to go home. It is no coincidence that pictures of these tents, and of hungry mothers breastfeeding in public (Gibbons 1997), are still a key source of Turkish-Cypriot nationalist propaganda imagery. In the years of relative 'calm' between 1964–7 and 1967–74, I would argue that the *subordination conflict* persisted, in as far as the legitimisation of violence persisted, not only as a means of attacking or defending oneself against the attacks of the perceived enemy, but more importantly as a facet of daily life. In other words, violence was experienced not only through the incidents of inter-communal strife, but as a feature of communal life as well, as the reconfiguration of nationalist fighters' units as paramilitary organisations became intertwined with the systems of governance[9] – both Turkish- and Greek-Cypriot ones. The 1974 coup, inspired and directed by the junta regime in Athens in the name of *enosis*, and the intervention of the Turkish military in the name of saving Turkish-Cypriots from slaughter are often seen as the culmination of this situation. Indeed, both of these were, according to many Cypriots, expected possibilities in the 1970s: the two failed coup attempts (1970 and 1971) preceding the one that succeeded in July 1974 were followed by widespread expectations on the part of Greek-Cypriots of Turkish invasions that did not occur. While the events of 1974 have often been seen as the culmination of intercommunal violence, which would suggest viewing them as symptomatic of the failure of local and international attempts to de-escalate the conflict, a review of the negotiation process suggests otherwise. In 1974, the negotiations between the Greek- and Turkish-Cypriot leaderships (conducted between Glafkos Clerides and Rauf Denktash respectively) that sought to end the violence and return to the coexistence framework of 1960, had almost reached a final agreement weeks before the coup took place. On the basis of this the coup should be seen as distinct from the trajectory of the intercommunal conflict, because it was primarily about the conflict *within* the Greek-Cypriot community. I claim this not to suggest that it was unrelated to the attempts to settle the violence through

[9] For an analysis of these links during this period, see Droushiotis (1996; 1998; 2002a; 2002b).

intercommunal negotiations but to emphasise, following from my argument about violence pervading between as well as within the two communities, that unlike the attacks of 1963 and 1967 which were directed against Turkish-Cypriots, the addressees of Greek-Cypriot violence in July 1974 were primarily Greek-Cypriots. Thus, while the negotiations up to that point suggest a relative success of the international community (mainly the UN which was facilitating the talks) in de-escalating the conflict, the coup could be seen as a prime example of the vulnerability of this success to being usurped by radical nationalist forces.

Up to this stage the EEC avoided involvement in the conflict, in spite of the fact that the Republic of Cyprus concluded an Association Agreement with it in 1972 – an agreement that entered into force on 1 July 1973.[10] By this time, the intercommunal conflict was already showing signs of intractability. The reason for this avoidance was that the agreement dealt almost exclusively with issues of trade and was complemented by a protocol providing the framework for EU–Cyprus relations, which was concluded only in 1987 (Gaudissart 1996: 11–12). The Customs Union was also agreed long before the stalemate of negotiations became plainly obvious (the relevant agreement was due for completion in 1977, but was extended first to 1987 and with the commencement of accession negotiations became part of the accession process). But by the time the Republic applied for EEC membership in 1990 the impasse-ridden status quo had become part of daily political rhetoric, and the argument that this new affiliation would 'act as a catalyst' to break the deadlock was gaining ground. In the same year the office of the European Delegation in Nicosia was opened and one year later a Joint Parliamentary Committee of European Parliamentarians (MEPs) and Cypriot Parliamentarians was formed and continued to meet twice a year up to accession.

At that point, the counter-argument for accession was voiced by the Turkish-Cypriot leadership, by now firmly grounded at the head of a government structure in the northern side of the island, that the Greek-Cypriot leadership claims were 'illegal', while the international community refused to recognise the state of the Turkish Republic of Northern Cyprus (TRNC), which it has, since 1983, proclaimed itself to be. The argument of this leadership rested on the 'illegality' of concluding such a union because it overwrote the Cypriot Constitution of 1960, which requires both communities on the island to agree before the state can join any other state. Should such a union be concluded, the argument

---

[10] Interestingly, this was the same time as Britain was preparing for its own membership (Ayres 1996: 39).

went, a 'solution' would be finalised in the form of a parallel union of the TRNC with Turkey.

To this, the Republic of Cyprus counter-argued that since the (now) EU is not a state there is no issue of contravening the 1960 Constitution. Thus, discussions regarding Cyprus's suitability for membership began in 1993, after the Commission decided to accept the Republic's application as one made on behalf of the island. The suitability for membership was decided in 1995 and negotiations began in 1998. They were concluded in December 2002 and the Accession Treaty was signed in April 2003. The accession of Cyprus to the EU took place on 1 May 2004 in what was hailed as the biggest round of enlargement to date, which included another nine countries.

In this context the particularity of the case of Cyprus lay in the fact that EU accession brought with it significant developments in the politics of the conflict. These developments culminated in the referenda that took place simultaneously on 24 April 2004 in both the north and the south parts of the island and sought the people's approval of the implementation of a UN-proposed plan (known as the 'Annan Plan') to end the division of the island and bring on a solution to the Cyprus conflict. Even though 65 per cent of the population in the north of the island approved the plan, 76 per cent of the population in the south rejected it, and thus it was not implemented.[11]

The relation of Cyprus's EU membership to this culmination of efforts to reunite the island was explicitly stated at various points in time. The timing of the referenda, which took place one week before the accession date, was explicitly decided on the presumption that had the reunification plan been supported by majorities on both sides, Cyprus would enter the EU as a united country. In this sense, the referenda could be seen as the result of concerted efforts on the parts of the UN, which brokered the agreement; the EU, which repeatedly made the point that it would prefer a united Cyprus joining in 2004; the Cypriot leaderships who subscribed to the arguments for reunification before accession (i.e. the Greek-Cypriot leadership in government during the period 1998–2003 and the Turkish-Cypriot leadership that took office in December 2003); and the governments of Greece, Turkey and the UK, which similarly supported this view of a 'European solution to the problem'.

In this sense, the period of the most intense EU involvement in the conflict (2002–4) is also the period that most closely adheres to the catalysis thesis. In this period, intense negotiations took place between

---

[11] Further details about the events in Cyprus around the period of the referenda and a commentary on the results can be found in Demetriou (2004a).

the communal leaderships, where 'the conflict' as a general umbrella term was broken down into its constituent *issue conflicts*, the Green Line that separated the two communities since 1974 became permeable to people who wanted to see 'the other', in terms of both people and places, bringing about a softening of the *identity conflict*, and the final solution plan was drafted, offering Cypriots a clear vision of what an 'end to the conflict' might look like. However, the failure to achieve reunification before accession is the fact that most obviously puts this catalysis theory into question. It is for this reason that I now turn to the presentations of the catalysis thesis prior to 2004.

Analysis, catalysis: the ups and downs of theorising EU impact

Ever since membership of Cyprus in the EC/EU began to be discussed in the political sphere, academic interest has been high. The argument that joining the EU would help bring about a solution to the political problem has been the main focus of this interest since the 1990s. Even if not all analyses agreed on their assessment of what kind of solution accession would catalyse, the catalysis thesis seems to have provided the sole focal point. Many of these analyses reflect the trends to which analyses of the conflict in general have been subject (Demetriou 2004c), with the chief concern being not whether, but what the EU would catalyse, i.e. unification or partition. It is thus extremely pertinent to look at this literature in some depth, primarily because it reflects the argumentation projected by the political elites of the two conflicting communities.

In this sense, it is interesting to note that the legalistic arguments, i.e. that membership would help safeguard international law (which upheld to a great extent Greek-Cypriot positions), were, from early on, a crucial part of these analyses. Papaneophytou, for instance, argued that the European Court of Justice's decision to prohibit imports from the northern part of the island was an indicator of what a future of EU membership might hold for Cyprus (Papaneophytou 1994: 90). While the theories supporting the Greek-Cypriot stand presented membership as a panacea to the various deadlocked components of the problem, the theories supporting the Turkish-Cypriot political stance warned of the dangers of accession – in terms of the act being illegal and the possibilities that it would catalyse the TRNC's union with Turkey (see for example Ertekün 1997; Mendelson 2001).

This hauling of the discourse into the *identity conflict* is not surprising: the catalysis thesis was, throughout its life, primarily championed by the Greek and Greek-Cypriot leaderships. Despite the fact that discussions of this 'catalytic effect' predated its official formulation as such, it is Yiannos Kranidiotis, Deputy Minister, until his death in 1999, of the Ministry of Foreign Affairs in Greece, who is credited with having set down the policy that guided Cyprus's accession process along the path of the 'catalysis' discourse. In a letter lobbying the EU's Ministers of Foreign Affairs in 1994, to support the EU's start of accession negotiations with Cyprus, he stated that:

[T]he examination of Cyprus' request for accession offers the EU its only opportunity to help the Secretary General of the UN in his efforts to find a solution through negotiations ... [to this effect] a clear and unequivocal message stating to all concerned that the EU is willing to begin accession negotiations with Cyprus on a specific date, could change the negative attitude of the Turkish side and act as an important pressure lever for a solution to be found and an end to 20 years of disappointment to ensue. (Kranidiotis 1999: 209–10)

The pointing of the finger of blame on the Turkish side may not have been biased at the time – yet it does show that the EU's role as a 'catalyst' was from the beginning made the prerogative of the Greek side in a discourse that perpetuated the *identity conflict*. In these terms, the EU, supporting the Greek-Cypriots, would act to put pressure on the Turkish and the Turkish-Cypriot leaderships (with Greece's role as advocate of the Republic within the EU quite clearly stated). In short then, the discourse of catalysis was inherently a biased one.[12] And it is in this sense that it can be said to have prompted the nationalist reactions from the Turkish side that focused – not only in terms of official political rhetoric but in more academic terms as well – on the 'impartiality' of EU involvement (Gazioğlu 1998; Moran 1999).[13]

The political focus of the argumentation is reflected in the comments that 'the economic argument is not the core element in the decision by the government of Cyprus to seek full membership of the EU. The motivation is mainly political, that is, it relates to the Cyprus problem' (Ayres 1996: 57). However, the translation of this argumentation in political and social science literature also entailed taking more critical views on the catalytic effect. Peristianis thus pointed out that although Greek-Cypriots 'seem to be some of the strongest supporters of joining the European Union ... they have pinned high hopes on joining the Union as a means of resolving

---

[12] Jakobsson-Hatay (2004) makes a similar point for the EU's approach to the Republic's accession process. While I would agree with her that presenting the EU as a 'catalyst' may have indeed complicated the EU's position of partiality, I would argue for the importance of maintaining a distinction between the partiality of *the discourse of catalysis* and that of *EU involvement* in Cyprus.

[13] See www.washington-report.org/backissues/0999/9909058.html.

the political problem ... [and] seem to believe that the resolution of the Cyprus problem will somehow be a magical outcome of accession into the European Union' (1998: 40). He further argued for a pathway of catalysis that passes through 'the enhancement of [mutual understanding and tolerance], which will be one of the greater benefits that will accrue to Cyprus, as a result of European Union accession' (1998: 40). For Mavratsas, the crucial element for catalysis to be effective is the modernisation of state institutions while he argues that Cyprus has a ' "European deficit" ... directly related to the weakness of civil society and the dominance of nationalist ideology' (1998: 73). On this basis, he also criticises the nationalist undertones of the Greek-Cypriot discourse of catalysis:

The situation would be entirely different if the Greek-Cypriot emphasis upon the earliest possible entry into the EU, independently of the solution of the Cyprus problem, was not motivated by nationalist axioms; and, perhaps more importantly, if the stress on Europe coexisted with a sincere and systematic attempt at building bridges of communication with the Turkish-Cypriots. The latter is absolutely essential if a viable settlement on Cyprus is ever to be achieved – and if Cyprus is to embark on a substantial process of modernization and Europeanization. (1998: 73–4)

The polarisation between the Greek side and the Turkish side that the catalysis thesis fostered was soon apparent and thus three years after sending the letter cited above, Kranidiotis was addressing an audience in Greece that included Turkish-Cypriot opposition politicians and grappling with the counter-catalytic arguments of the Turkish-Cypriot leadership head-on:

The prospect of accession is not a side road to perpetuating Greek-Cypriot domination, as the Denktash regime has often argued. On the contrary, it continues to constitute the only reliable and secure (in the interests of both communities) proposition and process that can act catalytically to finding a just and viable solution to the political problem. (Kranidiotis 1999: 250)

A turning point in the discussion were the decisions of the Helsinki European Council meeting in 1999, where it was stressed that:
  (i) the Union preferred a solution to be reached before accession and that at the time of accession Cyprus be a united country, but
  (ii) as long as the failure to reach such a solution did not fall on to the shoulders of the Greek-Cypriot side, Cyprus could accede before a solution and that
  (iii) at the same time, Turkey's membership was going to be considered. (European Council 1999: § 9.a and 9.b)

These decisions provided a perfect illustration of the catalysis thesis, spurring a new flurry of academic writing on the matter. However, the taking of sides in academia continued into the next decade and the lines between politics and analysis again became blurred in a different fashion. Chrysostomides's *Study in International Law* (2000) is in part concerned with combating illegality claims regarding Cyprus's application. Such vociferously 'officialised' political stands are presented in Ertekün (1997) and Mendelson in his capacity as QC (2001), who argue explicitly about the merits and justifiability of the view taken by the Turkish-Cypriot leadership at the time. In view of this stand, Chrysostomides's work almost equally explicitly presents the official Greek-Cypriot view on how beneficial EU membership would be for the eventual solution of the conflict. More tellingly, his publication in Greek on the matter (*In Defence of Tomorrow's Policy*), proclaimed in its title his aim to support Greek-Cypriot policies, not only as manifested at the time, but also in the nationalist turn they underwent after the rise to power of the Papadopoulos government whose spokesman he later became (Chrysostomides 2001).

The more critical analyses at this time turned to the opportunities that should be taken up if the accession process was to be catalytic, lending the thesis a good-use condition. Thus, Richmond noted that 'the EU does represent an excellent opportunity for a consensual solution to be found quickly … The EU is not a panacea' (2001a: 128). A diversification of the possibilities of good use soon became evident: in feminist writings possibilities of action against current power structures were foreseen as a consequence of accession (Agathangelou and Ling 1997; Cockburn 2004; Agathangelou 2005) while misuse of accession by paternalistic power structures already in place was warned against (Vassiliadou 2002). In terms of rapprochement, possibilities for use and abuse were also pointed out (Diez 2000). Yet, the conditionality of EU impact became much clearer as the process of accession reached its completion.

Solution and EU unbound

Although the EU's impact on the conflict seems to have gone through different phases of assessment in tandem with developments in the process of accession, there is one critical point (the referenda of 2004) that puts into question the entire frame of this thesis. In order to explain how membership would catalyse the solution of the Cyprus problem, in line with pre-accession rhetoric, the failure of reaching a solution prior to accession must be taken into account. In turn this also means explaining the change in the Greek-Cypriot stance with respect to the accession-solution rhetoric and the wider context of the nexus between EU norms and EU politics. What I will do below is outline the apparent effects of the EU's involvement in the conflict over the past decade, and up to the point of accession. On this basis I will argue that the process of accession and its relation to the eventual solution are best assessed on the basis of the use made by the leaderships of the two communities of the opportunities for solution that it offered, rather than on the basis of it being catalytic in itself.

Compulsory pathway

Perhaps the first example that springs to mind in speaking about the EU and its impact on Cyprus are the effects of the various decisions taken by the European Council during its most high-profile meetings on year-end. For Cyprus, such highpoints have been the 1997 Luxembourg meeting, the 1999 Helsinki meeting and the 2002 Copenhagen meeting.[14] The first was as important for launching Cyprus's accession process as for leaving Turkey out of the next enlargement round (European Commission 1997a: § 865) and was perceived as a blow to Turkish–EU relations and a victory for the Greek-Cypriot side (Christou 2004: 78–9). This perception might be one reason why the invitation of the Greek-Cypriot President to Turkish-Cypriots to attend the accession negotiations was rejected by the Turkish-Cypriot side in the following year – indeed, in that year, the Denktash regime banned all bicommunal activities on the island through refusing to allow crossings across the Green Line (Bertrand 2004), which had been taking place irregularly since 1989 (Chigas and Ganson 1997: 62). As a 'stick' to combat Turkish intransigence then, this set of decisions had a clear, adverse effect on the conflict's resolution – arguably, because the Turkish side refused to accept the 'stick' as an instrument of discipline.

In contrast, the threefold decisions of the Helsinki meeting outlined above had a clear and long-lasting positive effect in this direction and have marked an important turning point in the minds of politicians, which was reflected in interviews conducted for the present analysis (Markides 2002).[15] For the next four years, and until the final signing of the Accession Treaty in 2003, the two sides were engaged in intense

---

[14] What follows is a summary of the impact of the EU on the Cyprus conflict in terms of the pathways proposed in the project's theoretical framework. A more detailed analysis can be found in working paper no. 9 of the EUBorderConf working paper series (Demetriou 2004d).

[15] Interview, Ministry of Interior, Republic of Cyprus, Nicosia, September 2003; interview, Press and Information Office, Republic of Cyprus, Nicosia, December 2003; interview, 'Solution and EU Party' (ÇABP), northern Cyprus, Nicosia, January 2004; interview, Republic of Cyprus EU negotiation team pre-2004, Nicosia, April 2004; interview, 'Democratic Rally' (DISY) party, Nicosia, September 2004.

negotiations for a final settlement, producing the most comprehensive settlement plan brokered by the UN since the start of negotiations in the 1960s.

By comparison, the effects of the Copenhagen meeting could be classified as more indirect, in the sense that they produced a series of 'carrots' for the Cypriot communities: the Council's 'strong preference for accession to the European Union by a united Cyprus' and willingness to accommodate the terms of a settlement in the Treaty of Accession (European Council 2002: § I.4.10; § I.4.11) were confirmed and an invitation extended to the Commission 'to consider ways of promoting economic development of the northern part of Cyprus and bringing it closer to the Union' (European Council 2002: § I.4.12). That the meeting spurred huge pro-solution opposition demonstrations in northern Cyprus is an indication of their effectiveness (see below), especially in light of the subsequent breakdown of negotiations in the Hague in February 2003, when the Turkish-Cypriot leader walked out and was accused of intransigence.

Another series of 'compulsory pathway' effects can be seen in the implementation of decisions by other EU bodies following the failure to meet the deadline of April 2003 for reaching a solution that would guarantee a unified Cyprus entry to the EU. These were the adoption of Protocol 10 to the Act of Accession signed in April 2003, which stated, to the satisfaction of the Greek-Cypriot positions, that although Cyprus would join the EU as a whole, the adoption of the *acquis communautaire* would be suspended in those areas of the island outside the control of the authorities of the Republic (i.e. the north). It is at this time that an alternative rhetoric about a 'European solution to the problem' – which argued that Cyprus's prospects of solving the conflict would be better after its accession because the Greek-Cypriot side would have more bargaining power once in the EU as representative of the whole island – began to gain ground (Cleanthous 2002). In this sense, it could be argued that the dangers of misusing the EU's mechanisms of impact started to become evident. However, this was yet to become an issue, since the immediately apparent effect of signing the Treaty (incorporating Protocol 10) was the opening of the Green Line to crossers from north and south, which had for the previous thirty years marked the line of non-communication.

It was only in the final phase of negotiations that the disadvantages of the EU's previous 'carrot and stick' policies were made obvious. The Greek-Cypriot side, led since February 2003 by the intransigent Tassos Papadopoulos, entered negotiations from a position where the threat of 'sticks' from the part of the EU had been removed, accession was certain and the 'carrots' to be had were offered to the Turkish-Cypriot side. With the application of nationalist rhetoric in the presentation of the proposed solution to the Greek-Cypriot population, a public rejection of the solution was fostered and the Annan Plan was rejected at the Greek-Cypriot referendum of 24 April 2004. In this sense, the referendum showed the failings of the *compulsory* approach when incentives and disincentives are not available for use at all stages of the conflict resolution process (Demetriou 2004b), opening up the possibilities of the abuse of instruments that might originally have been developed to promote reconciliation.

The Green Line Regulation, adopted prior to Cyprus's accession and following the referendum failure, can be considered as another such instrument: while introducing the rather radical policy (from a Greek-Cypriot perspective) that non-Cypriot visa nationals could now legitimately enter the north 'from illegal ports' and cross to the south, its stipulations regarding trade raised Turkish-Cypriot expectations about its implementation and the prospects of achieving a level of trade activity quickly and in a way that would allow economic effects to be felt on a large scale. In the interviews collected from Turkish-Cypriot politicians there was agreement that the package of measures that the EU had proposed after the opening of the Green Line for supporting Turkish-Cypriots economically was unsatisfactory and had not been implemented in any way because of what they perceived as unwillingness by the Greek-Cypriots to actively promote such activities.[16] Additional amendments have been made to the Regulation since, but any substantial effects on trade were yet to be observed by October 2007. This casts such unwillingness as an example of a failure, at best, to effectively use the opportunities offered by this EU instrument to effect positive changes with regards to the conflict.

Enabling pathway

The abuse/misuse of EU-provided instruments for conflict resolution can be seen even more clearly under the lens of the *enabling impact* because it is from this viewpoint that the opportunities for policy change can best be examined and thus also the failure to take them up. For example, the Copenhagen Council meeting can be seen in just this light because even though it did not specifically aim at that, it provided the context that, had an agreement been reached in the discussions that took place between the

---

[16] Interview, 'New Cyprus Party' (YKP), northern Cyprus, Nicosia, December 2003; interview, ÇABP, northern Cyprus, Nicosia, January 2004; interview, 'Peace and Democracy Movement' (BDH), northern Cyprus, Nicosia, January 2004.

Greek, Greek-Cypriot and Turkish leaders present, could be used to legitimise whatever concessions each side would have been asked to make internally. The fact that at the end of the meeting both the Republic of Cyprus and Turkey came away with 'points' on their side could be used by both of them to explain such possible concessions for a solution. In turn, this context, and the possibilities of reaching an agreement made obvious through the local media focus on the three-way discussions on Cyprus, also prompted the Turkish-Cypriot opposition forces to arrange some of the most well-attended demonstrations against the regime and in favour of a solution to the problem and EU accession of the north. The meeting thus enabled the organisation of civil society activities that were later to prove of immense importance to the overturning of the political status quo in the northern part of the island, providing a unique example of 'good use' of EU policy instruments.

In contrast, the presence of EU officials in the negotiation process that led to the referenda of April 2004 could be seen as exemplary of the EU's willingness to use instruments at its disposal to enable positive change in a situation where these were not taken up by the Greek-Cypriot side. Although this presence had been an issue of considerable discussion between the negotiating sides, primarily because of the lack of trust towards the EU by the old Turkish-Cypriot leadership, the Greek-Cypriot side managed to have its demands for this presence met. The EU Commissioner for Enlargement attended the final days of the negotiation process, stating his hope that his presence would contribute to the reaching of an agreement. In parallel, European Parliament statements issued before the referenda urged the Turkish- and Greek-Cypriot peoples to vote in favour of the plan, stressing that the Union would accommodate the derogations from the *acquis communautaire* necessary to implement the final agreement.

Yet, the Greek-Cypriot side chose not to employ these statements in a campaign in favour of a positive referendum vote – instead, it used them in its rhetoric against the plan as proof that this was an imperialist plot that 'foreign powers', which now came to encompass the EU (formerly referred to as the 'large European family' welcoming Cyprus in its bosom), wanted to impose on Cypriots (read Greek-), despite the latter's better judgement. In contrast, in the campaign that followed (in which it was reported that the government employed various means of repressing the voicing of arguments in favour of the plan), EU instruments did provide mechanisms that enabled the pro-unification opposition in the south to expose the incompatibility of the lack of transparency that enveloped the government-led rejection campaign with EU norms and values: the main Greek-Cypriot opposition leader wrote to the President of the European Parliament complaining about the conduct of the government of the Republic with regard to freedom of speech and information during the pre-referendum period,[17] and received a reply indicating that the Parliament would initiate proceedings with a view to relevant sanctions against the Republic for not respecting 'the principles upon which the EU is founded'.[18] This however also allowed the government to build on the anti-imperialist argument, to depict the opposition as 'traitors', and to finally prompt the initiator of the complaint to withdraw his statements and the investigation proceedings to halt.

In these terms, it can also be argued that the Green Line Regulation was misused, in the sense that instead of forming the basis upon which the government of the Republic could campaign for the promotion of trade between the two sides, thus increasing economic ties and cultivating the trust of Turkish-Cypriot traders towards Greek-Cypriot politicians in the aftermath of the referendum, it was implemented by Greek-Cypriot authorities only half-heartedly.[19]

Connective pathway

At the same time this 'misuse' also affected the possibilities of strengthening the intercommunal connection offered by the Regulation as an instrument of the 'connective pathway' of impact. On the one hand, by delegating responsibility for goods certification in the north to the Turkish-Cypriot Chamber of Commerce, which also helped organise the pro-solution demonstrations in 2002, the Regulation 'officialised' channels of connection between the north and the EU. On the other hand, however, the failure of the Greek-Cypriot authorities to utilise this as a way of overcoming the stunting rhetoric of 'recognition' (of any official and non-official institutions based in the north) also limited the possibilities of further concerted EU attempts at maximising this connective impact.

This connective role has been somewhat more successful in areas not under direct influence of the authorities, such as the funding of independent bodies. Specific to Cyprus in this respect has been an emphasis on bicommunal projects (under the Civil Society Programme[20]), aiming to foster connections between civil society groups in the frame set up by USAID, UNDP and Fulbright. Other EU-funded programmes (LIFE,

---

[17] Nicos Anastassiades to Pat Cox, 21 April 2004, Nicosia: DISY.

[18] Pat Cox to Nicos Anastassiades, 22 April 2004, Brussels: European Parliament.

[19] Interview, ÇABP, northern Cyprus, Nicosia, January 2004; interview, BDH, northern Cyprus, Nicosia, January 2004.

[20] Such projects included research on topics as diverse as women in different Cypriot communities and the coastal environment.

LEONARDO DA VINCI, SOCRATES, Sixth Framework Programme) have had a more indirect impact on such connections by calling for Turkish-Cypriot participation, sometimes more explicitly than others. Similar calls for participation of applicants from both sides of the island have also been made in the case of EU-related job opportunities in Brussels and Cyprus. Yet Turkish-Cypriot politicians have claimed that the failure of the EU to make Turkish, which is one of the two official languages of the Republic of Cyprus, an official language of the EU has hampered the access of young Turkish-Cypriots to the EU-related job market and have blamed previous Greek-Cypriot governments for over-looking this issue during the negotiation process[21] – yet another example of failure to use the negotiations to ensure maximum connective and constructive effects. Responding to these criticisms, some of the Brussels-based jobs recently advertised have required that Turkish-Cypriot applicants exhibit fluency in one language less than would otherwise be the case. Through these efforts, the EU seems to be successfully following a *connective* path in its intervention in the conflict by actively providing solutions to problems that might otherwise be treated as legalistic puzzles (in the Greek-Cypriot side's pursuit of preventing recognition of the north as a state at all costs) and left unsolved to exemplify the Republic's government's 'benign neglect', as Herzfeld (1992: 12) terms such policies, towards Turkish-Cypriots.

In terms of funding, the greatest impact of the EU in the north at the time of writing is expected to come with the aid of €259 million, which have been pledged by the Union to help in the development of the north in the event of a solution. After the rejection of the solution plan by the Greek-Cypriot side, the European Commission decided to make these funds available to the north anyway, something to which the government in the south not only agreed, but which it also encouraged, according to its official statements. However, there then was the problem of how these funds were to reach the north, and whether their release to the Turkish-Cypriot side would be linked to an agreement allowing direct trade between the north and the EU or not. In October 2006 the first instalment of the aid was finally approved and will undoubtedly make a positive contribution to the improvement of the infrastructure and economy of the north and thus encourage the support of further EU initiatives and hopefully the continuing support for resolution of the conflict, but the debate over the distribution of the funds seems to suggest that this

---

[21] Interview, ÇABP, northern Cyprus, Nicosia, January 2004; interview, BDH, northern Cyprus, Nicosia, January 2004; interview, Turkish-Cypriot activist, Nicosia, September 2004.

connective pathway of impact, if misused, can also potentially create further friction between the conflict parties.

Constructive pathway

Finally, if the demonstrations of the Turkish-Cypriot opposition forces of 2002 and 2003 are considered an effect of the EU's involvement in Cyprus and if the changes they rendered possible in the political sphere are seen as a direct effect of the demonstrations, then what one is looking at is a prime example of *constructive* impact, even if this is largely realised on the level on which the 'EU' becomes a conceptual construct rather than a concrete actor in the form of one or more of its institutions and structures. The demonstrations, through asking for a solution and oppos-ing Denktash, established a connection between Turkish- and Greek-Cypriots who supported the same causes, even without being able to have contact with each other, and thus fostered a change of identification of the civil society of the conflicting parties from an ethnic (Greek/Turkish) to a political one (pro-solution and rejectionists). With the major policy shifts effected after the coming into power of these opposition forces, this impact was made further use of most impressively in the fast and well-executed revision of the history books used in Turkish-Cypriot high schools. The aim of this revision was quite explicitly the shift from an insulated and nationalist policy of fomenting the identities of future Turkish-Cypriot citizens to a policy aiming at preparing them for a Cyprus that would be much more open to the world, and marked locally by multiculturalism (see below).

By comparison, on the Greek-Cypriot side, a series of reluctant steps towards enabling constructive effects can be seen to take place in the spheres of education (Demetriou 2005) and civil society building (e.g. in the issue that arose when the President made statements to the effect that UNOPS- and USAID-funded projects aimed at undermining the polit-ical leadership). Yet at the same time, the fruition of such bicommunal activities has helped the debate around small and large political issues that centre on this 'change of scripts' from ethnic identification to political positioning in reference to the eventual solution. These debates were enabled not only through media discussions around the concepts of 'European values' and the role of Cyprus in the enlarged Europe, but also through public debates, academic and political, organised by rela-tively small but burgeoning civil society groups that used these focal points to raise and discuss political issues of local significance. As an example of the use made of the *constructive* pathway of involvement then, this could be said to be one where concepts related to 'EU',

'Europe' and Cyprus's new role as a member were used to propel the public debate about the various ways of impacting on the conflict, at the EU as well as the local level – despite governmental attempts to shift this discourse on 'European norms and values' back to the legalistic rhetoric that reigned through the earlier deadlocked phases of the conflict.

Conditions on 'use'

The impact of the EU on the conflict was made evident in a series of what could be classified as turning points in the three years preceding the island's accession: the 2002 demonstrations in the north; the finalisation of the solution plan; the referenda; and the accession itself. While the successes and failures of EU policies to affect a resolution of the conflict during these crucial periods have been discussed above, in this section I will be focusing on the causes of these variable outcomes through the lens of 'usage'. My main contention has been that any positive or negative outcomes ensuing from the EU's involvement in the conflict, whether direct or indirect, foreseen or unexpected, explicitly pursued or not, depended primarily on the ways in which this involvement was utilised by political actors on the island to augment or diminish possible positive effects. I further argue that this conditionality of 'use' was in turn intertwined with perceptions of the EU by local actors, and the consumption of EU (Brussels-generated) policy and rhetoric within local political structures.

In this sense, the various meanings attached to 'European norms and values', referred to in previous sections, exemplify the impact of 'use' on the determination of the effects of EU policies with respect to the conflict. As mentioned above, the problem of aiding development of the north in the aftermath of the accession of a divided Cyprus was a leading issue in discussions on the island and in Brussels throughout 2004 and 2005. Yet whereas EU diplomats may have seen 'reconciliation' as the fundamental 'European value', which Greek-Cypriots seem not to have embraced when rejecting the Annan Plan, the Greek-Cypriot governmental rhetoric placed emphasis on 'international law' and the guarantees it supplies against anything that could be construed as recognition of the TRNC as the first 'European norm' that must be respected. As a result, the €259 million the EU pledged for development of the north were held up in Brussels because of disputes between the government of the Republic and officials in the north and in the EU as to whether the funds should be channelled directly to the north (thus fostering Turkish-Cypriot trust in the EU and counteracting the disinterest in reconciliation with the Greek-Cypriot side that began to rise after the failure of the referendum, yet a move that would be seen by the Republic as tanta-mount to recognising the TRNC) or via the Republic's government in the south, as well as whether their disbursement would be linked to the lifting of trade restrictions between the north and the EU or not.

This difference in the interpretation of 'European norms and values' rests, I argue, not merely on a difference in perceptions between Cyprus and the relevant EU institutions (primarily the Commission) but on a shift in the interpretation of a 'European solution to the Cyprus problem' that the Republic's government has been advocating since the lodging of its membership application. The argumentation on how this solution would be achievable was initially based on the premise that the negotia-tion stalemate was the result of the intransigence of the Turkish side (see Kranidiotis's argument above), and that, once this impediment was removed, the accession process would be catalytic to the island's reuni-fication before accession. However, following the breaking of this intransigence under the pressure of the Turkish-Cypriot opposition, the Greek-Cypriot leadership that took power in 2003 argued that a European solution to the problem meant a solution that respected 'European norms and values' in full (that is, for the benefit of the Greek-Cypriot side), and that this could only be achieved after Cyprus had become a member.

This line of argument is well represented in a statement issued by the '1955–59 Fighters' Association'[22] on the occasion of the fiftieth anniver-sary since the beginning of their EOKA struggle. In it, they describe the Annan Plan as offering 'enslavement' and as contradicting 'the values of the UN and the European *acquis*' because it does not provide for the complete withdrawal of Turkish troops, the cancellation of Turkey's right of intervention and the removal of all 'settlers' (immigrants from Turkey in the north) from the island (*Politis* newspaper, 31 March 2005: 7). In this statement, 'European values' are represented by the *acquis commu-nautaire*, and presumably freedoms like those of movement and settle-ment that would guarantee the return of all Greek-Cypriot refugees to the north. Yet the Commission's statements that the EU would accommo-date derogations necessary to achieve a solution agreement as well as the principle of reconciliation on which the allowance of such derogations is based, are obviously not included in this definition of 'European values'. This view would also preclude EU legislation, declarations, resolutions and further instruments of the *acquis* that might, in application, also contradict other *acquis* instruments more in line with Greek-Cypriot

---

[22] The importance of this Association is that many of its members have held key govern-mental posts in successive governments since 1960.

positions. In this sense, the Green Line Regulation could be cited as a case in point, since the legitimisation of EU citizens arriving in Cyprus from the north was accepted by the government of the Republic, yet viewed with resentment by nationalist circles, within both the government and Greek-Cypriot civil society, because of its implications regarding recognition of airports in the north (no matter how tenuous the link). The resolution of such contradictions in turn requires a view of the EU as both ally and enemy, and thus a view of Cyprus as both within and outside the EU. It is exactly this ambivalent status that the shift in rhetoric before and after the referenda conferred on Cyprus: whereas in the years preceding accession the island's accession was celebrated by both government and opposition unequivocally as 'our incorporation into the large European family' [*i éndaxí mas sti megháli Evropaikí Ikoghénia*], following the Commission's and Parliament's backing of the Annan Plan, an adversarial rhetoric began to surface that separated 'the Europeans' who sought to impose imperialist plans, and the people of Cyprus, upon whom this imposition was sought. Over the months following the referendum (and Cyprus's accession) more distancing references to 'our European partners' [*i Evropéi edéri mas*] were in frequent use and noticeably more so than references to the 'large European family'.

Such negative views of the EU had in fact been articulated long before 2004, within a debate about the accession's possible negative effects on the conflict, which climaxed around the Helsinki and Copenhagen Summits. Most vociferously put forth by advocates of the Communist Party in Greece, this position presented the island's entry to the EU, in general, but especially in the form of its *de facto* division, as catalytic not of reunification but of partition, because it would be seen as an invitation to the EU to recognise the division. This 'Euro-partition argument' (that EU membership would solidify the partition rather than solve the conflict) was articulated by the far right as well as the far left, especially in Greece.[23]

While the exponents of this argument in Cyprus were never very vocal, they did propound similarly chauvinist positions (see references to historic

[23] See for example www.metromag.gr/issues/200302/article5.html, or the speech made on 26 February 1998 by the Secretary General of the Greek Communist Party criticising her government's policy ahead of the Helsinki meeting at www.kke.gr/politdrast/drasthr/ ell_tour_pap/el_tour_1.html, and on 27 March 2004 before the referendum at www.in.gr/news/article.asp?lngEntityID=526705. At http://anatolikos.com/politika/ ee2812.htm a journalist comments in the same vein on the outcomes of the Copenhagen Summit on 22 December 2002. An example of the response argument of the Greek-Cypriot government can be found at www.ekloges.com.cy/nqcontent.cfm? tt=article& a_id=10239, where Cyprus's accession to the EU in its divided form is presented as having prevented such a Euro-partition.

national triumphs that current governments fail to match and the view of Europeans as ruthless policy-makers who should be, but were not, stripped naked and ridiculed for their hypocritical anti-Hellenic projects), resulting in the similarly nationalist counter-arguments presented above that saw in the accession a guarantee that in the event of a solution, Greek-Cypriot demands, having by way of membership transformed themselves into EU demands, would be met. Thus, while this line of argument was initially submerged under a discourse that prioritised the breaking of Turkish intransigence and focused on concrete efforts to arrive at a solution through the renewed negotiation impetus, it later gave rise to an alternative discourse on the use that could be made of EU institutions to further Greek-Cypriot interests. And it is this discourse that guided governmental policy after the Greek-Cypriot elections of 2003.

It is thus precisely the mechanisms that made this shift possible that evidence the failure to realise the opportunities for solution offered by the EU's impact on the conflict. In other words, it is in the operationalisation of this shift that the failure to utilise such impact is to be found. Thus, the changing perceptions of the EU show the conditions upon which the pathways of impact operate. These are essentially 'conditions of use', pertaining to both direct and indirect impact, in the directions of both the political leadership and civil society. In these terms, the discursive shifts outlined above point to the moment when EU implements for conflict resolution became subject to catachresis by Greek-Cypriot nationalist rhetoric, thus allowing the government of the Republic and its civil society supporters to use them as impediments to a solution, while at the same time obstructing their use by pro-solution forces, within the political leadership and civil society in support of a solution. The branding, for example, of the political party leader who complained to the European Parliament is a case in point.

This catachrestic conduct comes into stark contrast with the utilisation by the civil society in the north of the prospect of EU accession as a good opportunity to amass support for a solution and remove the intransigent leadership from power. There are, of course, other aspects to the comparative economies of these discursive uses, most notable of which are the imagined 'costs and benefits' to the two communities of the implementation of the Annan Plan. Exemplary of this is the Greek-Cypriot nationalist argument that, in its final version, the Annan Plan benefited the Turkish side more than the Greek side and that the Turkish-Cypriot referendum succeeded not because the Turkish-Cypriots wanted reunification of the island but rather because they wanted the benefits of EU membership, which they had, after all, previously expended no effort to secure. This moralistic argument aside, the material costs and benefits of implementing the solution were incorporated into the pre-referendum debate, especially in the south. Reports supporting the view that material benefits would outweigh the costs (Vassiliou 2003), and the opposite view (Lordos 2004),[24] were discussed in greater length than detail. And this is precisely what is of concern here: that the catachresis of EU implements in the interests of nationalist rhetoric against a solution was in fact at the heart of, and overrode, any other of the shortcomings that these implements may have had in themselves as instruments of positive impact on the conflict.

In this context, the argument that Greek-Cypriot demands are better served within the framework of Cypriot membership of the EU before a solution has been finalised is perfectly justified because such a justification rests on the presupposition that the possibilities of catachresis can be realised. Indeed, I would argue that the policies of the Republic's government in the first year following the accession in regard to the solution of the problem were guided by just such a catachrestic logic. Examples of this are the Republic's attempts to stall policies aiming at integrating Turkish-Cypriots into the Republic and into the EU in any meaningful way, notwithstanding the fact that fostering such integration under the banner of 'citizenship' has been the government's explicit goal. And it has been a goal pursued vociferously because it is of national(ist) significance: it effectively bypasses the need for according Turkish-Cypriots (as citizens of the Republic of Cyprus) a political status other than that of a minority, while not even guaranteeing the special rights that would entail. Thus, apart from issuing passports and identification documents to the masses of interested Turkish-Cypriots relatively efficiently, the government has failed to fully implement, by mid-2005, the package of measures 'in support of Turkish-Cypriots' announced in May 2003, to facilitate trade with the north and across the Green Line between the north and the EU,[25] and to agree on a formula whereby EU aid pledged to the north would be channelled there in a way that would foster cooperation and trust. This logic can be said to have already been at work prior to the finalisation of the solution, when the opening of the border, via its timing

---

[24] For the reinterpretation of what was originally presented as a commentary of possible improvements that could be made to the Annan Plan in its earlier versions by the rejectionist Greek-Cypriot camp see http://unannanplan.agrino.org/economic_consequences.htm.

[25] It is important to note though, in relation to this point, the technical and infrastructural difficulties of the Turkish-Cypriot departments to respond effectively to the rigorous requirements set by the EU for standardised certification of products. An additional point, notwithstanding the above, is also the political significance of such trade, over its economic significance, keeping in mind the relatively low volume of trade that would be reached even in optimum conditions in relation to total EU figures.

with respect to EU accession, offered the possibility of using this indirect effect to promote the integration of the two parts of the island in reflection of the integration that was being finalised between the EU and Cyprus.

The differences between the two processes (i.e. integration of Cyprus within the EU and integration of Turkish-Cypriots into Greek-Cypriot society) are well illustrated in the parliamentary debates that took place on these two issues. By 2002 the focus of these discussions was almost exclusively on issues of accession and the passing of laws that would allow the negotiations with the EU to run smoothly. These matters were almost automatically 'declared urgent' (Parliament R.o.C. VIII.II. (12 September 2002)) and in most instances the relevant laws were approved with minimal discussion. This is in stark contrast to the meetings held after the opening of the border, where matters relating to regulating the crossing of Turkish-Cypriots from the north (e.g. regarding driving licences) were not only hotly debated, but also debated in terms of both process and content with decisions repeatedly postponed (Parliament R.o.C. VIII.II. (8 May 2003): 48).

Moreover, there are stark differences between this catachresis and the policy changes that the prospect of EU accession (despite its indefinite postponement following the failure of the referendum in the south) was used to legitimise in the north. The most spectacular of these policies was perhaps the already mentioned revision of the high-school history text-books that took place in record time in 2003–4, with the books finalised after the referendum and coming into use by September of that year. The books are used in replacement of older history textbooks that promoted a nationalist perspective (Serter 1970) and closely adhered to the official discourses, as they still did, by the time of writing, in the south. According to the Committee that undertook the revision of the books, this was done as an attempt to teach the history that the Turkish-Cypriot community has created on the island over the centuries to citizens who will grow to learn to think and question for themselves and contribute positively to the life of the community in the twenty-first century (KKTC 2004: viii). The ideological background of the textbooks, as well as their content, is one geared towards the goal of reunification of the island and from which the avoidance of nationalistic language is conspicuous throughout. In this sense, the production and introduction of the books can be taken as the clearest example of the EU's indirect impact on the conflict. The change of outlook on history that they seek to foster for the future generations of Turkish-Cypriots can be thought of, in terms of the theoretical framework, as an example of how changes in the conflict induced by the prospect of EU accession can enable leaderships to institute such major changes in the educational system. At the same time, such changes aim to foster different types of identities, where the concepts of 'peace' and 'reunification' are paramount to the formation of national/communal identification. In short, the introduction of these books shows the profound impact that the EU can have on border conflicts in terms of promoting a 'change of scripts'.

These revisions compare well with the more directly EU-induced changes in the educational policy in the south that produced, following adherence to EU guidelines, a report by the National Education Committee that recommended among other things the revision of history teaching, the revision of teaching in general to acknowledge Turkish-Cypriots and the introduction of Turkish-language teaching.[26] The report states that its goal is to make recommendations that respond to the changes within Greek-Cypriot society, which is now becoming a 'Euro-Cypriot society', and to review the prospects for modernising the educational system into the pluralist framework prescribed by the EU. However, the conclusions of the report point to a series of changes that are both substantial in terms of the content of the material that would need to be taught and formalistic in terms of the institutions that need to be put in place to oversee this process of change. These changes are envisioned in the much longer term, whereas the changes implemented in the Turkish-Cypriot educational system concentrate on the goal of social change that might indeed take a generation to become rooted, but is envisioned to start straight away. In this sense, the report of the Republic's Ministry of Education utilises the disadvantages of EU policy-making that enables great delay in their implementation because of the bureaucratic processes within which they are embedded. With the dynamics of the conflict changing as constantly and rapidly as they have been in the last few years, such delays are often counterproductive, in the sense that by the time specific changes are researched, discussed, approved and implemented, the educational or other policy requirements might already have changed.

Far from suggesting that it was the explicit aim of all those involved in these policy changes to use or abuse EU instruments to bring about or impede changes in the conflict, what I have aimed to show here is how the process of accession provided the opportunities, at particular points in time (through events taking place both locally and EU-wide), for the discourse on the relations between Cyprus and the EU to change and for a discourse to be cultivated that was less accommodating of the wider project of 'reconciliation' within which previous attempts at resolution

---

[26] The full report is available at www.moec.gov.cy/metarithmisi/f4.htm.

had been couched. If this is to be seen as a failure, then I would argue that it was a failure of both local and external actors.

Finally, some comments might be in order as regards the perception of the various EU actors on the ground. While this is explored by Pace in this volume (chapter 7), it should be pointed out here that in the island's media discourse, individual actors are not often visible, with the 'EU', the 'Commission' or the 'European Parliament' being the main references in presentations of the 'EU'. Exceptions to this are of course the individuals who have, at different points in time, been involved with Cyprus's accession, and specifically Günter Verheugen, the Commissioner for Enlargement during the period when the accession of the ten was finalised, and Leopold Maurer, Head of the EU negotiating team in the Cyprus accession negotiations. It is worth noting that while all of their visits to the island were well publicised and a positive profile projected for both of them by the media in the south, the view of these individuals in the north adhered largely to more general ideas about the 'EU'. Thus, while the 'EU' was seen by the Turkish-Cypriot leadership as partial in favour of the Greek-Cypriot side, meetings with its representatives were not forthcoming. A different situation emerged after the referenda, however, when the Commissioner for Enlargement was vilified by virtually all the media in the south, after making statements to the effect that the Greek-Cypriot President had 'cheated' him, implying that the Greek-Cypriot leadership had promised him a delivery of a positive Greek-Cypriot vote on the Plan that would unite the island before its official accession. By comparison to these public images of specific EU representatives, the EU representation on the island was in general terms rather low-profile. Yet, it should be said that it had, over the years, and under different heads, managed to gain the respect and support of a large number of civil society actors. More importantly, it had been successful in organising and supporting bicommunal events and meetings involving different levels of the local society and had played an important role in raising the confidence of the Turkish-Cypriot opposition in the EU. What has arisen from the interviews conducted, however, is that the concrete effects of what is generally perceived as commendable efforts to bring the communities together have been constrained by the legal tangle in which the conflict is embedded.

Understanding Cyprus, the EU and reconciliation

The analysis provided in this chapter regarding the EU's impact on the Cyprus conflict is summarised in Table 3.1.

When the UN official quoted at the beginning of this chapter stated that 'in Europe they don't understand', he was referring to a failure of the

Table 3.1: *Overview of EU influence on Cyprus*

Pathway	Main EU institution	Main addressee	Nature of influence	Facilitating factors
Compulsory	Council of Ministers; European Commission	Governments	Rulings, directives, regulations	Process of intense negotiations on resolution of the conflict and fundamental changes to Turkish-Cypriot official positions
Enabling	European Parliament; European Commission	Governments and officials	Resolutions, statements	Existence of UN plan offering framework for a final solution
Connective	European Commission	Local authorities; NGOs	Structural Funds; Community initiatives	Spirit of rapprochement cultivated through previous bicommunal efforts
Constructive	All: 'EU' as concept	Regional politicians	Principles, values	Opportunities for Turkish-Cypriots, articulated through demonstrations of opposition forces

EU officials he had spoken to, to understand the reasons for the Greek-Cypriot government's vehement rejection of the Annan Plan. Within the immediate context of the pre-referendum campaign this lack of understanding can easily be construed as a failure to empathise with Greek-Cypriot sensitivities and apprehensions regarding a solution that was not perceived to satisfy the key criteria that would guarantee a truly lasting peace on the island. This has been a key argument in post-referenda analyses that seek to 'explain the Greek-Cypriot vote' (e.g. Attalides 2004). These analyses share the presupposition of miscommunication between the Greek-Cypriot public that rejected the Annan Plan and the international community with the Greek-Cypriot governmental rhetoric, which bases its own rejection of the Plan on the public rejection it claimed to perceive prior to the finalisation of the negotiations. This is paradoxical in light of the fact that these analyses stem from long-term highly critical perspectives of Greek-Cypriot nationalist rhetoric (e.g. Attalides 1979).

Instead, there is a more fundamental aporia about the connections between the Greek-Cypriot government that had called for a 'resounding NO' to the referendum (after all, these statements were made before the popular official endorsement of that instruction) and the 'Greek-Cypriots' as a people who did not seem to have been taught the European meaning of 'reconciliation'. Admittedly, this latter proposition smacks of condescension and this is exactly what the government later built its rhetoric upon, arguing that the popular vote was not a passive one, and that there was an agency to this vote that arose out of a confrontation with the actual implications of this solution. This is an ongoing debate that cannot be ultimately resolved here because it involves wider consideration of what kind of agency is in question. What I want to argue is that if there was such a confrontation, it was a confrontation with the implications of any solution, not a particular one. For if the Annan Plan is to be seen as the most recent stage in a process that has seen increasingly detailed solution suggestions that fulfilled the requirements of a bicommunal, bizonal federation being tabled from 1977 onwards, which to variable degrees enjoyed the support of both leaderships (Sözen and Çarkoğlu 2004), then a rejection of the magnitude that ultimately ensued throws into question not merely the details of the stipulations of the Plan, but the essence of it. And in this sense it also puts into question the process by which leaderships have been representing people's wishes on the negotiating table and the realities of the negotiating table to the people.[27] As regards northern Cyprus, the first part was exactly what the demonstrations of 2002 questioned. What seems to be problematic at present is that in the south, these questions have never been asked.

Thus, with the removal of the obstacles to a solution in the north (i.e. above all the previous leadership) the EU played an indirect but yet vital role in the breaking of the deadlock. This was its best example of positive impact on the conflict. At the same time, the foreshadowing of the problems of nationalism and the power dynamics within the new Greek-Cypriot leadership that it brought about put in place the necessary conditions for the effective catachresis that ensued. In short, through its spectacular, albeit indirect, impact on the north, the 'EU', as a conceptual construct, raised expectations about its ability to solve the conflict irrespective of intransigence on the local leadership level to such an extent that the limits of this ability came out of focus. And it is these raised expectations that led to disillusionment when after the referendum, and after accession, and after the failure to deliver the imagined 'Europe' to

[27] Interview, UN official, Nicosia, April 2004.

the Turkish-Cypriot demonstrators the 'EU' was reimagined as a bureaucratic structure, as liable to abuse as local institutions.

In a wider context, this is a question of perceptions and the identification of Cyprus and the EU with respect to each other, both of which are far from static. What this chapter has attempted to do is to show that there was a process and a series of policies on both sides that prefigured the development of these perceptions, whereby the crucial question of whether the EU would inherit a perennial political problem or be proclaimed a 'peace catalyst' was constantly asked but never adequately answered. In the final instance, the ultimate answer had rested purely on 'good faith' towards the Greek-Cypriot government. It is this spectre of gross misjudgement that seems to have haunted Brussels officials and EU member state representatives, who alongside the urge to query Cypriots about their comprehension of 'reconciliation' also allegedly wondered whether 'this is what we are bringing into Europe'. In effect, this is nothing other than an aporia of catachresis. Writing in a daily newspaper on the issue of the government's performance since the referendum and EU accession, a former Minister of Foreign Affairs for the Republic, and MEP, declared: 'I honestly do not know what explanation to offer for the way in which we act and react on the international stage' (Kasoulides, *Politis [The Citizen]* newspaper, 13 April 2005). In the words of another Greek-Cypriot politician, in charge of EU affairs[28] prior to accession, the answer was a denial: 'we have actually denied Europe the ability to project the Union as a conflict-solving project'. The legacy of catachresis and failure to solve conflicts may not be new to the EU – the challenge will be to overcome both.

---

[28] Interview, EU negotiation team, Nicosia, April 2004.

4   Transforming the Greek–Turkish conflicts: the EU and 'what we make of it'!

Bahar Rumelili

Introduction

Greek–Turkish relations, in many ways, provide a fruitful case for scholars interested in the EU's role in the transformation of border conflicts.[1] First of all, it is a case where the impact of the EU is widely mentioned, but not yet comprehensively and systematically studied (Rumelili 2004a). Secondly, because the EU has been a factor in Greek–Turkish relations since the early 1970s, the case contains many useful insights about the historical evolution of the EU's role as a 'perturbator' of conflicts, and the conditions under which the EU can positively impact border conflicts. There is a clear puzzle in the EU involvement in Greek–Turkish conflicts: up until the late 1990s, the EU failed to have a positive impact. Countering the links made between European integration and peace, Greek–Turkish conflicts multiplied and intensified as Greece and Turkey developed closer institutional relations with the EU. However, clearly since 1999, we observe a promising *rapprochement* between Turkey and Greece within the EU context (Rumelili 2003a; 2004a). How the role of the EU changed from an additional forum for Greek–Turkish rivalry to a foundation for Greek–Turkish reconciliation is a very interesting empirical question that contains valuable insights for understanding the conditions for successful EU involvement in border conflicts.

---

[1] The research presented in this chapter was conducted as part of the EUBorderConf project, which was funded by the EU's Fifth Framework Programme and the British Academy. I would like to thank all my colleagues in this project, especially Thomas Diez, Stephan Stetter, Michelle Pace and Kemal Kirişci, for their stimulating input and criticism. In addition, I gratefully acknowledge the time and input of the many academics, policy-makers, civil society activists and informants in Turkey and Greece who have agreed to be interviewed for this project. I also thank Apostolos Agnantopoulos for his invaluable research assistance in the translation and analysis of Greek parliamentary debates. Some sections of this chapter are based on previous articles (Rumelili 2005a, 2007) and earlier versions have been published within the EUBorderConf Working Paper series. The title is a play on Wendt (1992).

This chapter will argue that the positive impact of the EU on Greek–Turkish relations has been realised through a complex interaction between domestic and EU-level conditions. My research has first of all indicated that the EU has made its positive impact on Greek–Turkish relations since 1999 not necessarily through the EU's independent, purposive agency but from the ways in which the EU, as a resource, symbol and a model, has been put to use by political and civil society actors in Turkey and Greece. The record of Greek–Turkish relations demonstrates that the EU can be and has in fact been just as effectively used to legitimise the perpetuation of conflicts at the domestic level. Therefore, what domestic actors choose to make of the EU is a very significant condition for EU impact on conflicts (cf. Demetriou this volume, chapter 3). In the Greek–Turkish case, it has been all the more important because Greece, as a member of the EU, has had the power to affect the Union's policies towards Turkey.

Domestic factors do not provide a sufficient explanation, because there have always been actors in both countries who sought to improve the bilateral relations, but their initiatives and efforts were always stymied by domestic opposition and setbacks in bilateral relations. The EU and, particularly, the nature of the EU's relations with Greece and Turkey, have set the structural conditions under which domestic actors define their identities and interests, and thus shaped the domestic balances of power. Greece's EC membership in 1981 turned the Greek–Turkish conflicts into a conflict between a member and a non-member state, and the resulting institutional asymmetry empowered the hardliners in both countries, who approached the EC/EU within the logic of alliance, and thus disabled the EU from having a positive impact. My research demonstrates that both the deepening of European integration in the 1990s and the EU's furthering of relations with Turkey have fundamentally altered the structural conditions set by the EU on policy-making in Turkey and Greece. This chapter will show how the EU's 1999 decision to grant Turkey candidacy status has unleashed various forms of positive EU impact: it has been the basis of an alternative Greek foreign policy, empowered the moderate elites in both countries, legitimised the governmental and civil society efforts directed at Greek–Turkish cooperation and conditioned significant changes in discourse.

In short, the positive impact of the EU on Greek–Turkish relations has depended on domestic actors, who are willing and able to use the EU framework as the basis for cooperation. And, in turn, those domestic actors have depended on the EU to provide the framework of incentives, ideas and norms within which they can ground, rationalise and legitimise their policy changes. In Greek–Turkish relations, this relationship of mutual dependency between domestic and EU-level conditions has been satisfied only after Turkey's EU membership candidacy.

The next section of this chapter will present a concise history of Greek–Turkish relations and outline the sources of dispute, arguing that since 1999, the Greek–Turkish conflicts have been transformed from an identity conflict to an issue conflict. The third section will chart the various forms of direct EU involvement in Greek–Turkish disputes since the early 1970s. Drawing on interviews and primary texts, the fourth section will investigate how the various forms of direct and indirect EU involvement have affected Greek–Turkish relations. The fifth section will discuss the domestic and EU-related conditions that have influenced the effectiveness of EU involvement. The final section will summarise the main conclusions and draw implications for EU policy from the Greek–Turkish experience.

A strategic identity conflict transformed

Greek–Turkish conflicts have long roots in history; however, the two states have also enjoyed periods of sustained cooperation. The current territories of Greece were under Ottoman rule roughly from the mid-fifteenth century until the Greek uprising in 1821. Through a series of expansions, Greece reached its present territories in 1920 (excluding the Dodecanese islands, which were ceded to Greece by Italy after the Second World War). Following the end of the First World War, and the invasion of the Ottoman Empire's territories by European powers, the Greek armies entered the present-day territories of Turkey and were defeated by the Turkish forces in the 1920–2 Turkish 'War of Independence'. The four centuries of Ottoman rule, the progressive expansion of Greek territories at the expense of the Ottoman Empire and the 1920–2 war all constitute bitter historical memories that continue to haunt present-day bilateral relations.

Ironically, following the 1920–2 war, bilateral relations between Greece and the newly established Republic of Turkey started out in a spirit of cooperation. The two countries signed the Peace Treaty of Lausanne in 1923 and enacted a forced exchange of the Muslim population in Greece with the Greek Orthodox population in Turkey.[2] In 1930, Kemal Ataturk and Eleutherios Venizelos adopted an agreement resolving their remaining differences over aspects of the Lausanne Treaty and initiated an era of

---

[2] Approximately 1.5 million people were forced to resettle. Despite its dire humanitarian consequences, the forced population exchange was considered a diplomatic success at the time.

extensive cooperation, which was to last until the 1950s. Starting in the mid-1950s, however, the relations between Greece and Turkey began to sour over the Cyprus question, and, with the reactivation of nationalist symbols and selective historical memories, turned into an entrenched identity conflict.[3] Following a brief period of improvement during the signing of the London and Zurich agreements, establishing the bicommunal Republic of Cyprus in 1959, the bilateral relations further deteriorated with the outbreak of communal violence between the Greek- and Turkish-Cypriots on the island. The two states came dangerously close to war over Cyprus in 1964 and during Turkey's 1974 military operation, which put approximately one-third of the island under Turkish control.

In the climate of mistrust and tension, certain differences about the maritime borders in the Aegean, which were uncommunicated before, began to be articulated as disputes, and securitised through a discourse which constructed the Other as expansionist. In particular, Turkey viewed the Greek positions as attempts to close off the Aegean as a 'Greek lake', and Greece perceived a Turkish strategy of encircling the Greek islands as attempts to separate them from Greece.[4] The two states engaged in various border-defining activities to mark their territories as they defined them, which frequently escalated the conflicts to conflicts of subordination. For example, the dispute over the continental shelf broke out in November 1973, when Turkey issued a licence for oil exploration in an area Greece argued was part of its continental shelf. The tensions escalated in July 1976, when Turkey sent the research vessel *Sismik 1* to the area to prospect for oil. In response, Greece called for an emergency meeting of the UN Security Council and instituted proceedings in the International Court of Justice (ICJ) against Turkey by unilateral application.[5] The issue flared up again when, in March 1986, the Greek government gave drilling rights to a private company. In March 1987, Turkey sent *Sismik 1* to drill in the same area accompanied by warships. The two states came to a near-war situation.

From Turkey's perspective, the issue of the continental shelf is interlinked with other sources of dispute in the Aegean, i.e. the territorial waters and airspace. However, Greece recognises only the continental shelf issue as a legitimate dispute and regards the others as unilateral

---

[3] This historical overview was compiled from many sources. See especially Aksu (2001), Moustakis (2003) and Athanassopoulou (1997).

[4] The border disputes were narrated as such on the websites of the Greek and Turkish Foreign Ministries as late as 2003. These accounts have later been changed. For a more detailed analysis, see Rumelili (2003c).

[5] However, the ICJ decided in December 1978 that it did not have jurisdiction to entertain the Greek application.

claims by Turkey against Greece's sovereign rights. Currently, both Greece and Turkey exercise a 6 nm breadth of territorial sea in the Aegean. However, the 1982 UN Convention on the Law of the Sea (UNCLOS) – to which Greece is a party but Turkey is not – provides that 'every state has the right to establish the breadth of its territorial sea up to a limit not exceeding 12 nm'. The dispute escalated in 1995 when UNCLOS came into force and was ratified by the Greek Parliament. In response, on 8 June 1995, the Turkish Parliament unanimously passed a resolution that it would view the expansion of territorial sea by Greece as a *casus belli*.

The airspace issue is a source of continuous tension in Greek–Turkish relations. Greece defined its airspace at a distance of 10 nm from its coasts in 1931 while maintaining a 6 nm territorial sea. While acknowledging that this constitutes an anomaly under international law, Greece defends this arrangement by arguing that it already has a right to 12 nm territorial sea and by pointing out that Turkey had not disputed the limits of Greek airspace until 1975. In order to mark their territories, the two states engage in dangerous border-defining activities in the Aegean airspace. Turkish military aircraft make routine flights in the additional 4 nm Greek national airspace, and they are always intercepted and harassed by Greek jets. Most recently, on 23 May 2006, a Greek pilot lost his life in a collision between Greek and Turkish fighter jets, an incident that was declared as an 'accident' by the two sides (*Milliyet* newspaper, 24 May 2006; see below). Previously, in 1996, a Turkish pilot had died in a similar incident.

Another issue that has brought Greece and Turkey recently to the brink of war is whether there are islands, islets or rocks in the Aegean close to the Turkish coast whose ownership has not been determined by previous international agreements. Since islands are entitled to territorial waters and possibly to continental shelves, this 'dispute' is very much interlinked with others in the Aegean. A crisis broke out over this issue in late December 1995, when the question of who was to assist a Turkish cargo boat that ran aground near the Imia/Kardak islets generated conflicting claims of sovereignty. Following an exchange of notes between the Foreign Ministries, the story was slipped to the Turkish and Greek press, and the mayor of Kalymnos, Turkish journalists and the Greek navy raced to hoist their country's flag on the islets. The arrival of Turkish commandos on the islets brought the two states very close to a military confrontation, which was avoided at the last minute by US intervention. Most recently, in April 2005, there was a twenty-six-hour standoff between Greek and Turkish coastguards near the islets (see below).

The militarisation of the east Aegean islands by Greece has been another cause of friction between Turkey and Greece, and has repeatedly caused problems within the NATO context. While Greece maintains that militarisation is necessary for self-defence, Turkey contends that the militarisation of the east Aegean islands by Greece constitutes a violation of the 1923 Lausanne Treaty and has consistently vetoed the inclusion of the Greek forces stationed on the islands in NATO exercises (Moustakis 2003).

The conflicts over Cyprus and the Aegean quickly captured other areas of societal interaction between Turkey and Greece. The Rum-Greek minority left in Turkey and the Muslim-Turkish minority left in Greece became targets of discriminatory practices, deportations and acts of violence (Rumelili 2005b). The most notable was the September 1955 looting of Rum-Greek homes and businesses by Turkish nationalist mobs incited by a false allegation that Ataturk's house in Thessalonica was burnt by the Greeks. The overtly ethnocentric education reproduced the stereotypes and a selective reading of history, which emphasised periods of conflict and hostility. The media and civil society took nationalist stances, pressuring the governments to adopt hardline positions, as in the Imia/Kardak crisis described above. Economic, cultural and social relations between the two countries remained at a minimal level. The few courageous initiatives in civil society cooperation remained vulnerable to political crises and in some instances to physical attack.

Therefore, starting with the mid-1950s, the Greek–Turkish conflicts have fluctuated between *identity conflicts* and *conflicts of subordination*, with war between the two states becoming very likely on numerous occasions. The military crises were usually followed by short-lived attempts at normalisation of relations, where threat communications subsided; however, the oppositional construction of identities remained. For example, after the 1976 crisis over the continental shelf, Greece and Turkey signed the Berne Declaration, where they undertook to discuss the issues of flight control and the delimitation of the continental shelf and refrain from unilateral actions that might impede the resolution of their bilateral problems. Similarly, the 1987 crisis over the Aegean continental shelf was followed by meetings between Greek and Turkish Premiers and Foreign Ministers, known as the 'Davos Process', where they agreed to promote cooperation in trade, tourism and communications, and signed a Memorandum of Understanding where they pledged to respect each other's sovereignty and territorial integrity. The 1996 crisis over the Imia/Kardak islets has been, according to many analysts, a 'blessing in disguise' (Athanassopoulou 1997) as it paved the way for the 1997 Madrid Declaration where the two states committed themselves not to use violence or undertake unilateral actions. After each of these initiatives, however, threat communications between Greece and Turkey quickly regained prevalence.

This chapter argues that the dramatic changes in Greek–Turkish relations witnessed after 1999 have resulted in the de-escalation of the conflict to the *issue conflict* level. Even though the two states have not yet arrived at a resolution of their disputes, in the positive atmosphere of evolving functional cooperation and the EU context, the Aegean disputes have, to some extent, been desecuritised, and begun to be articulated as differences that can be managed rather than as existential threats.[6] Since 1999, the two states have signed bilateral cooperation agreements on various issues, such as tourism promotion, fight against terrorism, removal of landmines along the border, illegal migration, incentives for trade and joint investment, and environmental and health issues. In addition, as confidence-building measures within the framework of NATO, Greece and Turkey have agreed to reduce and exchange information about military exercises. Most importantly, Turkey's EU membership has become the focal point of bilateral cooperation. Greece, that persistently vetoed any advances in the relations between Turkey and the EU in the past, has become the most ardent supporter of Turkey's EU membership. Despite changes of government in Turkey (2002) and Greece (2004), the issue of bilateral relations was never politicised during the election campaigns. Official visits have become routine, and the officials of the two countries have not missed an opportunity to meet on the sidelines of various NATO, EU and UN meetings.

Progress towards the resolution of bilateral disputes has been slow; since 2002, thirty-plus rounds of secret negotiations have taken place at the technical level between the two Foreign Ministries. In mid-2004, there were increasing reports in the press that the two sides were very close to an agreement. However, the negotiation process was stalled in late 2004, mainly due to the Greek government's decision not to insist on the 2004 deadline stipulated by the 1999 Helsinki European Council (see below). Despite the fact that the Aegean border disputes have not yet been resolved, there are clear indications that issues that would have easily escalated into serious crises in the past are now carefully contained by the elites. For example, when the airspace violations issue flared up in May and June 2003, with allegations of the harassment of an Olympic Airways passenger jet by Turkish warplanes, the two governments quietly handled the situation in the midst of escalatory pressures from the media

---

[6] Officials of both states have made public pronouncements that they no longer see the other as a threat. See, for example, *Kathimerini* newspaper (English edn), 19 November 2002.

and military circles (Rumelili 2003b). Similarly, in April 2005, Greek and Turkish Foreign Ministers concluded an agreement on confidence-building measures in the Aegean during a twenty-six-hour standoff between Greek and Turkish coastguard boats near the Imia/Kardak islets. In response to the death of a Greek pilot during a dogfight in May 2006, Greek and Turkish Foreign Ministers made a joint statement expressing their regret and agreed that the incident 'must not affect the two countries' target of improving their relations' (*Kathimerini* newspaper, 24 May 2006). Consequently, the 'red line' establishing direct communication between the two countries' militaries was put into operation (*Zaman* newspaper, 9 June 2006).

Also after 1999, Greece and Turkey have successfully managed to isolate their bilateral relations as much as possible from the ups and downs experienced in the Cyprus problem in the wake of Cyprus's EU membership in 2004 and afterwards. Both states have declared support for the UN-sponsored Annan Plan for the reunification of the island prior to EU membership, albeit arguably Turkey exercised greater pressure on the Turkish-Cypriot leadership for the acceptance of the Plan than Greece (Onis and Yilmaz 2008). The Greek-Cypriot rejection of the Annan Plan in public referendum and its subsequent EU membership have reinforced the uncertainties in the Greece–Turkey–Cyprus–EU quadrangle, and left the process in a stalemate. However, the entire process has also demonstrated the strength of the Greek–Turkish *rapprochement*.

As a result of the improved atmosphere at the political level, transnational contacts between Turkey and Greece have multiplied, both in form and in number. The annual bilateral trade between the two countries exceeded 1 billion dollars. The number of people visiting Turkey from Greece and vice versa has increased tremendously. Many cultural activities, festivals, concerts and joint theatre productions have been organised. Numerous youth exchanges have taken place. New organisations directed at Greek–Turkish cooperation have been established, the activities of existing organisations have been diversified and various joint projects between Greek and Turkish NGOs have been initiated (Rumelili 2005a).

EU involvement

The EEC/EC/EU has always been a factor in Greek–Turkish conflicts, and the Greek–Turkish disputes have been a concern for European policy-makers from the beginnings of European integration. Both Greece and Turkey expressed interest in the fledgling European Economic Community in 1959, only two years after its inception.

Greece became an associate member in 1961 and Turkey in 1963. The first direct intervention of the EC in Greek–Turkish conflicts took place during the 1974 Cyprus crisis. Following the coup on the island by the Greek junta, the EC member states issued a joint communiqué reaffirming their support for the independence of Cyprus; and after the first Turkish military operation in July 1974, launched two démarches calling for an end to all military operations, and issued a joint statement asking for a ceasefire. However, the EC could not do anything to prevent the renewal of hostilities on the island in August 1974 (Tsakaloyannis 1980).

When Greece applied for full membership of the EC in 1975, the Council of Ministers communicated its concern for maintaining an equitable relationship with Greece and Turkey by explicitly assuring the Turkish government that the Greek application would not affect Turkey's rights. In addition, in its opinion on the Greek application, the European Commission expressed its concern about importing conflicts and recommended a pre-accession period that would allow, among other things, for the settlement of Greek–Turkish disputes. However, the Commission Opinion was overruled in the Council of Ministers' meeting in February 1976 by extensive Greek lobbying. At the time the European Community was rather conservative about its potential role in conflict resolution, preferring to ignore disputes among member states (Meinardus 1991; Stephanou and Tsardanides 1991). Yet, when the first crisis over the Aegean continental shelf erupted with the dispatch of *Sismik 1* on 24 July 1976, the President of the Council of Ministers flew to Athens to dissuade the Greeks from putting into effect their threat to remove the Turkish ship by force (Tsakaloyannis 1980).

With Greece's EC membership in 1981, Greece acquired the institutional capacity to influence EU policy-making on Greek–Turkish issues and relations with Turkey. The extent of Greece's influence, however, has been overrated (cf. Aksu 2001). Greece has been constrained by general EU norms and principles and its limited bargaining power within the Council, although its influence has been stronger than that of other EU institutions, such as the European Parliament (Ugur 1999; Pace this volume, ch. 7).

In 1986, Greece vetoed the resumption of the association relationship between Turkey and the EC and the release of aid, which had been frozen in response to the 1980 military coup in Turkey (Guvenc 1998/9). When the Council overrode the Greek veto through a majority decision, Greece pursued the case further by bringing cases against the Council and the Commission in the European Court of Justice. In April 1987, when Turkey applied for EC membership, Greece was again the only member state that openly opposed referring the application to the Commission for an Opinion (Guvenc 1998/9). Meanwhile, in May 1987, the European Parliament passed a resolution which called on Greece and Turkey to refer the question of the delimitation of the Aegean Sea continental shelf to the ICJ. A subsequent European Parliament's resolution on Cyprus in May 1988 stated that Turkey's unlawful occupation of northern Cyprus presented a major stumbling block to the normalisation of relations with Turkey. The European Commission's Opinion on Turkey's application in 1989 stated that Turkey was not ready for membership, and pointed out that the Greek–Turkish conflict as well as the Cyprus problem constituted negative factors for Turkey's admission.

In the 1990s, Greek opposition began to create increasing problems for an EU that wanted to advance relations with Turkey within the framework of a Customs Union Agreement. In addition, Greece's bargaining power within the Community began to decline because of Greece's divergence from its partners on a variety of foreign policy issues. The most serious divergence occurred in 1994 when the Greek government imposed a unilateral trade embargo on the Republic of Macedonia because of the name-recognition issue. The European Commission took the case to the European Court of Justice requesting an emergency interim ruling. However, the ECJ refused the Commission's request to order Athens to end the blockade (Featherstone 1994).

In this period, the EU increasingly began to resort to the strategy of linking together progress on Cyprus's and Turkey's relations with the Community. In December 1994, the Customs Union Agreement between the EU and Turkey could not be finalised due to Greece's opposition, and Greece lifted its veto in March 1995 only after the EU offered Greece the side-payment of pledging to start membership negotiations with Cyprus. As Turkey intensified its pursuit of EU membership in the context of deteriorating Greek–Turkish relations, the Union directed a series of communications to Turkey on Greek–Turkish disputes. A European Parliament resolution on Turkey, dated 18 January 1996, 'deplored the declaration made by [Turkish Prime Minister] Tansu Ciller on the possible incorporation of the northern part of Cyprus into Turkey in relation to Cyprus' future accession to the European Union' (European Parliament 1996a).

In reaction to the 1996 Imia/Kardak crisis, the EU took a firmer line towards Turkey in solidarity with Greece. In February 1996, the European Parliament adopted a resolution, which stated that Greek boundaries were the EU's international boundaries, so any intervention would be accepted as an infringement upon the EU's sovereign rights (European Parliament 1996b). In July 1996, the European Council warned that 'the relations between Turkey and the EU have to be based on a clear commitment to the principle of respect for international law and agreements, the relevant international practice, and the sovereignty and the territorial integrity of the member states and of Turkey' (Council of the European Union 1996). In addition, the Council called for restraint and the pursuit of dialogue, and proposed the establishment of a crisis-prevention mechanism as well as the submission of the dispute to the ICJ. However, the Council of Ministers rejected a motion by Athens that the financial aid promised to Turkey by the EU to facilitate the implementation of the Customs Union be tied to conditions about the Greek–Turkish disputes. After Greece blocked the first financial assistance package to Turkey and the release of the EU Mediterranean Aid Programme, the EU reminded Greece that these attempts to block the financial aid to Turkey might affect the negotiations on Cyprus's accession.

Initially, it was primarily Greece that, as a 'concerned member state', insisted on subjecting Turkey's relations with the EC/EU to conditions on Greek–Turkish disputes, and influenced EU decision-making in that direction. However, it is also the case that the principle of conflict resolution strongly resonated with the normative basis of the EU. Therefore, in the late 1990s, as the EU developed, acquired confidence and began to face a multiplicity of potentially problematic border disputes in its eastern enlargement, the resolution of border disputes prior to membership in the EU became an integral part of the EU's membership conditionality framework. The Agenda 2000 document, released by the European Commission in July 1997, stated:

Enlargement should not mean importing border conflicts. The prospect of accession acts as a powerful incentive for the states concerned to settle any border dispute. (European Commission 1997b: 67)

In the late 1990s, the deteriorating relations with Greece, coupled with Turkey's deficiencies in human rights and democratic governance, took its toll on Turkey's EU membership bid. The 30 October 1996 European Commission *Report on Developments in Relations with Turkey* noted that 'the tension in the Aegean in particular has cast a shadow over relations between the EU and Turkey' (European Commission 1996). In April 1997, Dutch Foreign Minister Van Mierlo advanced a proposal as the holder of the EU Presidency to establish a committee of wise men to study the pending problems between Turkey and Greece. The 29 April 1997 EC–Turkey Association Council Conclusions stated that 'continued strengthening of relations [between Turkey and the EU] depended [among other things] on an improvement in relations between one of the member states and Turkey through settlement of their differences in accordance with international law' (EU Bulletin 1997: 1.4.74.). Consequently, EU–Turkey relations hit bottom during the Luxembourg European Council on 12–13 December 1997, where the EU did not grant Turkey candidacy status while further advancing its relations with other candidate states. The Presidency conclusions noted that the 'strengthening of Turkey's links with the EU depends on ... the establishment of satisfactory and stable relations between Greece and Turkey' (European Council 1997). Angered by the stipulation of a change in Greek–Turkish relations as a condition, Turkey froze its relations with the EU.

By autumn 1999, the Greek objective of joining the Economic and Monetary Union (EMU) combined with the changing attitudes in EU capitals towards relations with Turkey to bring about a fundamental change in Greek policy towards Turkey and altered the nature of EU involvement in Greek–Turkish relations. During the Helsinki European Council on 10–11 December 1999, in line with the prevailing positive spirit, Greece chose not to use its veto against the EU's decision to grant Turkey candidacy status. In addition to granting Turkey candidacy status, the Helsinki Council decisions established the peaceful resolution of outstanding border disputes as a Community principle and urged candidate states 'to make every effort' to resolve any outstanding disputes, and if these efforts failed, to bring the disputes before the ICJ (European Council 1999). The European Council also set the end of 2004 as the latest date by which it would review the situation relating to outstanding disputes and their repercussions on the accession process. Incorporated into Turkey's Accession Partnership Agreement and National Programme – albeit with some ambiguity – the Helsinki Council decisions linked progress on Turkey's membership with the resolution of its border conflicts with Greece.

With the approval of Turkey's Accession Partnership, the European Commission introduced two forms of funding that were directed at Greek–Turkish civic cooperation. The first was the Civil Society Development Programme, introduced in 2002, with a budget of €8 million for two years to promote Greek–Turkish civic dialogue at the grass roots and local levels, and to enhance the capacity of NGOs in Turkey. The second form of funding was the €35 million package to support cross-border cooperation between Greece and Turkey for 2004–6.

Believing that Turkey's EU accession process would be a stronger incentive for the resolution of bilateral disputes than the pressure of a deadline, the Greek government announced in the spring of 2004 that it would not insist on the 2004 deadline set by the Helsinki European Council and that it was willing to extend the negotiations beyond that date. Accordingly, the 16–17 December 2004 Brussels European Council conclusions, in addition to deciding to start accession negotiations with Turkey on 3 October 2005, 'welcomed the improvement in Turkey's relations with its neighbours and its readiness to continue to work with the concerned Member States towards resolution of outstanding border disputes', and stated that 'unresolved disputes having repercussions on the accession process, should *if necessary* be brought to the International Court of Justice for settlement' (European Council 2005: 5; emphasis added). This change clearly demonstrates the extent of member state influence on the EU's conflict resolution policy especially if the member state is a party to the conflict. Even though the opposition in Greece has vehemently criticised this policy change (*Kathimerini* newspaper, English edn, 22 November 2004), both sides expect Greek–Turkish relations to retain their positive course in the following years.[7]

Pathways of EU involvement

The previous overview suggests that the EU has continuously been a factor in Greek–Turkish relations since the early 1970s. This section will examine various forms of EU involvement in Greek–Turkish relations, using the analytical categories of *compulsory, enabling, connective* and *constructive* influence developed by Diez, Stetter and Albert (this volume, Introduction). Drawing on newspaper reviews, interviews with policy-makers and civil society leaders, and analysis of parliamentary debates in Turkey and Greece, this section will also analyse how and the extent to which the EU has impacted on policy-making, actor identities, perceptions, interests and prevalent discourses.

Compulsory influence

The EC/EU has used the incentive of membership to prod Greece and Turkey to resolve their disputes in two periods. As the previous overview suggests, in the period from Greece's application in 1975 to its membership in 1981, the influence was directed towards Greece in a weak, disorganised and non-institutionalised fashion. While the Commission recommended a pre-accession period, which would allow Greece to settle its disputes with Turkey, this recommendation was overruled in the Council of Ministers. Therefore, the EC could not take full advantage

---

[7] Interviews conducted by author in Ankara in March 2004 and in Athens in February 2005.

of Greece's membership application process to exert its compulsory influence on Greece. Nevertheless, the desire to secure EC membership led Greek policy-makers to restrain themselves from escalatory policies, and pursue attempts at dialogue during this application period.[8] Couloumbis and Yannas (1994) argue that how the Greek Prime Minister Karamanlis chose to handle Greek–Turkish relations following the Turkish invasion of Cyprus in 1974 reflected 'the deep impact that the prospect of EU accession exercised on post-1974 Greek foreign policy'. When the first Aegean continental shelf crisis erupted in 1976, as a result of EC pressure Karamanlis chose to deal with the crisis by taking the issue to the UN Security Council and the ICJ, rather than by military means (Arvanitopoulos 1994; Tsakaloyannis 1980). In addition, the period from Greece's application in 1975 to its membership in 1981 was marked by several attempts at dialogue, such as the 1976 Berne Declaration, which were mainly driven by Karamanlis's desire to secure Greek membership of the EC (Pridham 1991). However, these proved to be only short-term and tactical improvements in bilateral relations. As will be elaborated in the next section, the perception of Turkey as the primary security threat, and of the EC as a deterrence mechanism against Turkey, remained.

Starting with Turkey's membership application to the EC in 1987, the EC/EU's compulsory influence has been directed towards Turkey in an increasingly stronger and systematic fashion. However, the linkage between the Greek–Turkish disputes and Turkey's membership prospects was not accepted by Turkey and brought about only temporary or tactical policy changes until 1999. For example, following Turkey's application for EC membership in 1987, Greek–Turkish relations enjoyed another temporary period of improvement. Replicating the earlier Greek pattern, Turkey's reaction to the second crisis over the continental shelf in 1987 was restrained as it occurred right before Turkey filed its application for membership in the EC (Pridham 1991). Aware that improved relations with Greece were necessary to prevent a Greek veto and to strengthen Turkey's membership prospects in the EC, Turkey's Prime Minister Ozal adroitly defused the crisis and actively pursued dialogue with Greece (Birand 1991; Pridham 1991). However, this promising dialogue, known as the 'Davos Process', could not be sustained due to the uncooperative attitude of public opinion and the press in the two countries.

---

[8] This period also coincided with the return of Greece to democratic rule. However, democratisation has not led to a major change in Greece's foreign policy towards Turkey.

In the 1990s, several initiatives undertaken by Turkey can be linked to the EU's compulsory influence. However, these initiatives lacked a basis in policy change, were mainly intended for international consumption and were subsequently denied or diluted in front of domestic audiences. Often, the domestic criticism following these initiatives led policy-makers to counteract them afterwards with conflict-enhancing communications and behaviour. For example, it can be argued that the carrot of a Customs Union Agreement led Turkey to tacitly accept in March 1995 the start of accession negotiations with Cyprus. Even though some policy-makers at the time saw no problem in Cyprus joining the EU if a prior solution was reached on the island, this tacit acceptance was not grounded in a change in Turkey's Cyprus policy and was subsequently denied.[9] Consequently, when the Turkish media released the details of the deal to the public, it became the focal point of opposition, who criticised the government for 'selling off' Cyprus (*Cumhuriyet*, 10 December 1995). The government denied any change of policy on Cyprus and, in order to regain domestic legitimacy, was compelled to take some initiatives, which in turn fuelled the perceptions of threat in Greece and Cyprus. On 28 December 1995, Turkey and the Turkish Republic of Northern Cyprus (TRNC) issued a joint declaration that Cyprus should join the EU only simultaneously with Turkey and set up an Association Council that would take measures to achieve the partial integration of TRNC with Turkey.

Similarly, following the Imia/Kardak crisis, widespread international criticism led the new Turkish government into launching a peace proposal initiative to Greece in advance of the scheduled meeting of the EU–Turkey Association Council.[10] In a press conference in March 1996, Prime Minister Yilmaz called for unconditional talks with Greece to sort out problems relating to the Aegean and, marking a significant departure from the established Turkish policy, indicated Turkey's willingness to take the issues to the ICJ if the talks were to fail. In a follow-up debate in the Turkish Grand National Assembly (TGNA), however, this initiative became the subject of heated criticism from opposition deputies, who charged the government with bypassing the Foreign Ministry, undermining Turkey's resolute stance on the Kardak issue (*sic*), 'indexing' Turkish–Greek relations to the EU and naively trusting Turkey's

---

[9] Prof. Emre Gonensay, Turkish Foreign Minister (March–June 1996). Interviewed by author (Istanbul, 25 February 2004).

[10] Gunduz Aktan, member of Parliament and former Turkish Ambassador to Greece. Interviewed by author (Ankara, 4 March 2004). Aktan highlighted that it was not solely EU pressure, but the coupling of criticism from the EU with widespread international criticism that prompted the Turkish government to act.

interests to international institutions (like the ICJ) (TGNA 1996a). In the end, this widely publicised 'peace initiative' from the Turkish side did not lead to an improvement in bilateral relations and even produced hardened positions (Rumelili 2004c).

Therefore, we see that while the EC/EU had established a linkage between Turkey's membership and the resolution of its border disputes with Greece since Turkey's membership application in 1987, it was not able to exercise effective compulsory influence on Turkish policy towards Greece until after 1999. Even though some Turkish policy-makers were pressured to accept certain things and compelled to undertake certain initiatives, they were not able to 'sell' these to the wider Turkish elite and public. In front of domestic audiences, Turkish policy-makers were always careful to deny accusations that they acted because of EU pressure.[11] Acting on the basis of EU pressure could not be rationalised or legitimised because the Turkish elite did not perceive credible prospects in the EU, and due to Greece's membership the EU's involvement in Greek–Turkish relations was perceived as biased.

On the other hand, the 1999 Helsinki European Council decisions, by granting Turkey EU candidacy status, strengthened the incentives and persuasive elements in the EU's interventions, and has led to a major change in Turkish policy (Rumelili 2004c). Turkey has accepted EU involvement in Greek–Turkish disputes in the form of linking the resolution of Greek–Turkish disputes to Turkey's membership process, and prescribing a certain calendar and a conflict resolution framework. It is not known whether there has been a concomitant change in the Turkish position on the Aegean disputes because of the secret nature of Greek–Turkish negotiations; however, there has certainly been a change in the Turkish policy on Cyprus.

The Turkish elite began to perceive credible membership prospects only after the 1999 decision on Turkey's candidacy and my interviews indicate that a certain segment of the Turkish elite perceive themselves to have been induced by the candidacy carrot into this policy change towards Greece and the EU. As Gunduz Aktan, a former Turkish ambassador to Greece, remarked: 'We are pursuing these negotiations with Greece because we want to be in the EU.'[12] Nesrin Bayazit, Director General of Bilateral Relations with Greece in the Turkish Foreign

---

[11] See, for example, Foreign Minister Gonensay's response to accusations that Prime Minister Yilmaz's peace initiative to Greece in March 1996 was induced by and therefore specifically timed ahead of the EU–Turkey Association Council Meeting (TGNA 1996a).

[12] Interviewed by author (Ankara, 4 March 2004).

Ministry, has chosen to express this compulsory influence in less stark terms:

It is a fact that without Greece's positive stance – I am not saying if it does not just use its veto – it will not be possible for Turkey to enter the EU. We have to assess this realistically, and we are doing so. Greece is one of the countries that has to be on our side.[13]

In addition, critics tend to link the policy change to the EU's compulsory influence and caution that Turkey is creating the impression that 'it will do anything for the EU'.[14] However, as will be discussed in the next section, most Turkish policy-makers have expressed themselves as having been enabled rather than coerced/induced into this policy change. Thus, the Helsinki Council decisions have influenced Turkish elites holding more moderate and hardline positions with respect to the Greek–Turkish issues in different ways and facilitated the formation of a broad coalition. The candidacy status has functioned both as a carrot and as a legitimiser. While the carrot served to 'buy off' the hardliners into accepting EU involvement in Greek–Turkish disputes, the candidacy status also enabled the moderates to legitimise a European framework for the resolution of Greek–Turkish disputes.

Enabling influence

The EEC/EC/EU has always been a major reference point in the making of Greek and Turkish foreign policies vis-à-vis each other. However, prior to 1999, it has been a reference point for the legitimisation of conflict-enhancing policies. As rival states, Greece and Turkey approached their relations with the EEC in a competitive way from the very beginning. For example, in 1959, Turkey launched an application for associate membership to the EEC only after and mainly because of Greece's application. According to Birand (2000), Turkey's decision to apply was motivated by the policy of not leaving Greece alone in any Western international organisation.

Following Turkey's military operation in Cyprus in 1974, a foreign policy consensus emerged in Greece that Turkey posed a revisionist threat in the Aegean, Thrace and Cyprus (Triantaphyllou 2001; for a critical account, Heraclides 2001). In this context, membership in the EC was perceived as and valued for having provided Greece with security and

---

[13] Interviewed by author (Ankara, 3 March 2004).
[14] Dr Enis Tulca, Galatasaray University. Interviewed by author (Istanbul, 14 February 2004).

negotiating leverage in its dealings with Turkey; in short, as the logic of alliances predicts (Valinakis 1994; Tsakonas and Tournikiotis 2003). Hence, within the EC, the established Greek strategy of the deterrence of Turkey (Platias 2000) found new means of implementation. Greece pursued a policy of negative conditionality towards Turkey, blocking its relations with the EU until Turkey offered some concessions and/or agreed to the endorsement of the Greek positions by the EU (Couloumbis 1994; Yannas 1994).

The use of the EU lever as a short-term instrument of pressure against Turkey remained attractive to the Greek elite because it was generally regarded as successful[15] and politically less risky and more rewarding than alternative policies (Veremis 2001). The institutional asymmetry created by Greece's membership and Turkey's non-membership in the EU rendered this policy of negative conditionality not only possible, but also successful and legitimate. At the same time, the proponents of alternative policies towards Turkey were placed on uncertain and shaky ground. This disabling effect on the moderates in Greece can be clearly seen in the period between 1996 and 1999. While Costas Simitis, who assumed the governing PASOK's leadership in 1996, advocated a fundamental change in Greek foreign policy towards actively supporting Turkey's European orientation, on many occasions he had to give in to the hardliners, who favoured the continuation of the exclusionary policies of negative conditionality.[16] For example, following the 1997 EU Presidency proposal to establish a committee of wise men to study the problems between Turkey and Greece, thirty-two MPs from the governing PASOK Party addressed an open letter to Simitis stating their opposition to any discussion on the substance of the Greek–Turkish problems and the lifting of the Greek veto on Turkey in the EU (*Milliyet*, 22 April 1997). As a result of this pressure, the Greek government diluted the wise men proposal and retained the Greek veto on EU funds to Turkey (Rumelili 2004c).

According to Greek (and also Turkish) policy-makers and analysts, the Greek government's *volte face* to support Turkey's European orientation, as epitomised in the 1999 Helsinki Council decisions, constitutes a major

[15] Alkis Courcoulas, Istanbul Bureau Chief of Athens News Agency. Interviewed by author (Istanbul, 25 May 2004).
[16] Dimitris Droutsas, Chief Foreign Policy Advisor to George Papandreou on Greek–Turkish and Turkey–EU relations. Interviewed by author (Athens, 21 February 2005).

'turning point' in Greek foreign policy.[17] The EU has enabled this change in several ways. At a more fundamental level, European integration has been a 'powerful agent for the domestication of foreign policy and for the softening and broadening of national security toward low politics and economics' in Greece (Keridis 2001). These longer-term influences of Europeanisation on Greek policy-making, however, have taken a long time to mature and bear fruit (Ioakimidis 1994; Pettifer 1994), and began to generate changes in Greece's Turkey policy only in the late 1990s.

The longer-term influences of Europeanisation on Greek policy-making have been unleashed by the more immediate enabling influences of the EU. According to Kostas Ifantis, professor at the University of Athens and Head of the Policy Planning Unit at the Greek Foreign Ministry, it was the changing structural conditions at the EU level in the 1990s that led Greece into aligning its foreign policy with its EU partners.[18] The prevalent perception that the EU is moving forward generated fears of being left behind. Further integration with the EU became a reference point to legitimise the pursuit of alternative policies with respect to Turkey, when it became apparent in the late 1990s that Greece was far from fulfilling the conditions to join the EMU. After 1996, accession to the Eurozone came to be represented as a national goal in Greece that would bring about 'a strong Greece within a strong Europe' and ensure that Greece 'remains in the core' in what is increasingly becoming a 'multi-speed Europe' (Hellenic Parliament 1999b: 2363, 2400). As Ifantis aptly put it: 'In order to gain membership of the EMU, Greece had to bargain. In order to bargain effectively, Greece had to improve relations with Turkey.'[19]

A 'real' and 'substantive' EU membership perspective for Turkey has been the crucial element in the logic upon which the alternative policy of supporting Turkey's Europeanisation has been formulated and advocated in Greece. For Greece to eliminate the Turkish threat, Turkey needs to Europeanise and commit to certain principles within a European framework. For Turkey to Europeanise, the EU must be both willing and able to offer Turkey a 'real' membership perspective.[20] This logic therefore legitimises, and renders rational, that Greece should work towards bringing its main rival into the European Union. However, the logic is

---

[17] According to Couloumbis and Tziampiris (2002), the unanimous, if conditional, decision to invite Turkey to become an EU candidate during the 1999 Helsinki Summit marks 'the end of history' for Greece.

[18] Interviewed by author (Athens, 22 February 2005).

[19] Interviewed by author (Athens, 22 February 2005).

[20] Dimitris Droutsas. Interviewed by author (Athens, 21 February 2005).

doomed to fail if the EU does not offer a membership perspective to Turkey: the exclusion of Turkey from the EU would make it much more difficult – if not impossible – for Turkey to Europeanise. As Alkis Courcoulas surmised in 2004, 'if Turkey is not given a date [to start accession negotiations] in December, Greece's Turkey policy would lose its foundation'.[21]

By the autumn of 1999, these longer-term and more immediate ena-bling influences of the EU combined with a cabinet change and the atmosphere following the deadly earthquakes in Izmit and Athens to bring about a 'turning point' in Greek policy towards Turkey. Following the removal of three hardline Ministers from the Greek cabinet because of their responsibility in the crisis triggered by the abduction of PKK leader Abdullah Ocalan, the moderate George Papandreou was placed in the foreign ministerial post, and he was able to fully put into practice the alternative policy of engagement that actively supported the European orientation of Turkey. The deadly earthquakes in Izmit and Athens, respectively in August and September 1999, also brought out feelings of empathy and solidarity between the Greek and Turkish peo-ple, and allowed the leaders 'to claim a popular mandate for changing policies historically supported by a large majority on both sides' (Gundogdu 2001).

After Helsinki, the continuing *rapprochement* in Greek–Turkish rela-tions and Turkey's progress on the membership track enabled the con-solidation of this policy at the domestic level, and generated a broad domestic coalition in support of it in Greece. While the main opposition party, New Democracy, had criticised the government in 1999 for failing to tie the candidacy carrot to certain preconditions (Hellenic Parliament 1999b), it later admitted that the strategy was right and continued it after forming the government in 2004.[22] Most Greek analysts believe that the Helsinki strategy is built on the 'right assumptions'.[23] Whereas the hard-liners want Turkey to remain on the membership track because they believe they will thereby be able to control Turkey with the EU stick, the moderates support Turkish membership because they believe it will socialise Turkey into changing its foreign policy along EU norms. This domestic coalition has proven flexible enough to survive potentially serious crises in bilateral relations, such as in May 2003 (Rumelili

---

[21] Interviewed by author (Istanbul, 14 February 2004).
[22] Dr Panagiotis Tsakonas, University of the Aegean. Interviewed by author (Athens, 25 February 2005).
[23] Prof. Theodore Couloumbis, Director of the Hellenic Foundation for European and Foreign Policy. Interviewed by author (Athens, 25 February 2005).

2004c). In addition, the EU's inclusive approach towards Turkey has rendered the policy of negative conditionality less possible, less successful and less legitimate. The more the EU commits to Turkey's membership, the more Greece loses its power within the Union to block Turkey's path, and it can exercise a veto only at great cost to its reputation.[24] This awareness was highly visible among Greek policy-makers in the lead-up to the Brussels Summit (Bourdaras 2004).

Like Greece, Turkey has perceived the EC/EU within the logic of alliance, but as an alliance that it is not a part of. Mirroring Greece, the prevailing perception among Turkish policy-makers has been that Greece is pursuing a revisionist policy against Turkey (Gunduz 2001; Bilge 2000). Greece's membership has created and sustained the understanding in Turkey that the EC/EU has been 'captured' by a hostile Greece, and therefore cannot be impartial with respect to Greek–Turkish issues (Aksu 2001). In other words, the EU was perceived as just another platform through which Greece pursued its revisionist agenda with respect to Turkey. Under these perceptual conditions, alternative policies could not be legitimised by reference to the EU, because their critics would automatically frame them as concessions to Greece.

In addition, prior to 1999, the perceived ambivalence of the EU to Turkish membership has incapacitated the EU from becoming a reference point for policy change in Turkey in many areas, including Greek–Turkish relations (Diez and Rumelili 2004). The EU's direct interventions in Greek–Turkish relations, through statements and warnings that the Cyprus problem and Greek–Turkish disputes would adversely affect EU–Turkey relations, were negatively interpreted as broader reflections of a European reluctance to admit Turkey into Europe (Ugur 1999). The EU's exclusionary stance towards Turkey also fuelled a dominant conviction in Turkish political culture that 'Europe' is conspiring to weaken and dismember Turkey, aptly called the 'Sevres syndrome' after the 'Sevres Treaty', which conceded large parts of the Ottoman Empire to European powers after the First World War (Kirisci and Carkoglu 2003). This prevalent conviction has hindered the EU's impact on sensitive, sovereignty-related issues. In a particularly telling episode in February 2002, the Representative of the EU Commission to Turkey, Karen Fogg, was made the personal target of accusations that the EU was undermining Turkish interests in Cyprus and sponsoring secessionist activity in Kurdish-dominated south-eastern Turkey.

---

[24] Kostas Ifantis, interviewed by author (Athens, 22 February 2005).

In this perceptual environment, the EU's various interventions in Greek–Turkish disputes had become reference points in legitimising the continuation of non-compromising positions with respect to Greece. For example, in a follow-up debate on the Luxembourg European Council decisions in the TGNA, MPs from various political parties were united in characterising the EU as 'an organisation that implements Greek policy', and 'strongly condemning the EU's tendency to see itself as [an impartial] party in Greek–Turkish disputes', warning of the 'dangerous consequences of this imprudent tendency' (TGNA 1998). It is interesting how Bulent Akarcali explained why the EU could not be a conflict resolution mechanism for the disputes between Turkey and Greece:

After the EU tells Turkey to unilaterally resolve its disputes with Greece, why would Greece cooperate with us? ... Continuing its disputes with Turkey is to Greece's advantage ... Like Germany and Poland ... Turkey could have resolved its border disputes in the Aegean within the EU context. If there is friendship, that is the right thing to do. But if friendship has been unilaterally destroyed, then it is up to us to decide what is worth it and what is not. (TGNA 1998)

Since 1999, the prospect of EU membership has been a reference point in triggering a process of reform and transformation in Turkey in all areas of politics, including foreign policy (Diez and Rumelili 2004). In the 1990s, Turkey perceived nearly all of its neighbours as security threats, and pursued policies of deterrence. The present government, on the other hand, has adopted 'zero-problems with neighbours' as the guiding maxim of its foreign policy.[25] The EU's December 1999 decision to grant Turkey candidacy status has undermined the above-cited perceptions of an unreliable EU in collaboration with a hostile Greece. As a result, Turkey has first tacitly, and then more explicitly, accepted a linkage between Turkey's EU membership process and the resolution of Greek–Turkish disputes, and actively maintained the détente with Greece through various confidence-building measures and cooperation agreements. Nothing would demonstrate the changed perceptions of Greece and the EU better than Turkey's willingness to accept Greece's guidance on EU matters.[26]

This foreign policy change in Turkey was facilitated by the prospect of EU membership and the concomitant positive identification with the EU. The EU began to function both as a legitimate reference point and as an

---

[25] Prof. Ahmet Davudoglu, Chief Foreign Policy Advisor to Recep Tayyip Erdogan. Speaking at the Greek–Turkish Forum (Ankara, 17 November 2003).
[26] See Joint Declaration on Turkey–Greece Cooperation in EU Matters (Ankara, 6 April 2001) in www.mfa.gov.tr.

attractive carrot, enabling the moderates to justify policy change, to convince the sceptics and to silence their opponents. The prospect of co-membership in the EU with Greece offered to Turkish policy-makers a perspective for an alternative future when the border disputes with Greece would lose their meaning. As Nesrin Bayazit recounts: 'Once Turkey is in the EU, the problems with Greece will be resolved. We give the example of France and Germany. Many issues are resolved within the EU in the long-term.'[27] Thus, the perception of the EU as a successful security community has served to legitimise among the Turkish elite the joint efforts to gain membership in the EU and to resolve the outstanding disputes with Greece.

Connective influence

Civil cooperation between Greece and Turkey remained weak until the late 1990s because the civil society in both countries was underdeveloped and the Greek–Turkish activities particularly lacked legitimacy because of the ongoing conflicts. Groups – among them businessmen, journalists, artists and activists – dedicated to the intensification of transnational relations remained small, isolated minorities in both societies, and their activities were often subjected to criticism and, in a few instances, to physical attack. Although following the 1996 Imia/Kardak crisis civil society efforts intensified, they remained vulnerable to crises at the governmental level and were easily disrupted. For example, in reaction to Ocalan's capture on his way out of the Greek embassy in Kenya, Turkish businessmen unilaterally cancelled the scheduled meeting of the Turkish–Greek Business Council and 'even the most pro-Greek business personalities felt the need to make anti-Greek statements' (Ozel 2004: 167).

Civil society cooperation between the two countries had received a boost following the deadly earthquakes that hit Izmit and Athens respectively in August and September 1999. The extent of suffering generated feelings of popular empathy, and Greek and Turkish rescue teams, doctors and humanitarian workers got the chance to work together in a highly emotional setting. Since then – taking also advantage of the improved relations at the political level – transnational contacts between the two countries have multiplied both in form and in number. Turkish and Greek governments have developed and strengthened these transnational linkages by concluding a series of cooperation agreements on tourism,

[27] Interviewed by author (Ankara, 3 March 2004).

incentives for joint investment, environmental protection, economic cooperation, scientific and technological cooperation, customs services, maritime transport, culture, species protection, agriculture and on the exemption from double-taxation.

While this growing civil cooperation was undeniably initiated at the bilateral level through the active agency of political and civil society actors in Turkey and Greece, the EU has influenced this process in several ways. My interviews indicate that policy-makers in Greece and Turkey have consciously drawn from the EU model in choosing functional cooperation as their main strategy in improving bilateral relations.

A very wide spectrum of agreements in trade, energy, tourism, environment … This is a European framework as well. Civil society approach was the basis of reconciliation between Germany and France.[28]

In addition, its December 1999 decision to grant Turkey membership candidacy enabled the EU to help consolidate transnational cooperation. First of all, the institutional status of candidacy made Turkey eligible for many additional forms of EU funding, and thus allowed the EU to directly support the development of civil society in Turkey and assist Greek–Turkish civil initiatives.[29] The availability of EU funding has been important especially for Turkish NGOs, which are more dependent on foreign funding than their counterparts in Greece (M. Belge 2004). The EU has specifically supported local and grass-roots organisations, which would have difficulty accessing other forms of funding, and encouraged the formation of new partnerships between Greek and Turkish organisations.[30]

The EU-funded Greek–Turkish Civic Dialogue Programme first granted three macro-grants to organisations that are already active in Greek–Turkish issues – European Centre for Common Ground, Women's Initiative for Peace and AEGEE-Ankara – to run demonstration/cooperation projects. Afterwards, the Programme has also organised three workshops – two in Istanbul and one in Athens – with the aim of bringing together civil society actors from both sides to design joint

---

[28] Interview requested to be anonymous. Conducted by author (Athens, 24 February 2005).

[29] It is important to note that the nature of its relations with Turkey initially posed institutional limitations to the EU's ability to financially support the development of civil society in Turkey and direct funds to Greek–Turkish initiatives. For example, while the Greek–Turkish civil society activity peaked following the 1999 earthquakes, the Representation of the European Commission in Ankara was able to obtain funding and initiate its Greek–Turkish Civic Dialogue Programme only in 2002.

[30] Rana Birden, Greek–Turkish Civic Dialogue Programme, Representation of the European Commission to Ankara. Interviewed by author (Ankara, 18 November 2003).

projects. The funded projects focus on many issues, including protection of endangered species, women's rights, fight against women trafficking, rural development, peace education, study of the 1923 population exchange, joint theatre productions, and tourism promotion and development (www.stgp.org). The Cross-Border Cooperation Programme between Turkey and Greece, initiated in 2004, has allocated funds to various projects between Greek and Turkish municipalities in the northern Aegean, including projects on cooperation in the production and marketing of olives and olive oil, the development of Kaz Dagi National Park in Turkey as a centre for eco-tourism, the modernisation of the border crossing and the renovation of a Greek Orthodox church in Ayvalik, Turkey (*Aksam* newspaper, 19 April 2005).

With respect to the implementation of these programmes by the Representation of the European Commission in Ankara, civil society actors have noted the bureaucratic limitations and the continuing elitism as concerns. For example, as the director of an EU-funded Greek–Turkish project noted:

> The Commission gives us money but limits the activities that we can do. It says that I am providing this money for civil society development in Turkey, you cannot organise an activity in Greece ... [The Greeks] complain that they always have to come to Turkey ... In the beginning, it was extremely difficult to apply for these funds. They accepted applications only in English. Now they have translated the forms into Turkish. This thing needs to go beyond the NGOs based in the few major cities of Turkey.[31]

More importantly, the EU's connective influence has manifested itself in Turkey's EU membership becoming a common denominator or reference point for activists in Turkey and Greece. The activists working for Greek–Turkish cooperation mostly support Turkey's membership in the EU. In fact, when asked to discuss the impact of the EU on their activities, my interviewees – both Greek and Turkish – generally mentioned their support for Turkey's EU membership.[32] The EU dimension of the Greek–Turkish relationship is also an important additional motivating factor, especially for the Turkish activists, to work for Greek–Turkish cooperation. They perceive themselves and are also perceived by others as not only working for Greek–Turkish cooperation but also for Turkey's membership in the EU. The VEN Volunteers Association, for example, states this very explicitly in its mission statement:

---

[31] Interviewed by author (Ankara, 1 March 2004).
[32] Fotini Sianou, Political Association for Women, WINPEACE member. Interviewed by author (Athens, 12 March 2004), and Taciser Belge, Founding Member of Helsinki Citizens' Assembly. Interviewed by author (Istanbul, 9 February 2004).

It became apparent that the common denominator of our vision was to contribute to Turkey's process of European Union membership and this vision directed us to reorient ourselves. The active members all agreed that the most important advantage for Turkey in the EU membership process would be the establishment of strong and healthy relations between Turkey and Greece. (Tarikahya 2004)

Furthermore, with the Greek–Turkish border being an EU border, the EU's border regime shapes the nature of the EU's influence on transnational relations between Turkey and Greece. The 1995 EU–Turkey Customs Union Agreement has been a turning point in opening the Greek–Turkish border to trade and investment flows. The real rise in Greek–Turkish trade, however, has occurred after the improvement in bilateral relations, reaching $1.3 billion in 2003. Yet, the Schengen border system constitutes an important impediment to the further development of cross-border links. The strict and costly visa regime puts both the Turkish businessmen and exporters doing business in Greece and the Greek tourism sector at a disadvantage. There are ongoing attempts by local politicians and the Greek Foreign Ministry to raise this issue at the EU level and ask for the relaxation of the visa regime to encourage more travellers from the Turkish mainland to the Greek islands (Papandreou 2003).

Constructive influence

As identity conflicts, Greek–Turkish disputes have been articulated through representations of Greek and Turkish identities as oppositional and antagonistic towards each other. Such representations are validated by a selective reading of history in the two countries, and reproduced through the nationalist educational systems. At the beginning, this chapter made the argument that, since 1999, Greek–Turkish conflicts have de-escalated to issue conflicts. It is necessary to underline at this point that such conflict de-escalation does not and cannot amount to a rapid and total disappearance of oppositional and antagonistic identity constructions; due to the very nature of discursive change, this process is slow, indeterminate and always contested. Therefore, this section of the chapter will chart out the nature and extent of the discursive change that has accompanied the conflict de-escalation in Greek–Turkish relations, and analyse the role of the EU in that change.

An analysis of the Greek media, parliamentary debates and other relevant texts prior to 1999 reveals a prevalent construction of Turkey as inherently aggressive and provocative. For example, in a debate in the Greek Parliament on 6 November 1997, Karamanlis explained as the leader of the main opposition party, New Democracy, that 'Turkey has a very clear policy ... in breach of international law, aggressive, provocative, dangerous, consistent and timeless. It advances its own objectives ... chooses the time' (Hellenic Parliament 1997: 1250). Another major characteristic of the discourse on Turkey is the depiction of Turkey as monolithic and unable to change. During the same debate, Karamanlis added that 'there is a systematic policy from the other side which everyone pursues' (Hellenic Parliament 1997: 1250) and Tsovolas, leader of the opposition party Democratic and Social Movement (DIKKI), noted that the 'Turkish political system and the Turkish economy do not allow for a different type of relations ... This system can never become democratic' (Hellenic Parliament 1997: 1269).

In this period, the constructive influence of the EU discourse manifested itself in the representations of Turkey also as inherently non-European and unable to Europeanise (Rumelili 2003a). It was argued, for example, in the Greek daily *Ta Nea* that 'Turkey's Europeanness stems from geo-political and geo-strategic factors ... In actuality, Turks are closer to Asia by civilisation, thinking, language, and instinct' (Dountas 1995). A Turkey constructed as such can be disciplined only through the compulsory influence of the EU. The political debates in Greece prior to 1999 thus revolved around the question of whether Greece could convince other EU member states to direct this compulsory influence in a concerted way or whether it should resort to the veto. There was little if any discussion of the possible enabling influence of the EU on Turkey (i.e. Hellenic Parliament 1999a).

Prior to 1999, the question of how to relate to Turkey within the EU context was further complicated by the ambivalent approach towards Europe and the EU in the Greek discourse. According to Herzfeld (1987: 7), this stems from Greece's 'paradoxical status in the Eurocentric ideology'. Ascribed the identity of the living ancestors of the European civilisation, Greece has had to continuously live out the perceived imbalance between its mythical past and its present backwardness in relation to the contemporary states of Europe (Herzfeld 1987: 19). Prior to 1999, representations of the EU in Greek discourse, on the one hand, positively identified with the EU as the centre of civilisation that includes Greece and excludes Turkey. However, on occasions where the EU was perceived as favouring Turkey against Greece, positive identification quickly gave way to the construction of the EU as imperialist and hostile. For example, the Athens daily *Niki* characterised the EU's conclusion of the Customs Union Agreement with Turkey as an 'unethical policy': 'The Europeans, who bear responsibility for the Turkish barbarism against the Greeks and Armenians at the turn of the century, have returned back to their imperialist roots' (*Niki* newspaper, 12 December 1995).

The de-escalation of Greek–Turkish conflicts within the EU context in the post-1999 period was made possible by, and made visible, three fundamental changes in the Greek discourses on Turkey and the EU. The first was the shift from monolithic to more pluralist perceptions and representations of Turkey, while still employing the European/non-European distinction. Zoulas argued in the Greek daily *Kathimerini*: 'Greece's Foreign Minister is deeply convinced that there are two Turkeys. One is the Turkey of Prime Minister Recep Tayyip Erdogan: *pro-European*, moderate and flexible. The other is that of Turkish Chief of Staff Gen. Hilmi Ozkok: typically *eastern*, intransigent and aggressive' (Zoulas 2003).

Secondly, the representation of Turkey as pluralistic and able to change has made possible its construction as susceptible to the EU's enabling influence. This representation has become prevalent in Greece to such an extent that almost everything about Turkey has been made sense of within the discourse of 'Europeanisation'. To justify the policy change towards Turkey, Prime Minister Simitis argued in the Greek Parliament on 15 December 1999 that '[W]e have opened the door to Turkey because we believe that the Europeanisation of Turkey would favour everyone' (Hellenic Parliament 1999b: 2364). Similarly, the political turmoil in Turkey and even conflict-enhancing behaviour towards Greece are represented as a 'Europeanisation crisis' (Ioakimidis 2002).

Thirdly, the policy change towards Turkey has been grounded in a more positive identification with Europe and the EU. Reflecting a complete identification, the Greek Foreign Ministry spokesman Koumoutsakos reportedly said during the December 2004 Brussels European Council that 'whatever is European is also Greek and whatever is Greek is also European' (Bourdaras 2004). Similarly, the Greek daily *Kathimerini* commended the Greek Prime Minister for attempting 'to behave like a European leader, and not a Balkan leader' during his visit to the USA in January 2002 (*Kathimerini* newspaper, 16 January 2002). Greek policy-makers have repeatedly justified their policy change towards Turkey by reference to European norms. In fact, the Greek Foreign Minister Papandreou explained the policy change in December 2002 as: 'Our experience in Europe has taught us that the stability of our neighbour gives us strength' (Papandreou 2002).

In Turkey, prior to the improvement in relations with Greece, the prevalent representation of Greece was as a 'neighbour' and an 'ally' (in name only) that 'has made a habit of hostility towards Turkey' (TGNA 1996b) and 'lives off' (TGNA 1996a) its problems with Turkey. The Greek policy of using the EU as a lever against Turkey has been made sense of in terms of the dominant metaphor of Greece as 'the spoiled kid of Europe', which implies immaturity, undeservedness and abuse of position. Therefore, Greece was identified at best as a 'fake-European' (Rumelili 2003a). Thus, as in Greece, Europe served as the basic denominator of identity, reflecting the EU's constructive influence.

Also in Turkey as in Greece, these constructions of Greece and the EU were rooted in an ambivalent identification with Europe and the West in general. There is a fundamental tension in Turkish discourse, emanating from the simultaneous construction of Europe as an aspiration and as a threat (Rumelili 2004c). The construction of the EU as a threat flourishes on the memories of the dismemberment of the Ottoman Empire at the hands of European powers (i.e. Sevres syndrome), while the desire to validate Turkey's identity as modern and European constitutes the EU as an aspiration. The deteriorating state of Turkey's relations with Greece and the EU prior to 1999 have legitimated and reproduced the constructions of the EU as a threat. For example, during a debate in the Turkish Parliament on 20 April 1996, in opposing the referral of the Greek–Turkish disputes to the ICJ, Opposition MP Ali Dincer made an analogy with how Mosul was 'taken away ... by international institutions ... even though Turkey was right' (TGNA 1996a). Within this historically inspired discourse, many representations of Greece and the EU assumed as natural that the EU would support (Christian) Greece in relation to (Muslim) Turkey. Kislali argued in the Turkish daily *Cumhuriyet*: 'We have to accept that whether due to efforts of the Greek lobby in the USA, or stemming from a close culture like in the EU, the West favours the Greek side' (Kislali 1999).

The improvement in Greek–Turkish relations after 1999 made visible, and in turn was made possible by, two significant changes in the Turkish discourses on Greece and the EU. The first was the ensuing positive identification with the EU, such that the constructions of the EU as an aspiration gained prevalence over the constructions of the EU as a threat. Turkey's new identity position as an EU candidate also facilitated the gradual internalisation of EU norms and procedures on the resolution of border disputes as a requirement of European identity and a neutral basis on which to build a cooperative relationship with Greece. Turenc argued in the Turkish daily *Hurriyet*:

[S]eeing the benefits of sharing common values and interests will bring the two countries closer to each other with every passing day. No one can believe that Turkey and Greece, who have come together in the same family, will remain foes from now on. (Turenc 1999)

The second important discursive change was the shift towards the construction of Greece as a 'full, mature and rational' European state, and in a lot of ways as a 'model' for Turkey. Kohen argued in the Turkish daily *Milliyet* that 'it is also difficult not to admire Greece's current position within the Union ... just a few years ago certain EU circles harshly criticised its weak economy and uncooperative attitude ... Let's admit that the pragmatic, progressive policies of the Simitis administration have played an important role in Greece's successful rise within the EU ranks' (Kohen 2003). Coupled with the unwavering Greek support for Turkey's EU membership, this construction of Greek identity has facilitated the perception of Greek behaviour towards Turkey in the EU context in less hostile and conspiratorial terms.

The above analysis makes clear that the EU exercises a strong constructive influence on Greek–Turkish relations because the discourse of 'Europe' as a collective identity has consistently been the authoritative reference point in the construction of Greek and Turkish identities vis-à-vis each other. However, the discourse of 'Europe' has authorised and validated two conflicting identity discourses on Self and Other in Turkey and Greece. One is the conflict-enhancing discourse that differentiates the 'European' Greece from the 'non-European' Turkey, which was dominant prior to 1999, and served to legitimise the Greek-threat perceptions and aggravate Turkey's identity insecurity. The other is the conflict-diminishing discourse that positions Greece and Turkey as 'European' and 'Europeanising', which has become prevalent following Turkey's EU candidacy and the improvement in Greek–Turkish relations.

However, the nature of the EU's relations with Turkey and Greece has structurally conditioned which of these two very conflicting identity discourses will be validated within the broader discourse of 'Europe'. Before 1999, the EU's exclusionary discourse on Turkey, and Turkey's ambivalent institutional position, reproduced and validated the conflict-enhancing discourse based on the European/non-European distinction. Turkey's EU membership candidacy, on the other hand, has legitimised the construction of Greek and Turkish identities as 'European' and 'Europeanising' (Rumelili 2003a).

Conditions of EU impact

The positive impact of the EU on the Greek–Turkish conflicts, a case of an identity conflict on EU borders between a long-time EU member and an associated state desirous of EU membership, has been realised through a complex interaction between domestic and EU-related conditions. The previous section broadly referred to these conditions in discussing the various forms of EU influence and their impact on Greek–Turkish relations in different time periods. This section will present these conditions in a more comprehensive fashion, and evaluate their relative significance.

Firstly, the EU's offer of a credible membership perspective to Turkey stands as the critical condition that has facilitated multiple forms of positive EU influence on Greek–Turkish relations. In Turkey, the credible EU membership perspective brought together a strong domestic coalition in favour of reform, and induced and legitimated wide-ranging policy changes in many areas, including Cyprus and the resolution of Greek–Turkish disputes within the EU framework. In Greece, it has been a facilitating condition for the rethinking of Greek policy towards Turkey. The advancement of institutional relations through the candidacy framework has enabled the EU to direct greater amounts of funding to Turkish civil society and to Greek–Turkish initiatives. And finally, the identity positions entailed in the candidacy status have directed Greek and Turkish discourses towards less oppositional and antagonistic identity constructions.

Secondly, given the extent of member state influence on the EU's external relations, the policy change in Greece towards Turkey and the EU has been a mutually constitutive condition for the EU's positive impact on Greek–Turkish relations. If there had not been a policy change towards supporting Turkey's European orientation in Greece, then the EU would face institutional obstacles in furthering relations with Turkey. In addition, Greece would insist on subjecting those relations to very strict conditions, which ultimately would not be accepted by Turkey, as was the case during the 1997 Luxembourg European Council. While itself an important condition for EU impact, this policy change in Greece was, as has been discussed previously, also enabled by the EU – through the longer-term influences of Europeanisation and the structural pressures generated by the deepening European integration, and the developing EU–Turkey relationship.

Thirdly, the existence of constituencies that actively promote Greek–Turkish cooperation in the two countries has also facilitated the EU's positive impact. The positive atmosphere that arose between the two societies following the 1999 earthquakes has been a necessary condition especially for the following connective influence of the EU. In the absence of supportive constituencies and established networks, EU-funding programmes would have had no foundation to build upon and might even have backfired. In addition, and as was noted in the introduction, the EU's positive impact on Greek–Turkish relations has been realised through the willingness of domestic actors to use the EU as a model, symbol and resource. Therefore, the fact that the constituencies that promote Greek–Turkish cooperation have also advocated closer integration with the EU has greatly facilitated the EU's impact.

Finally, corroborating conflict resolution activities of other international institutions, such as NATO, and third-party actors, such as the United States, have facilitated the EU's impact on the Greek–Turkish conflicts. If these other actors had taken different positions on the disputes, or engaged in activities that undermined or overtook the EU's role, then the EU's impact on Greek–Turkish relations would have been much smaller.

Conclusions and implications for EU policy

Greek–Turkish conflicts have constituted a conflict resolution challenge for the EU dating back to the beginnings of European integration. This chapter showed that while the EU has possessed important instruments to influence Greek–Turkish relations, it has not been able to exercise that influence independently of what the Greek and Turkish domestic actors have chosen to make out of the EU. Therefore, until the late 1990s, the EU has actually had a conflict-enhancing impact on Greek–Turkish relations, because certain domestic and EU-related conditions have empowered those domestic actors in Turkey and Greece who have perceived the EU within the logic of alliance and used it as an additional battleground in their ongoing rivalry. Only after 1999 has the EU begun to have a consistent conflict-diminishing impact on Greek–Turkish relations because Turkey's EU membership candidacy has empowered the domestic actors in both Turkey and Greece who have sought to use the EU as a framework for long-term conflict transformation.

My research on how the EU has contributed to the post-1999 improvement in Greek–Turkish relations shows that the enabling impact of the EU has been the most pervasive and manifested itself in different ways. Not only has the EU, and more specifically Turkey's EU candidacy, been the reference point in the formulation and legitimisation of alternative foreign policies in Greece and in Turkey, it has also served as the common denominator in building strong domestic coalitions at the political and civil society level. Due to Greece's EU membership, the EU's compulsory influence has been directed at Turkey in an asymmetric fashion, and my research indicates that, contrary to expectations, the compulsory pathway has played only a complementary role in relation to the more pervasive enabling influence of the EU. In both Turkey and Greece, the compulsory influence of the EU on Turkey has served to 'buy off' the hardliners and bring them into the domestic coalition in favour of policy change.

While in Turkey, the membership carrot has induced those actors to negotiate with Greece within the EU framework, in Greece, the availability of the EU stick against Turkey has convinced the hardliners to support Turkey's EU accession process. The connective influence of the EU has been, thus far, relatively minor and limited to certain sectors of the society. However, cross-border links and functional cooperation have been actively promoted by the Greek and Turkish governments, who have claimed to have taken the EU as a model in their endeavours. And finally, though very significant, the EU's constructive influence on Greek–Turkish relations has been, thus far, ambivalent because while certain elements in EU discourse have authorised starkly oppositional identity constructions in Turkey and Greece, other elements have validated less antagonistic identity positions. Turkey's EU membership candidacy, to the extent that it has had a transformative effect on the overall EU discourses on 'Europe and Turkey' and 'Europe and its others', carries the potential to tilt the EU's constructive influence to the positive, conflict-diminishing direction.

Table 4.1 provides an overview of the forms of EU influence on Greek–Turkish relations.

Greek–Turkish relations are a case of conflict on EU borders. As such, the EU's lengthy experience with Greek–Turkish relations contains important lessons for how the EU should approach and handle the other conflicts that it faces around its new borders (Rumelili 2007). With the 2004 enlargement of the EU and the Greek-Cypriot rejection of the Annan Plan for the reunification of Cyprus, the Cyprus conflict and Russia's relations with the Baltic states have similarly been situated on EU borders (see Demetriou and Joenniemi in this volume, chapters 3 and 5). In the case of Greek–Turkish conflicts, the EU's decision to grant Turkey candidacy status has paved the way for positive EU impact. Therefore, the obvious policy implication to be drawn from the Greek–Turkish experience is that the EU should build close institutional and identity relations with outsider states if it desires to have a positive impact on (potential) conflicts on its external borders.

To some extent, this is sought to be realised through the European Neighbourhood Policy (ENP), which promises to EU's 'neighbours' privileged relations and, possibly, a certain degree of economic and political integration with the EU.[33] However, the experience of Greek–Turkish conflicts points to some serious shortcomings of this policy, as it stands. Firstly, the ENP replaces the distinction between insiders and outsiders

---

[33] This section largely draws on Rumelili (2007).

Table 4.1: *Overview of EU influence on the Greek–Turkish conflicts*

Pathway	Main EU institution		Main addressee		Instrument of influence		Condition of influence	
	Greece	*Turkey*	*Greece*	*Turkey*	*Greece*	*Turkey*	*Greece*	*Turkey*
Compulsory	N/A (at least since 1981)	Council of Ministers	N/A	Government	N/A	Membership criteria	N/A	Credibility of membership carrot
Enabling	Council of Ministers	Council of Ministers	Government and political elite	Government and political elite	Pressures of integration	European norms as requirements of European identity	Positive identification with the EU	Positive identification with the EU
Connective	European Commission	European Commission	NGOs; local authorities	NGOs; local authorities	Structural funds; Interreg	Pre-accession funding	Relative openness of the EU border	Relative openness of the EU border
Constructive	All	All	Political elite and opinion makers	Political elite and opinion makers	Discourse on European identity	Discourse on European identity	Nature of EU discourse on conflict parties	Nature of EU discourse on conflict parties

with another clear-cut dichotomy between members and neighbours in terms of both institutional and identity relations. The alternative does not necessarily entail committing to further enlargement, but offering to neighbours a more nuanced, but also clearly defined, gradation of integration/cooperation relations on a differentiated basis. More importantly, this gradation of relations needs to be grounded in an identity discourse that rejects any sharp distinction between Europeans and non-Europeans. Then, just as it did in the case of Turkey–Greece, the prospect of a higher degree of integration with the EU can induce the outsider state to change its policies, while, at the same time, providing the basis for an alternative policy to the insider state. Secondly, the ENP includes no safeguards against possible attempts by a member state to adversely affect the EU's relations with a particular neighbouring state, as a strategy in their ongoing conflicts. Though the Strategy Paper states that 'it is of utmost importance that the Institutions and Member States act in a consistent and coherent way' (European Commission 2004) in the implementation of the ENP, there is no set of general principles which will govern the member state's relations with the EU's neighbours.

5   Border issues in Europe's North

Pertti Joenniemi

Overview of the conflict

Towards shared space

This chapter covers Europe's North in a region-specific perspective, exploring the European Union's role as a 'perpetuator' of conflicts in a broader, regional context.[1] In the first place, as the relevant issues of the post-Cold War period have been – almost without exception – dealt with in a fairly peaceful fashion, the proper term to be used might be disputes rather than conflicts. It is also worth noting that although the EU broadly covers the region, the intra-regional forces seem to have impacted on the various conflictual issues at least as forcefully as the EU.

In general, Europe's North has been quite quick in capitalising on the option of change that opened up with the end of the Cold War. Having been profoundly divided by the conflict between East and West with region-formation not even existing as an idea (with the exception of Nordic cooperation), the North has not merely caught up with the rest of Europe, it has, in fact, turned into one of the most regionalised parts of the continent. Borders, previously seen as lines of exclusion and defence, have changed in meaning with the emergence of a rich patchwork of various Euro-regions, trans-boundary arrangements, cross-border projects and contacts of twinning. Old divides and suspicions have to a large extent been replaced by building a new sense of regional community as exemplified by Baltic Sea cooperation, Barents Euro-Arctic cooperation and Arctic cooperation. In most cases the impact of the EU has been

---

[1] I would like to acknowledge the assistance and contributions of Andrey Makarychev and Sergei Prozorov in the writing of this chapter. They both worked at DIIS in 2004 carrying out research on border issues in Europe's North. This chapter covers a relatively large geographic area in which, unlike in the other case studies, not 'one', but, strictly speaking, four different 'cases' are encountered. Thus, while it seeks to retain the structure of the other case study chapters, it does need to pay some tribute to the fact that four, not one, cases are covered and that unlike in the other cases the EU has become a conflict party itself in one of the cases (Kaliningrad).

contextual, with 'Europeanisation' playing a considerable role, although as to actorness the EU has for the most part remained a player among others.

More generally, various statist arrangements that push politics beyond concerns about security by embracing ideas of debordering, multiplicity and regionality, have been complemented by civil society-related initiatives with NGOs, local municipalities and actors such as cities becoming engaged in a multitude of transnational linkages, particularly between the Nordic and Baltic countries. Alongside an idealism that has strived to reach beyond security, there has also been a more security-oriented concern with creating stability within northern Europe. This became an issue in the early 1990s following the break-up of Yugoslavia and concerns that the Baltic Sea region should not turn into a 'northern Balkans'. In this respect, questions of security became conducive to solving a range of conflictual issues in peaceful ways and by promoting, in this context, cooperation and regionalisation in the North. Whereas during the Cold War questions of 'security' were a reason to avoid too much interaction, more recently security has become precisely a reason to cooperate. Instead of staying aloof, there has – in line with the latter type of thinking – been an aspiration for shared space, and this despite the fact that according to Huntingtonian-style perceptions deep dividing lines should have unfolded precisely along the EU's northern borders.

As to the ideational underpinnings of the policies pursued, two elements need to be considered (cf. Browning and Joenniemi 2005). Firstly, for the Baltic states and Poland traditional *realpolitik* concerns of alliance building against a possible resurgent Russian threat have been evident.[2] In this respect, plugging into regional cooperation projects promoted by the Nordic countries and Germany was seen as one way of escaping the Russian sphere of influence, while at the same time making the Baltic states and Poland eligible for future EU and NATO membership. Thus, the 1990s' discourse of 'returning to Europe' was always understood as leaving something threatening and 'non/less-European' (Russia) behind (see Jæger 1997). In opposition to the construction of any unifying identities, 'Europeanisation' was thus understood in a rather traditional, power-political and divisive manner with the policies pursued being impacted on by 'old energies, injuries and differences' (Mälksoo 2006: 279).

Secondly, however, throughout the 1990s there was also a strong emphasis on more liberal institutionalist approaches to security (cf. Archer

---

[2] For a description, see Emerson *et al.* (2005).

2005). Instead of an emphasis on zero-sum gains, security has been reconfigured and represented in terms of ideas of cooperative, collective and comprehensive security. This reflects a twofold realisation: firstly, that state security is best achieved through building trust with each other; and, secondly, that with the end of the Cold War a range of new and pressing 'soft security' issues that now appeared on the regional agenda (e.g. economic, environmental, social and public health issues) could only be effectively tackled through cooperative action. Indeed, throughout the 1990s the Nordic states and Germany (and later the EU) promoted a certain strategic blurring of these realist and liberal logics of security, with the (liberal) belief being that by promoting cooperation over common 'soft security' issues, qualitative gains might also be made in the 'hard security' realm by fostering trust and cooperative relationships between Russia and the Baltic states, and between Russia and its Western neighbours more generally. The institutionalist element to this approach became clearest in the creation of the Council of the Baltic Sea States (1992), the Barents Euro-Arctic Council (1993) and the Arctic Council (1996) as forums for dialogue between the states and various other entities within the region, but also as (potential) symbols of shared interests and identities.

Obviously, the vision of European integration (as well as NATO membership in the case of the Baltic states and Poland) has helped to tone down conflictual issues and settle questions of identity. This has taken place to the extent that the region has gained features of a 'security community'. However, it has to be noted concerning regionalisation, that for much of the 1990s the EU's approach to the region remained rather limited. That is to say that while the Union's presence in northern Europe did increase markedly with Finland's and Sweden's membership in 1995 and with the 'Europe whole and free' aspiration providing guidelines for the policies to be pursued in a region-specific context, the EU was slow in developing (in addition to enlargement) a distinct approach and set of policies towards the region as a whole. The furthest the EU went in this regard was the 1996 Baltic Sea Region Initiative, which was fairly limited in essence. As such, the EU's northern members (and northern actors more generally) were provided with considerable space and opportunity to take the lead and shape the EU's northern agenda, a task most notably taken on by Finland with its 1997 proposals for the Northern Dimension (ND) initiative. In aiming at promoting active regional and cross-border cooperation in a bottom-up fashion, the initiative raised, among other things, the question of how to think about the new common EU–Russian border and what could be done in order to avoid isolating Russia in the context of an increasingly integrated North.

While the 1990s stood out as a period of stabilisation, more recent policies have often been described as representing a 'normalisation' (cf. Stålvant 2005; Mälksoo 2006) and as a rather pragmatic turn. Arguably, with concerns about security declining, there has been more space for discourses about the EU's *duty* to avoid the emergence of new, dividing borders and to bring about stability and progress in the region as well as various themes pertaining to the *opportunities* being opened up. The dual enlargement is there and hence the major security concerns of countries such as Poland and the Baltic states have been alleviated with security declining as a policy-relevant argument in a region-specific context. It has, instead, been thematised quite differently in the discourse on the War on Terror, and, with the prominence of the latter theme, more future-oriented and spatially quite different as well as broader – if not global – issues have figured high on the political agendas. The change in emphasis is notable also in the sense that Russia, in the latter context, comes out as a 'strategic partner' – rather than being seen as a potential territorial threat in the region – in the fight against terrorism and transnational crime. With terrorism seen as something that tends to change our lives dramatically, Russia is treated (and aspires to be treated) in inclusive terms.

Although being usually considered as something of a marginal area in European politics, the successes of the post-Cold War years have clearly increased the weight of Europe's North. Riding actively on the idea of integration has allowed it to some extent to shape the development of European political space. More recently, however, this impact appears to have been in decline. This is primarily because the EU, for some time at least, appeared to try to narrow the space available for region-specific initiatives. The Northern Dimension (ND) has increasingly gained the appearance – with Poland and the Baltic states having achieved EU membership – of being a core instrument in EU–Russian relations, and it also appears that the EU is on its way to establishing a centralised framework in the form of the European Neighbourhood Policy (ENP), a policy introduced in 2004. Initially it appeared that the ND was on its way to becoming subordinated to the more centralised and bilaterally oriented ENP, and secondly, the EU appeared to aim at precluding outsiders from having an equal voice in policy formulations and agenda setting as to the unfolding of political space in Europe's North. If true, these tendencies would imply that the space available for heterogeneous approaches with a variety of voices – including those belonging to the Union's 'partners' – is closing down. The EU's northern boundaries would in such a context become more restrictive. Borders would be managed rather than over-come, with the option of new memberships being closed down with the introduction of the new Neighbourhood Policy (ENP).

The issues involved

With the enlarging European Union having advanced towards Russia's borders, the question of compatibility between the positions held by the EU and those of Russia has become increasingly relevant. It appears on this account – as the increasing presence of the EU also in Europe's North tends to contribute to a process of desecuritisation – that there exists some degree of compatibility. The relations have thus in general unfolded in a reasonably positive manner, albeit some sticking points are there and remain to be sorted out.

We may identify two types of conflictual dispositions in EU–Russian relations that spill over beyond the narrow issues in interstate relations into the wider social space and acquire characteristics of 'identity conflicts'. The problematic of the 'Schengen curtain', related to the expansion of the Schengen visa regime for Russians in the course of EU enlargement, is capable of developing into a conflict discourse on Russia's exclusion from Europe and jeopardising the EU's own efforts at stimulating regional cooperation along the EU–Russian borders. The interpretation of this contradiction in the EU stance vis-à-vis Russia may be found in the dilemma between 'external' and 'internal' security projects of the EU, whereby the logic of regional integration clashes with a 'soft-securitising' uniform approach to borders (Browning 2003).

Secondly, the widespread perception of Russia's passive or subordinate status in cooperative regional arrangements with the EU has resulted in the efforts to reconstitute the North-western Federal District as an active political subject, encountering the EU with an autonomous development strategy for the Russian North-west. In the extreme case, the lack of recognition of Russia as a legitimate political subject with its own interests that need not necessarily coincide with those of the EU brings forth a discourse of self-exclusion from European integration, grounded in the reaffirmed principle of state sovereignty. The Russian position therefore oscillates between two, at first glance opposed, stances of the problematisation of exclusion from the European space and the affirmative self-exclusion: the dissatisfaction with the present format of EU–Russian cooperation leads to the disillusionment with the very idea of Russia's greater integration with the EU and the renewed valorisation of sovereign autonomy.[3]

Notably, there have not been any serious eruptions of conflicts in Europe's North for quite some time, although some tensions remain, as indicated by the Bronze Soldier statue disputes in Tallinn in 2007. One may

---

[3] For a more detailed analysis of these conflictual dispositions see Prozorov (2005a).

further note that the border issues that are there pertain mostly to the relations between respective EU countries and Russia rather than the EU and Russia as such. Moreover, the tension tends to be latent rather than overt. There is, along these lines, the Karelian 'question', part of the relations between Finland and Russia. It pertains to demands of restitution occasionally raised in the sphere of the Finnish civil society and covers territories ceded by Finland to the Soviet Union according to the Paris Peace Treaty in 1948 in the aftermath of World War II. Similarly, the contested Estonian–Russian borderlands as regards the Pechora/Petserimaa and East of Narva regions as well as the Abrene/Pytalova area between Latvia and Russia in the direction of Pskov all pertain to historical disputes. In the case of both the Estonian–Russian (1999) and Latvian–Russian (1998) borders, treaties have been negotiated and initially approved but have only come into force in the Latvian–Russian case.

In the case of the border treaty between Latvia and Russia, the ratification was for a while postponed by Russia based on the argument that Latvia's government insists – by issuing a declaration to the 1920 peace treaty – on references to previous history that might open the gate for claims of restitution. In the case of the border treaty between Estonia and Russia, it was negotiated between the governments and ratified by the Estonian Parliament, although Russia felt itself compelled to pull its signature from the treaty when the Estonian Parliament added a reference to past injustices to the preamble. These failures notwithstanding (which pertain to identities and interpretations of past history rather than the border as such), Russia has declared itself ready to reopen the case with Estonia, and the EU has urged Russia to do so in order for the border treaty to be ratified.

The question of Kaliningrad has a quality of its own. It does so in pertaining, primarily, to the EU–Russian relationship at large (although it has an impact on Polish–Russian and Lithuanian–Russian relations as well). This is to say that the Union does not occupy a position of an external perturbator but is to be viewed as a conflict actor in being an integral part of the overall setting. As to the background of the Kaliningrad 'puzzle', history plays a certain role but it is also closely related to current issues and terms of interaction. In the case of the 'puzzle', there are quite concrete issues involved, although they also relate to the identities of the relevant actors, including those of the EU and Russia. Moreover, in the case of Russia there also appear to be fears present of being, more generally, offered a position of subordination within the order emerging in the North and the new, integration-oriented Europe.

In the context of EU–Russian relations, Kaliningrad has so far been approached and treated as a question mainly about the terms of transit and in that regard a compromise was found in 2002 through a variety of technical solutions. The Karelian 'question' has not been on the official agendas in the first place, and in the case of the Estonian–Russian border, the parties seem arguably to be moving in the direction of a solution acceptable to the respective governments and parliaments. Looking ahead, it appears that Europe's North is heading towards a situation with largely all the pending issues settled and the EU–Russian relationship in general being the more important issue to be sorted out. The overall order of the region increasingly points in the direction of a concentric, EU-driven one, with Russia showing signs of being basically able to live with the options offered, although placing its own 'common spaces' agenda on the table and aspiring, in general, after a recognition of its alleged exceptionality as a 'special partner' and a more inclusive position of true partnership within the unfolding order.

The Karelian 'question' As to the requests for restitution raised in the sphere of the Finnish civil society, the areas included mainly cover the Karelian Isthmus.[4] It is fairly unknown internationally and does not stand out as a major theme on the European agenda, neither is it a pressing one in current Finnish–Russian relations. Regarding the positions of the states involved, Finland has refrained from any border claims (although it has expressed its preparedness to discuss the issue if that would turn out to be acceptable to Russia as well) whereas Russia basically denies the existence of the issue in the first place. Since the demise of the Soviet Union, the issue has been addressed in the discourse of the civil society in Finland. The Karelian Association, representing people (and their descendants) that fled from the areas handed over by Finland to Russia, has been an active social agent in the promotion of the issue.[5] A major item on the agenda of the association consists of a call for restitution. The areas handed over are claimed back on the basis that the ceding of the areas was unjust in the first place and that the injustice should be rectified (see Forsberg 1995b; Joenniemi 1998).

The position of the Russian Federation on the Karelian issue has been one of denial. The stance has hardly changed since the Soviet period, although the reasoning behind such a view has moved from the geostrategic considerations that led to the occupation during the war towards the concern that raising the border issue with Finland would open up the

---

[4] Information on the issue is available particularly from the Karelian Institute, University of Joensuu, see www.joensuu.fi/ktl/index.php. Interviews have been carried out in the context of the EUBorderConf project particularly with Director Ilkka Liikanen and the former Director of the Regional Council, Tarja Cronberg.

[5] For information on the association, see www.karjalanliitto.fi.

Pandora's box of border revisions and weaken the new fragile Russian state. Thus, while President Yeltsin officially denounced the Soviet annexation in a speech in 1994, the federal policy line since 1992 has been that no border issues exist between Russia and Finland. Instead of focusing on restitution, efforts have been made to enhance cross-border cooperation and to make the border more transparent and less securitised (see Aleksandrov 2001). These efforts were initiated immediately in the aftermath of the dissolution of the Soviet Union and premised on a Neighbourhood Agreement between the Russian Federation and Finland, signed in January 1992.

The Putin Presidency has been marked by some changes in this position. Initially, in one of his interviews to the Finnish press, President Putin suggested that even the discussion of the border issue endangered relations between the two countries (Ahtiainen 2000). However, since his state visit to Finland in 2001, Putin has adopted a different line. Changing borders by returning those parts of Karelia ceded to the Soviet Union is, in his view, not the best way to resolve the problems, although those calling for a restoration of Karelia are not to be ignored. Thus, instead of any revision he advocated integration and cooperation.[6] Putin hence appears to aim at reorienting the discussion away from the dichotomous and zero-sum logic of a border dispute towards integrative and joint arrangements, with borders changing from divisive lines to sites of cooperation. In this manner the issue is shifted from the 'high' to the 'low' political agenda, and the Russian regions bordering on Finland, particularly the Republic of Karelia, acquire a voice in the new arrangements, as opposed to the interstate border dispute, in which the regions do not have any jurisdiction at all.

The increasing impact of an EU logic thus appears to contribute to a deproblematisation of the border. Political decisions are not taken with regard to the border *per se* (either restrictive or facilitative, e.g. the abolition of visa controls). Instead, the function of borders is reconstructed in the new cooperative context. In contrast to the more ambitious – if vague – visions of 'debordering', the concept of border deproblematisation does not emphasise the irrelevance of the border, let alone its disappearance, but rather marks the change at a discursive level, whereby the political significance of the border becomes diminished and border regions become framed as zones of interaction, devoid of identity-related disaccord.[7] The border thus ceases to be the privileged marker of identity and the object of contentious political discourses, while it retains its

---

[6] See *Helsingin Sanomat*: www.helsinki-hs.net/news.asp?id=20010904IE3.
[7] These points are stressed in the EUBorderConf study on the issue, see Prozorov (2004b).

significance in the domain of depoliticised interaction – or interaction of a European nature – as both a recognised obstacle and a source of opportunity.

The Karelian Republic, one of the twenty-one republics within the Russian Federation, has for its part actively contributed to a deproblematisation of the border. One of the features of Karelian policy in the 1990s has been the active establishment of international links, primarily with bordering Finland but also through membership in the multiple regional arrangements in the North of Europe (e.g. Barents Euro-Arctic Region, Council of Baltic Sea States (see Aleksandrov 2001; Shlyamin 2002)). Throughout the 1990s, the leadership of the Republic of Karelia prioritised the development of cross-border cooperation with Finland at the same time as it maintained the federal line on the impossibility of raising the issue of a border revision. One might venture that the 'anti-revisionist' and 'integrationist' stances are in fact related insofar as the Republic's 'strategy of cooperation' is hampered by any reconstruction of the border area as a 'zone of conflict', whether in the Finnish discourse of restitution or in the Russian 'counter-discourse' of entrenchment that gives federal-level publicity to the Republic, but framed negatively as the 'bastion' of Russian statehood in the North-west.[8]

Since Finland's entry into the EU in 1995, EU frameworks of cross-border cooperation (Interreg and TACIS, including the TACIS CBC (Cross-Border Cooperation) sub-programme) have – as a form of border deproblematisation – to a great extent supplanted bilateral programmes with Finland as the primary format of cooperation. In 1998 the Karelian government launched the proposal of establishing a Euregio Karelia as an 'umbrella project' utilising the opportunities of the 'peripheral border area' status. Officially inaugurated in 2000, Euregio Karelia comprises the Republic of Karelia and the Finnish provinces of North Ostrobothnia, Kainuu and North Karelia (Prozorov 2004b).

The basic principle of the project is the formation of what the Karelian Programme of Cross-Border Cooperation refers to as 'the *culture of transparent borders*', making cross-border contacts in trade, science, culture and tourism a 'natural activity in the everyday life' of the border communities (Republic of Karelia 2001: 3.2). This principle exemplifies the operation of the *enabling impact* of the EU logic of border deproblematisation: the institutional framework of the Euregio provides a new institutional platform, at which border issues may be discussed and joint policy solutions devised.

---

[8] For a more detailed discussion of this point see Prozorov (2004c).

The Euregio's programme on fostering the development of a 'cross-border civil and information society', which envisions the intensification of cross-border contacts between both experts and citizens' organisations, explicitly invokes the argument about the *'connective impact'* of such societal interfaces on conflict transformation: '[the programme will] create opportunities at the level of individual citizens and communities for interaction, changing attitudes and pursuing more in-depth co-operation in order to prevent *border-related conflicts* and thereby at the local level *promote security between states'* (Euregio Karelia 2002: 12).

The optimistic scenario for the Euregio is that it will ultimately also have a *constructive impact* on the border region, leading to the constitution of a new transnational macro-regional identity that thoroughly deproblematises the Karelian issue (cf. Cronberg 2003). Borders could, in the best of cases, turn into integrated borderlands, spaces rather than lines. Elements of this vision are already there and the EU may in this sense be said to have been moderately successful in displacing the Finnish–Russian border dispute with the new discursive site of trans-border cooperation. Euregio Karelia exemplifies the region-building logic that sidelines the issue of territorial restitution (whose resolution at the official level is unrealistic in any case) by offering a concrete plateau for trans-boundary regional integration. Moreover, it is within the EU logic that the border question, which in the statist logic belongs squarely to the competence of national authorities, becomes reinscribed within the 'low' political framework of cooperation across and beyond the border.

The Estonian–Russian border Estonia's return to independence in 1991 raised and activated the question of its eastern border. In practice the question has been settled, albeit the formal conclusion of a border treaty between Estonia and Russia is still pending.

The contest regarding the eastern bank of the river Narva and the Pechora/Petserimaa has a long history, and the question was already imminent in the context of Russian–Estonian relations when Estonia declared independence in 1918. The solution then consisted of Russia recognising that these two areas belong to Estonia. The solution was later confirmed in the Peace Treaty signed in Tartu in 1920. The agreement unravelled, however, in the context of World War II with Estonia being annexed – after German withdrawal – by the Soviet Union, and the Red Army returning to the area in 1944. The two regions were then both divided, with parts of Petserimaa ceded to the Pskov Oblast and the mainly rural district behind the Narva river to the Leningrad Oblast (Jääts 1995). The question to be settled at the end of the 1980s was thus whether Estonia's regained independence should imply a restorationist return to the borders of the Tartu Peace Treaty of 1920 or, instead, imply staying with the borders of the Soviet period. The implications in terms of identity are obvious in the case of both Estonia and Russia.

Estonia took the stand that the Tartu Peace Treaty should form the basis of relations with Russia, although the prevailing situation was viewed as a *de facto* reality. Russia held, instead, that the Tartu treaty was no longer in force with Estonia having been annexed to the USSR in 1944 (Aalto 2003c: 27–37). Negotiations started in 1992 only to end in stalemate in 1994. Russia leaned in the direction of demarcating the border unilaterally on the basis of the *de facto* situation, while Estonia held the view that it could take a more flexible stand on the various practical issues if the relevance of the Tartu Peace Treaty was recognised. With no progress in sight, President Yeltsin gave an order in 1994 to demarcate the Estonian–Russian border without consulting the Estonian representatives.

For Russia, Estonia's independence in 1991 created mixed feelings to start with, and it would have been politically difficult to return to the borders that were there prior to 1944, in particular as the population of the regions in question was mainly Russian-speaking. If a split was to emerge, then it should follow the *de facto* border that was already there (confirming indirectly that Soviet rule since 1944 rested on legal grounds). Estonian opinion was more divided, with considerable support also for the view that to have a border agreed upon was more important than the question of where exactly it was running (Jääts 1995: 198).

As to the border areas themselves, life changed considerably with the domestic border shifting to an interstate one and a previously quite nominal border being altered into an internal and contested one, with security and identity-related issues high on the agenda. Also, the mutual interdependence of the border areas had already been quite high before the change to a form of 'cross-border interaction' (Viktorova 2001). A previously uniform and uniting infrastructure was cut into two distinct parts, as in the case of water and electricity supply to the towns of Narva and Ivangorod located on different sides of the River Narva.[9] More generally, a relatively homogeneous population was divided so that over time divisions into 'us' and 'them' started to emerge in place of previous local unity (Berg and Ehin 2006). The emergence of a divisive border was initially interpreted by the local actors as an endeavour to subordinate and discipline the border regions, and this also went for the ways according to

---

[9] Information is available on the website of the Peipsi Center for Transboundary Cooperation (CTC), see www.ctc.ee.

which the policies of the EU were interpreted (Berg and Oras 2003: 56; Ehin and Mikenberg 2003).

As a result of the emergence of more divisive borders, the border regions have turned into socio-economic problem areas characterised by high unemployment, low income levels, significant out-migration and gradually also a considerable difference in living standards because of the growth experienced on the Estonian side of the border (Lunden 2002: 140; Berg and Ehin 2006). It should be noted, however, that the subject positions appear to be far more conflictual among the statist actors than at various local levels, with regional, municipal and local actors representing more conciliatory and cooperation-friendly aspirations. More recently, some attempts to initiate cross-border cooperation have taken place, with considerable help from NGO actors such as the Peipsi Center for Transboundary Cooperation (Viktorova 2001), although they have not yet matured to a considerable degree.[10]

In addition to the border being contested and the fact that there is a lack of a finally agreed treaty, the negative consequences also pertain to Russia's introduction of double tariffs on some products in 1995. Estonia was thus deprived of its previous most favoured trading status, although the double tariffs have later been abolished due to Estonia's EU membership. More generally, the Estonian–Russian cooperation has been placed in the context of the EU–Russia Partnership and Cooperation Agreement (PCA), i.e. it has become part of the agreed nature of EU–Russian relations.

Although a formal treaty does still not exist, some agreement has none-theless been reached. In order to facilitate cooperation across the border, a simplified border-crossing regime was installed between 1991 and 2000. It stood out as an exemption from the general visa regime in force between Estonia and Russia, with residents (some 20,000 in total) being allowed to travel under a temporary regime. Due to humanitarian concerns, residents living in areas near the border were allowed to visit close relatives, attend churches and visit cemeteries on the other side through the use of special permits handed over by local authorities. However, with Estonia turning into a candidate country, pressure increased to abolish this system. Yet, instead of abolishing it at the time of accession, Estonia chose – in line with the Schengen requirements – to implement a full visa

---

[10] For information covering the views of the Pskov regional authorities, see www.invest. pskov.ru/euroregion.php?lang=ru. For the views of one of those involved, see the interview given to Pskovskoe Agenstvo Informatsii by Alexei Ignatiev, Head of the Russian arm of the East–West Institute, www.informpskov.ru/interviews/7361.html. See also Makarychev (2005b).

regime with Russia in 2000. In order to compensate for the loss of privileges for local residents, a new agreement between Estonia and Russia stipulated that both sides can issue up to 4,000 multi-entry visas annually to those border-region residents who have a compelling need to cross the border on a regular basis. The visas are issued free of charge and are valid for one year.

Notably, the lack of a border treaty did not stand out as an obstacle to prevent Estonia from joining the EU and NATO, although both these actors have a policy which stipulates that countries joining should be devoid of open border disputes with their neighbours. However, in the case of Estonia (and Latvia), the reading was that it was the Russian party which was to be blamed for lack of progress. Russia was taken to have deliberately, for tactical reasons, linked the border issue to other issues such as Estonia's and Latvia's aspirations for NATO membership as well as the situation of the Russian-speakers in Estonia. For its own part, the EU appears to endeavour to unpack such linkages by dealing with the various issues separately. Together with a number of other actors such as the Council of Europe and the Organization for Security and Co-operation in Europe (OSCE), the Union has used its leverage for minority rights to be properly protected, with Russian-speakers being increasingly integrated into Estonian society.

In general, the fact that Estonia's Russia-policy basically resides in an EU–Russia context and that Russia mainly deals with various Estonia-related questions through the EU–Russia channel has taken much heat out of bilateral Estonia–Russia relations. As to Estonia's eastern border, the principal issues have largely evaporated with Estonia having withdrawn its insistence on starting on the basis of the Tartu Peace Treaty. Approving the *de facto* borders as a point of departure has been conducive to the establishment of a functioning border regime (cf. Mikenberg 2005). In line with EU membership understood primarily as a form of protection-seeking, Estonia has favoured the establishment of unambiguous borders rather than opted for any 'fuzzy' borders conducive to various forms of cross- and trans-border cooperation (Berg and Ehin 2006). Another way of putting it would be to say that the parties aspire after a firm border to serve as a marker of identity and an object of non-contentious political discourses.

The Latvian–Russian border The story of the Latvian–Russian border is in many ways similar to the Estonian–Russian one, with instability and disaccord having long historical roots. The town of Abrene (Pytalovo) and its rural districts were included in Latvia when it declared its independence through its National Council in 1918, and recognised as part of Latvia in the Peace Treaty signed with Russia in 1920. Arguably, the Soviet authorities did not consider the peace treaties with the Baltic states as legally binding (Anderson 1990; Dauksts and Puga 1995: 181), and after the return of the Red Army to Latvia in 1944, the border was changed by incorporating the town of Abrene and six rural districts into the territory of the USSR. With Latvia being annexed into the Soviet Union the border became nominal and lost its interstate meaning. This changed again when Latvia regained independence in 1991 in the sense that a border had to be drawn and demarcated to indicate the existence of two different sovereign entities, Russia and Latvia.

Like Estonia, Latvia started from the assumption that with independence it had returned to the *de jure* borders of 1918 and the ones stipulated in the Peace Treaty of 1920. The town of Abrene and its surroundings were thus part of Latvia for which international recognition was desired, although territorial issues did not rank very high on the agenda, with questions such as the withdrawal of Russian troops having higher priority. One reason for this could be that the border drawn at least to some extent followed ethnic and linguistic lines with the population on the Latvian side consisting mainly of Latvians (Bleiere and Henins 2004: 9). Negotiations were conducted with Russia and an interstate agreement was signed in 1991 in order to settle various pending issues, although the question of the contested area remained unsettled (according to a Russian interpretation, the agreement to observe the territorial integrity of each other implied that Latvia accepted the *de facto* border). Latvia feared – as did Estonia – that Russia still regarded it as its 'near abroad', with subordination as a potential outcome, whereas Latvia saw itself as being on its way to 'returning home', i.e. to becoming part of the Western camp with a clear difference in relation to Russia.

In order to alleviate at least some of the difficulties caused by the new border – imposed by the states with some local resistance – a provisional interstate agreement was signed in 1994, with Latvia having withdrawn its earlier claims as to the restoration of the Abrene region. The agreement included, among other things, a special list allowing the crossing of the border for humanitarian reasons. This practice was terminated in the year 2000, due to Schengen-related pressures, and instead a system based on visas free of charge for people from the border region with a need to regularly cross the border was prepared. Furthermore, a border agreement (with negotiations completed in 1998), an agreement on cross-border cooperation as well as an agreement on cooperation in case of natural disasters were negotiated, although not yet signed and ratified. The border treaty is there, and – as stated by Arkady Moshes (1999: 18) – 'Russia recognises that the treaty is mostly ready, but keeps linking the solution with the general state of relations and further progress on the Russophone issue.' The double tariffs – a system also imposed by Russia on Latvia – have disappeared with the trade regime becoming part of EU–Russian relations.

Overall, the border issue also appears to be fading into the background in the Latvian–Russian case, among other reasons because Latvia joined the EU and NATO (with the latter membership also becoming less controversial in the sphere of Latvian–Russian relations than was perhaps expected some time ago). 'Europeanisation' has not implied a return to traditional power politics and instead a more integration-oriented logic has made itself felt. With the EU border and trade regime becoming more important, the agenda has become far less securitised, albeit the competence of the relevant actors to take advantage of the various EU-related options for the initiation of various forms of cross-border cooperation seems to have remained limited (Bleiere and Henins 2004).[11] The EU, for its part, has not (until mid-2005 with the failures to sign and ratify an agreed treaty) taken a stand on the border issue as such but has rather acted by keeping various issues distinct from each other. The EU's reading during the accession period, i.e. that Russia was to blame, and the acceptance of Latvia's membership in 2002 despite the border issue remaining open also foreclosed the option of the EU returning to the issue. It has become hard for the EU to pressure the parties of the dispute to change their views, particularly those of Latvia (or Estonia). Like in the case of Estonia, the Union has encouraged Latvia to guarantee minority rights and enticed it to move away from a strict nation-state ideal towards a multinational society model, thereby endeavouring to impact on the discursive framework that has caused much strain on Latvian–Russian as well as on intra-Latvian relations. As in the Estonian–Russian case, the EU in this instance also appears to aim for an increasing tolerance for diversity within the existing political constellation rather than to opt for the transformation of identities through 'Europeanisation' or some other post-nationalist and border-altering formula.

Approaching the end of 2005, at least for a while the prospect for the border treaty being finally signed and ratified appeared to have improved. Latvia's President accepted Russia's invitation to attend the festivities celebrating the Allied victory and the end of World War II in Moscow, in summer 2005. The expectations were high that a border treaty might be signed on that occasion. However, progress stalled with Latvia insisting

---

[11] Information is also available on the website of the Pskov-Livonia Euregio between Latvia, Estonia and Russia, see www.aluksne.lv/cbc/EN/padome.htm.

that reference to historical issues should be included in the treaty. This setback notwithstanding, pressures intensified to settle the remaining issues and the treaty came into force in 2007. It was in the interests of both the EU and Russia to terminate the abnormal situation that had been there for quite some time. For Russia, a major concern is that any movement towards visa-free transit (with the EU regarding the proposal as something to be considered, although implemented only in the long run) gets stalled with the EU–Russian border remaining (formally) unclear in the case of Estonia.

The Kaliningrad 'puzzle' Of the various border-related issues located in Europe's North, Kaliningrad has been met with far more interest and scrutiny than any other case. It has, in contrast to the other border-related issues pertaining to Europe's North, also attracted considerable international attention and has occasionally broken into the sphere of high politics creating explicit strains in EU–Russian relations (Joenniemi and Makarychev 2004).[12]

There has, in general, been little agreement concerning the essence of the issue. While for some authors issues of dissidence, territorial belonging and the various military-strategic aspects – including fears of excessive military developments – have been of prime importance (see for example Lachowski 1998; Pedersen 1998; Donnelly 2000; Krickus 2002), most contributions have dealt with Kaliningrad's position between the EU and Russia, focusing on issues of political stability as well as on various economic and social questions that follow from the Oblast's position as an exclave/enclave (Batt 2003; Wellmann 2003). The problem has quite often been depicted as one of open borders turning into lines of exclusion with the EU's enlargement. This recalls the situation that Kaliningrad enjoyed relatively open borders since the demise of the Soviet Union (Fairlie and Sergounin 2001) and has done so particularly in relation to Lithuania and Poland. Yet, with the Union's enlargement, it has been confronted with stricter border practices. The new member states have been compelled to implement the so-called 'Schengen system' of tighter controls at the EU's external borders, along with the Union's common visa regime. More generally, the case of Kaliningrad blurs conceptual barriers and identity-related approaches by constituting a kind of 'little Russia' encircled by the Union, and a part of Russia that is

---

[12] Information on the Kaliningrad issue is particularly available from the Schleswig-Holstein Peace Research Institute, see www.schiff.uni-kiel.de. See also Joenniemi and Makarychev (2004).

considerably exposed to the rules and regulations – including the border policies – of the EU (cf. Baxendale *et al.* 2000).

That is to say that although issues of transit have been very much at the forefront and the effort has been one of treating Kaliningrad as a single-conflict item, the problem nonetheless stems more generally from Kaliningrad turning – with the Union's enlargement – into an overlapping entity that blurs a variety of geographic and conceptual boundaries. The problem does not relate (as is the case between Estonia and Russia and Latvia and Russia) to the location of the border but to its nature and the way it functions. Above all, it has become difficult to distinguish clearly between the inside and the outside as Russia and the EU are increasingly entangled in the context of Kaliningrad (Makarychev 2005a). Consequently, two somewhat different understandings of political space are brought into contact with each other. The EU has, in this context, emphasised options for the 'opening up' of economically depressed regions in the light of the prospects of enlargement, whereas Russia – and the Kaliningraders themselves – fear that the consequences might boil down to even further restrictions of movement as well as impoverishment and marginalisation.

Initially Russia suggested that Kaliningrad could become a 'pilot region' in the development of EU–Russian relations. The Russian side called, as a starting point for negotiations, for a visa-free regime operating along fixed train and bus routes, with a special permit system for travel by car. It was stressed that a lack of free communication between mainland Russia and Kaliningrad would entail a division of Russia's sovereignty. Moreover, actors within the Kaliningrad regional administration also called for Kaliningrad's greater internationalisation and for its partial inclusion within the EU's economic space, in ways similar to Norway's EEA arrangement. During the year 2002, Russia's leadership actively exerted pressure in order for the EU to abandon its strict policies of bordering. Proposals that aimed at an unrestricted movement between the Oblast and the rest of Russia were aired. In August 2002, President Putin made an entirely new opening to facilitate the settlement of the dispute by advocating that the system of visas might be totally abandoned between the EU and Russia. The Kaliningrad issue was, in general, purported as one determining the future of Russia's relations with the EU (cf. Joenniemi 2003: 50–1). Through the rhetoric employed – putting forward, among other things, the argument that the resolution of the Kaliningrad transit affair stands as a litmus test for the future of EU–Russian relations – Russia endeavoured to present itself, in the context of the Kaliningrad dispute, as an advocate of human rights and freedom of movement whereas the Union was depicted as holding back and restraining freedom. The EU was portrayed as standing for restrictions and narrowing issues down to very technical measures of bordering. In contrast, Russia was taken to stand for integration, inclusive solutions and recommendations to do away with barriers, while the EU was depicted as standing for limitations and engaged in separating the 'ins' and the 'outs'. Instead of using openness in order to spread its peaceful norms and practices, the EU was accused of aspiring after firm borders in order to be protected from external risks and ills. While Russia showed itself as aiming to break previous conceptual constraints and to search for new departures, the Union was accused of endeavouring to stick to established concepts, which it saw as 'natural' and given, and to insist on implementing a pre-given set of policies to be imposed on Russia.

Russia's challenge thus rested on raising questions that refer to the very nature of the EU and not just to a particular set of policies. By framing the debate on Kaliningrad in terms of openness, freedom of movement, defending human rights and doing away with barriers and moves of exclusion, Russia drew attention to fundamental issues. It played, in fact, on the tension inherent in the Union's aim of extending its peace mission through openness and doing away with divisive borders, and the search for protection against various external risks and ills through strict bordering.

The Union thus found itself torn between, on the one hand, a promise to pay attention to Russia's views and proposals concerning possible solutions and, on the other hand, a rather fixed understanding as to the nature of the Kaliningrad issue and how best to solve it.

For its part, the EU admitted in a communiqué issued by the Commission in 2001 that the problem of increased isolation was, in some of its aspects, related to the Union's enlargement, although Kaliningrad was in general seen as an integral part of Russia, with Russia responsible for the various ills ascribed to the region. It was conceded that enlargement, although viewed as something basically positive, might in the case of Kaliningrad also entail some adverse effects. In other words, the EU agreed to position itself as a party to the dispute. If the Union's enlargement implied problems for Kaliningrad rather than offering solutions, the EU announced its preparedness to talk things over. However, at the same time the policies pursued remained rather cautious, with the EU insisting adamantly that those travelling in transit would need to carry a valid international passport and to be furnished with a visa. The challenge in the case of the EU, it seems, was not just one of achieving a satisfactory solution as to borders and border management. It also had aspects of an internal challenge relating to the essence of the Union.

The question at stake was thus not merely one of restoring a balance between positive cross-border cooperation and protection against risks, such as the spread of crime, diseases and environmental problems. As borders are sites that have constitutive effects, the solution was unavoidably broader as to its consequences. It pointed to the figure of the EU, the nature of EU–Russian relations, Russia's urge to gain recognition as a 'special' partner, as well as to the future of the overall European configuration.

In the end – in November 2002 – the Union decided upon the use of a 'Facilitated Transit Document' (FTD) for 'all the Russian citizens who travel frequently and directly between Kaliningrad and the Russian mainland'. Russia, for its part, found this basically technical solution satisfactory. It was introduced in July 2003 (see Holtom 2005). As part of the deal, the Russian Duma ratified the Russian–Lithuanian border treaty (which had been pending like those with Estonia and Latvia) and approved a Readmission Agreement. The Union, for its part, promised to consider the dropping of visa requirement in EU–Russian relations, and in this sense the FTD was cast as a 'temporary measure' before the EU–Russian visa-free travel regime was established. Although some smaller matters relating to the control of transit goods and military equipment remained to be sorted out, both the EU and Russia consider the transit issue to be solved. Although not signalling an end to the Kaliningrad 'puzzle' as such, matters appear to be 'back to normal' in EU–Russian relations in this respect. Eastern enlargement has proven to entail considerable – although not insurmountable – problems for the relations between the Union and Russia, as the process has required new bordering practices instead of implementing the declared stance of 'no more dividing lines in Europe'.

The emerging EU order: a contested issue

Obviously, as to borders and border disputes in the northern part of Europe, the crucial questions to explore consist of the policies of the EU and the way EU–Russian relations are bound to unfold in this context.

As to Russia, the Union has aspired after somewhat closer relations, as evidenced by the Partnership and Cooperation Agreement (PCA), the Common Strategy and the agreement on four common freedoms, four common spaces (on economics, external security, internal security, and research and education), concluded in May 2005. Moreover, there is the ENP, although there Russia is included only for the part of the European Neighbourhood Partnership Instrument (ENPI) which aims at narrowing down the various border-related funds and programmes to one single instrument by 2008.

The aim has, in general, been one of promoting structural economic reforms in order to contribute to the emergence of a functioning market economy; to promote flows of trade and investment; and to help bind Russia into a closer and more productive two-way political relationship with the West (Gowan 2000: 21). The endeavour could also be seen as one of trying to 'Europeanise' or 'civilise' Russia. Once drawn into the EU order, a key question appears to become whether Russia is assigned the position of a 'semi-insider' (a non-member, yet partially included and thereby also furnished with a legitimate voice in the intra-EU dialogue, albeit not a semi-insider in the sense of being a member like for example Denmark or the UK but then opting out of some of the joint policies) or whether it is allotted the post of a 'close outsider' (an entity behind the outer border engaged in a number of cooperative endeavours but deprived of a legitimate voice as to intra-EU affairs) in the context of a Brussels-centred concentric Europe (Aalto 2003b).

Besides following its universally applied standard rules, the Union has also pursued region-specific policies that might allow for special arrangements and exceptions in a regionalised form. Arrangements such as the Karelian Euregio allow for equality in the process of decision-making and allow Russia to influence, for example, the use of EU-related finances (Cronberg 2002). The insistence on the Schengen Convention rules relates to the first, more statist and all-European category, whereas the EU's Northern Dimension initiative stands for the latter, more regionalist approach in being tuned to the more spontaneous and less rule-bound forms of cooperation. More recently, with the emergence (since 2003) of the European Neighbourhood Policy (ENP), the policies pursued appear to display a fairly clear distinction between the 'ins' and the 'outs' with the EU aspiring after proximity policies that place all neighbourhoods within the same framework. Yet it has to be noted that regarding Europe's North the EU has simultaneously agreed to a 'new Northern Dimension', approved at an EU–Russia summit in Helsinki in December 2006,[13] which promises Russia full equality as a partner within that arrangement. Whereas the ENP stands for exclusion through inclusions (with neighbours exempted from membership but invited to share 'everything but institutions'), the 'new Northern Dimension' seems to address Russia differently and in a rather inclusive manner in comparison to other non-accession countries in the Union's vicinity.

Russia has, for its part, adopted a basically positive view on the EU and the 'shared values' of democracy, respect for human rights and individual

---

[13] See http://ec.europa.eu/external_relations/north_dm/doc/frame_pol_1106.pdf.

liberties as spelled out in a number of joint documents. The level of engagement as well as awareness about the essence of the EU has left much still to be hoped for, but basically, Russia has pursued constructive policies. The views on the EU's border policies vary in a similar manner: there are hopes that the lowering of borders will energise some of Russia's north-western regions, yet there are also fears that the Union's enlargement will lead to political encirclement and exclusion, and consequently banishment to the fringes of Europe.

Russia has in general favoured uniform policies that treat the different parts of the country in a similar fashion, and has been worried about exceptions and differentiation. The fear has been that policies extending special favours to parts of the country might bring about internal tensions, dividing lines and dissidence. The discussion on Kaliningrad as a free trade area in the context of the four common spaces is a case in point. It appears that Russia has basically been pressing for a kind of centralised and state-based order, and has – until recently with the acceptance of the new Northern Dimension – been hesitant to opt for a regionalising strategy, one that would increase the permeability of borders and bring about differentiation within Russia. Consequently, the reactions to the EU's Northern Dimension have been lukewarm (although the reading could also be that Russia is critical about the lack of initiative content-wise, including the claim that there has been too little factual regionalisation; cf. Aalto 2002:156; Joenniemi and Sergounin 2003: 37–41). On occasions Russia has itself proposed localising solutions such as developing Kaliningrad into a 'pilot region' for EU–Russian cooperation. This is to say that at least in the case of Kaliningrad, Russia has argued for open and porous borders with the semi-integration of Kaliningrad into the EU. This would then provide, in a larger perspective, Russia with the position of a semi-insider, 'piggy-backing' on the Kaliningrad 'puzzle'.

What kind of entities?

Besides being different in size, amount of population as well as economic weight, the EU and Russia differ in terms of the processes underway: the EU is enlarging whereas Russia has shrunk with the demise of the Soviet Union and aspires after stability following considerable turmoil. The Union has considerable subjectivity in the constitution of an empire-type concentric Europe whereas the Russian role has so far remained modest concerning the emerging features of post-Cold War Europe.

There are also significant qualitative differences in the sense that it is commonplace to comprehend the European Union as being intimately related to globalisation. It is part and parcel of an age that renders strict territorial delineations and borders obsolete. The borders between the entities included become – much of the thinking goes – as useless as the medieval city walls when the feudal era came to an end (Denieul 1997: 10).

Whereas the EU is slotted in a postmodern category and seen as an entity aspiring after postnationalist solutions (cf. Ruggie 1993), Russia is taken to be rather modern in essence (Haukkala 2003: 276). EU governance has multiple tiers: there is a considerable dispersion of powers between the local, regional, national/federal, European and international domains. Legal sovereignty is dispersed and the economic structures are highly internationalised, as are many non-governmental activities. Subjective identities of the individual are becoming multiple, and the internal perimeters are highly permeable, even non-existent for many practical purposes (cf. Emerson 2002: 7). Concepts such as 'shared sovereignty' or 'reducing the importance of borders' are not seen as representing a threat to the EU's identity.[14]

Russia, on the other hand, remains sovereignty-geared and similar conceptualisations as referred to in the EU's case above are thus in a Russian reading – particularly within the influential 'realist' and geopolitical schools (cf. Joenniemi and Sergounin 2003: 28–37) – seen as problematic, if not dangerous. They are taken to undermine established self-understandings in bringing about disharmony and lack of clarity. 'Few in the Kremlin would have questioned the assumption that the sovereign state is the basic means of comprehensively organising modern political life,' claims Andrey Makarychev (2000: 26).

It has to be added, however, that the departures to be traced do not seem to lead to a constellation where the EU advocates open borders, ambivalent statehood and fuzzy spaces, whereas Russia opts for rigid and protective arrangements in areas where the two entities increasingly encounter each other. On occasions it has, in fact, been Russia that has stood for open and inclusive solutions while the EU aspires after the establishment of firm and largely exclusive borders. Kaliningrad is a case in point, with Russia advocating a continuance of the openness that was there for quite some time in the aftermath of the Cold War. Russia has also adopted an assertive stance in opting for a dismissal of visas between Russia and the EU, and aspires thereby after an at least *de facto* partial inclusion into the Schengen system, i.e. an EU-established order.

This is to say that particularly in the case of Kaliningrad Russia seems to be able to live with being basically compelled to adapt to EU rules. The constitutive role of the EU is recognised provided that it is a negotiated

---

[14] For a critique of these assumptions see Prozorov (2005b).

and mutually agreed one in a manner that provides Russia with a considerable degree of subjectivity. And, more generally, there are no clear signs that the lack of a far-reaching meeting of minds in border-related issues would lead to a vicious circle of mutual expectations in EU–Russian relations (Haukkala 2003: 276). This also applies to the Kaliningrad puzzle and the border disputes that have been there in Estonian–Russian and Latvian–Russian relations. It seems that in all three cases a system either has been or is on its way to being put into place and implemented based on an agreement between Russia and the EU, indicating that compromises are possible. The Karelian 'question' has been kept off the agenda altogether. The EU's emphasis on borders conducive to cooperation as well as cross-border contacts, and yet protective in view of the various adverse effects such as international crime, illegal immigration, and illicit drugs and arms trade, appears to meet some understanding. One may doubt whether Russia is eligible for inclusion into the Schengen system at large or even some aspects of it through a skipping of visas, but in any case the Russian proposal for joining in appears to indicate that the logics of the two entities as to borders and border practices are not that far from each other. The meeting of minds that appears to be there in the context of the 'new Northern Dimension' confirms this point.

To the extent that the border issues reflect a contest over order between the EU and Russia – as argued by Pami Aalto (2003a: 256) – it tends to be a relatively mild one, with Russia searching for recognition of its actorness rather than revolting against the imposed order as such. With the exception of the 'left-conservative' political orientation, which calls for a decisive break with Russia's perennial quest for the recognition of its 'Europeanness', the Russian discourse on relations with Europe has been content to criticise select EU policies as unjustly exclusive without abandoning the overall 'European orientation' in foreign policy.[15] By appealing to aspects that from the Union's perspective are bound to be fully legitimate – and which function as a 'mirror' that forces the Union to be confronted with the impact of its own policies – Russia has been able to bolster its claim pertaining to a subjectivity as a semi-insider and aspire after a negotiated settlement regarding carefully delimited issues.

The Union's approach

The European Union is, as to one of the underlying logics, essentially a peace project and this is also reflected in the Union's approach to borders.

---

[15] For a more detailed discussion of this theme see Prozorov (2005a). For the analysis of the left-conservative position see Prozorov (2005c).

Borders are not seen as inhabiting the terrain of classical geopolitics, of state versus state, and of war and peace, or geographical territory understood as a power resource. The policies pursued do not aim at drawing lines in order to allocate territories or to inscribe a new order among states or, as stated by William Walters (2002: 564): 'Schengen is not about political power understood as confrontations between territorial power containers' (see also Rupnik 1994; O'Down and Wilson 1996).

Thus, in the context of the enlargement process, the EU strives to expand its 'area of freedom, security and justice', in order to create what the former President of the EU Commission, Romano Prodi, called: 'a wider European area offering peace, stability and prosperity to all: a new European order' (quoted in Grabbe 2000: 519). Arguably, the aim is to do away with the borders inside the Union, to have the flows of capital, goods and people effortlessly traverse these borders and to avoid the emergence of sharp and divisive borders at the outer edges of the Union. And still, the outer borders are conceptualised as regulatory instruments necessary for the delineation of the internal sphere of freedoms, as most clearly recently demonstrated by the emergence of the ENP. While internal borders are losing in significance, the emphasis is increasingly on external perimeters. There is, in this sense, a 'double move' (Walters 2002: 561) with the efforts to establish internal freedoms being accompanied by a set of political anxieties about the ability of borders to keep out various ills such as crime, illegal migration and terrorism (Geddes 1999; Andreas and Snyder 2000; see also Koslowski 2001). Similar moves and concerns also label the northern borders of the Union and in particular those with Russia (Eskelinen *et al.* 1999) as likely permanent outside borders at the fringes of a concentric Europe.

Over recent years the EU has increasingly operated on the assumption that the Union should have an all-encompassing, continuous external border. The aspiration for uniform policies vis-à-vis the adjacent regions in the form of the above-mentioned ENP – an approach coined in the context of the latest round of enlargement – points in the same direction.

The goal of more standardised and centre-driven policies is also visible in the context of the Union's eastern enlargement. Applicant countries are assumed to apply the Schengen *acquis* in full without flexibility (cf. den Boer 2002). The aspiration towards uniform policies has certainly been there, and to some extent it has also been successful, although it still seems true to argue that the Union continues to aspire after 'variable geometry' rather than uniformity. This latter endeavour is visible also in the sphere of border policies. There is the Schengen Accord but there are also Schengen-related opt-outs (UK, Ireland), and there are non-member opt-ins in the form of the EEA partners (Iceland, Liechtenstein and

Norway). Some countries move faster in implementation with the Amsterdam Treaty allowing for 'flexible integration'.

The upshot of all this, as stated by Thomas Christiansen and Knud-Erik Jørgensen (2000: 74), is 'that there is no single border to the EU complex that might be said to delimit a single administrative space, defining at one stroke population, territory and *raison d'être* of the policy. Instead, membership and space, which are defined by different policies, overlap. The walls "erected" by individual policies intersect.' This is what the EU now tries to remedy, it seems, with the help of the ENP as the complexity appears to have become too much for the EU to handle, albeit probably some flexibility will be retained in the future – as is already indicated by the fact that Russia will largely remain outside the ENP with its own 'strategic' relationship to the EU, as is also indicated by the 'new Northern Dimension'.

Christopher Browning (2003) has been able to straighten out the record in a study on the EU's policies vis-à-vis Kaliningrad. He points out that the Union is struggling with two conflicting aims. On the one hand it aims to prevent the infiltration of crime and illegal immigration from the Russian exclave in order to be able to preserve its own internal freedoms. On the other hand the aim is to foster the Union's external security as well as to enhance relations between the EU and Russia.

The Union has, in this context, clearly prioritised its internal security, and acts in this sense very much according to a 'modern' logic in which the problem of Kaliningrad is more about managing than abandoning the boundary. This logic, Browning claims (2003: 550), stands in clear tension with the widespread view that 'the EU's *raison d'être* is that of securing peace within Europe, the achievement which has been frequently applauded'. The Union's aim, in order to overcome Europe's divisions, has been one of promoting cross-border networks as well as multiple overlapping local, regional and European identities to meliorate the exclusive nationalisms of the past. Internally – he remarks – the result of the avoidance of a major clash, above all between France and Germany, has been the emergence of a 'neomedieval/postmodern' space in which the nation-state divide between borders and governance has become increasingly fuzzy, the aim being to lock peoples of the EU into a sense of common destiny. However, while the understanding of the EU as a peace project has resulted in a certain 'postmodernisation' of the EU internally, Browning (2003: 550) further contends that this is not the case as to the Union's external relations. With the outside being seen as unstable and potentially threatening, the EU has tended to conceptualise its outer edge in rather modernist ways. The security of the insiders and those on the outside is disconnected by claiming that the outsiders have to sort out their own problems. The needs of the Kaliningraders are perceived as being different from those of the EU. The peace policies, in their original form, are restricted to the internal sphere and not seen as applicable as such or to be extended to the nearby regions. Moreover, adapting to localised and regionalised solutions for example in the context of the Northern Dimension is precluded. There is an inability to think in truly regional terms as the Union fails, Browning argues (2003: 551), to comprehend the people in northern Europe as equal. With the operation of a distinction between 'us' and 'them' and the consequent bordering practices, regional solutions are seen as potentially contaminating clear-cut identities, leaving uniform and unambiguous policies as the only option available.

In this context, the border turns into a first line of defence, which requires among other things that the applicant countries apply the Schengen *acquis* and have to shore up the eastern borders that they share with non-members. Kaliningrad – Browning notes (2003: 570) – forces open this tension in the EU's external relations, that is between the Union's desire to fulfil its peace mission and the negative effects of its desire for modernist exclusionary borders to protect itself from external threats. In sum, according to Browning (2003: 571), 'the consequence of this perceptual frame ... may actually be to undermine peace and stability in Europe'.

In other words, the framing of internal/external security draws upon and reproduces rather modernist understandings of subjectivity, central to which is the notion that subjects require clearly demarcated territorial spaces and borders over which they exercise sovereign control. And this conflation of identity, territory and sovereignty in turn tends to lead to the reification of selfhood and the negative characterisation of those outside the borders of the EU as potential threats to the EU's security. There is little space for outsiders to join the construction of an integration-related Europe and gain subjectivity and a legitimate voice in the constitutive discourse pertaining to the configuration that unfolds.

It seems clear against this background that the EU as a peace project comes to a halt in being restricted and bordered above all in order to constitute its internal sphere. Consequently, the Union is not able to project its peace-related identity – with the discourses pertaining to *duty* and *opportunity* being downgraded due to *security*-related concerns – across the new borders. This shortcoming and restraint show themselves clearly in the case of Kaliningrad, and the EU has also refrained from developing any regionalising policies in relation to the relevant Russian regions such as Karelia, Pskov, St Petersburg and Leningrad as well as Murmansk (the initiatives that are there are local and supported by neighbouring countries). In sum, it could be concluded that the EU has not been especially forthcoming as to northern Europe and Russia in particular, regarding joint and unifying conceptualisations of cooperation. There has been some *negotiation* but not much of a *dialogue*. The clash on Kaliningrad demonstrated with particular clarity that the EU and Russia still remain apart from each other (cf. Potemkina 2003), although the conflicts at stake have remained limited and have also offered an inroad into mutual recognition. The prevailing state of affairs has been depicted by David Gowan (2000: 13) as follows: 'the EU and Russia have been talking past each other, but at least they do so in the same room'.

Russian perceptions

Russia remains outside the sphere of EU members or applicants but is compelled – due to a variety of reasons – to devise a policy of its own vis-à-vis joint borders with the EU. Finland's membership in 1995 implied that a joint EU–Russian border emerged, with Finland applying stringent EU policies. Norway has been drawn into the same sphere due to an inclusion into the Schengen *acquis*, and Latvia as well as Estonia have been pursuing EU-related border policies already as EU applicants and since 2004 as members of the EU. Similarly, the policies of Lithuania and Poland are relevant because of the location of Kaliningrad as a Russian exclave. Moreover, Russia's 'strategic relationship' with the EU and the fact that some 50 per cent of its foreign trade is now with the EU after the latter's enlargement, also serve to highlight the importance of the issue of joint borders.

Generally, it appears that a certain duality can be found in the Russian views on political space and borders. Firstly, there is a strong modern legacy with emphasis on strict territorial control, one of linking the nation (identity) to the territorial state (cf. Trenin 2002). National identity is elevated above all other alternatives, and there is, consequently, little tolerance for any overlapping, loosely bordered spaces (Morozov 2002: 42). Security – and the inviolability of borders – has in this context been elevated to a matter of high priority. Secondly, there are more postmodern departures to be traced. These tend to surface once Russia is confronted with the task of relating to an increasingly globalised and regionalised world (the latter challenge is particularly distinct in northern Europe and in view of the joint borders with the EU). Although the modern approaches pertaining to realist and geopolitical worldviews appear to prevail, in some instances the latter type of more pluralist approaches have also found their way to the political agenda (cf. Joenniemi and Sergounin 2003: 28–37).

Still, more often than not, the Russian administration has been rather suspicious of the concepts of globalisation as well as regionalisation, and in this context of porous borders. Although perceiving itself as profoundly European and with 'Europe' as an integral part of its self-understanding, this is not the type of Europe that Russia opts for. Consequently, the disinclination and inability to project itself into the form that contemporary Europe takes also bring about features of self-exclusion. Moreover, representing the 'true' Europe carried with it the concept of a 'false' Europe with the latter category reserved particularly for the Baltic countries, above all Estonia and Latvia (see Prozorov 2004a and 2004b; Morozov 2004). This is to say that to a certain degree the spatial and temporal logics of Russia and the EU differ from each other. While the EU is primarily concerned with enlargement and regionalisation as crucial aspects of its external policies, the Russian worries tend to relate to a possible loss of identity and, on a more practical level, processes of disintegration that might follow from getting excessively involved in European integration.

Thus, regionalisation and fuzzy borders tend to be, more often than not, perceived negatively in the Russian discourse on Europeanisation. This has also been due to fears of chaos and separatist tendencies. As such this approach is perhaps not that surprising taking into account Russian traditional views as well as the experiences of the Yeltsin period – one characterised by a considerable freedom for the regions to grasp power – and the disorder that followed. Over recent years Russia has moved towards a strengthening of 'vertical power', depriving the regions of influence, and region-building in a more administrative manner in the form of the seven federal districts or 'super-regions' established on the orders of President Putin, and more recently the decision to strengthen the position of the federal administration in the appointment of regional governors.

Yet, aside from the dominant modernist stance, some innovative approaches on flexible borders and overlapping political spaces have also been aired in an EU–Russia context. For example, in the late 1990s President Yeltsin proposed a joint patrolling and handling of the border with Finland, i.e. then the only border with the EU (for the proposals merely to be rejected out of hand in Finland without any discussion on the merits of the proposal). In a similar vein, Prime Minister Chernomyrdin advocated in 1998 a 'Baltic Schengen', i.e. an arrangement that would override the exclusionary practices of the Schengen regime. If the Schengen system could be extended to Norway and Iceland (as well as Greenland and the Faroe Islands which are parts of Denmark, yet remain outside the EU), why could one not think of also including Russia, at least regionally, within the sphere of the system? A Baltic Schengen would form an intermediary space that would link the EU and Russia, rather than separate them. However, the proposal was met with almost total silence around the Baltic Rim. It did not contribute to Russia's subjectivity in the constitution of a post-Cold War northern Europe. In order to gain subjectivity, escape a passive and subordinate status and become recognised as a legitimate and active political subject, Russia has also aimed to encounter the EU more generally by providing Russia's North-west with an autonomous and active role in the sphere of regionalisation and cross-border cooperation (Prozorov 2004b).

The Russian criticism concerning the EU's Northern Dimension can be interpreted in a similar manner. Russia has basically been in favour of the initiative. However, there has also been the complaint that the ND has largely failed to break down borders by giving Russian partners an equal voice and creating effective sub-regional spaces through processes of linking and debordering (Aalto 2002: 153; Browning 2002: 38). As Deputy Prime Minister Viktor Khristenko (2001) has put it, while the Northern Dimension can be seen as a 'brave political experiment' calling for 'unconventional decisions' to promote sub-regional cooperation that ultimately might develop into 'a common European social and economic space', in practice Russia has until recently been largely excluded from decision-making in the context of the initiative. It may be added, however, that Russia has also to a considerable extent refrained from putting forward initiatives of its own (except downgrading 'soft security' issues prioritised by the EU and trying to upgrade investments into the infrastructure of Russian regions) in order to provide further substance to the process and to deepen the ND dialogue that calls for region-specific measures of cooperation rather than some general, all-encompassing moves pertaining to EU–Russian relations. Still, it has to be noted that Russia took active part in the preparations of the 'new Northern Dimension' and seems to be leaning in the direction of engaging itself more actively in regional cooperation in Europe's North.

It could be argued, against the general background of Russia's rather heavy modernist legacy and self-understanding, that there have been quite a few efforts to explore new ground. The ideas and initiatives that point in a different direction have all been coined in relation to the challenges posed by the EU. Moreover, they have usually been northern Europe specific in character (the proposal to skip visas in general stands as an exception here). The initiatives launched have not always been very well thought out, it seems, or pursued systematically. Still, they have been there, and the EU has, for its part, put forward a regionalist framework in the form of accepting the placement of the Northern Dimension on its

agenda, through participation in the Baltic as well as Barents coopera-
tions and more recently by approving the jointly agreed technical frame
for handling transit between Kaliningrad and mainland Russia. The
assertive policies occasionally pursued by Russia have every now and
then paid off.

The four pathways

Compulsory impact

With the two waves of enlargement and basically only Russia outside EU
membership and void of any prospects of joining, the Union has turned
into a crucial factor in Europe's North. The Baltic Sea, for example, has
more recently been viewed as the Union's 'internal sea'. Still, it may be
observed that the EU's policy has remained largely indirect as to the
region as a whole and is not to be compared for example to the top-
down type of aspirations that the Union has been displaying in Europe's
South through the initiation of the Barcelona Process and the Euro-
Mediterranean Partnership (EMP). The fact that no northern European
country is bound to sign an Action Plan in the context of the Union's
Neighbourhood Policy, with Russia being positioned outside the
ENP, will further contribute to the Union's concerted impact remaining
relatively modest, although the conclusion of negotiations on the four
common spaces and, later, the renegotiation of the Partnership and
Cooperation Agreement with Russia might to some extent remedy this
state of affairs.

A broadly shared strategy in view of the Karelian 'question' has been to
keep it off the agenda in the first place, i.e. avoid the use – in the case of the
EU – of any 'carrots' or 'sticks'. This has been rather easy as the dispute is
a latent one pertaining largely to aspects of Finnish civil society, with
Finland never having raised the question in order not to legitimate the
issue and to internationalise it beyond the bilateral Finnish–Russian
relations. It may be noted, however, that Finland's accession to the EU
has further solidified the 'anti-restitutionist' stance in Finnish politics,
further marginalising the societal advocates of the 'return of Karelia'. At
the same time, the EU has decided not to offer the 'carrot' of the
integration of (and thus easier access to) TACIS and Interreg funding,
restricting the operation of the Euregio to economically modest projects
and thereby limiting the integrative capacity of the Euregio.

In a somewhat similar fashion – having declined to play down Estonia's
and Latvia's plea for membership due to the lack of a border treaty in the
context of the accession talks – the inroad for a compulsory impact on

border issues has narrowed down to very little. Thus, the issue has been mainly left to the countries concerned to handle bilaterally. Only recently have there been signs of the EU pushing the parties to pass the last hurdles. The border issues notwithstanding, the compulsory impact has been there in the case of Estonia and Latvia in the sense of the EU stressing the importance of minority rights as regards the Russian-speaking population. Overall, the pending Estonian–Russian border treaty and the human rights issues have been treated separately on their own merits.

The Kaliningrad dispute deviates from the general pattern in the context of the Union's policies vis-à-vis Europe's North. The recognition that the EU's enlargement may impact on the exclave/enclave not only positively but also in a negative fashion has furnished the EU with the posture of a *party to the dispute*. That recognition opened up for negotiations particularly on the issue of transit. Moreover, the EU has also been compelled to concede that the Schengen *acquis* is not to be exported as such to apply to the case of Kaliningrad. By compromising on the requirement that visas are always needed in crossing the border (through the proposal pertaining to the 'Facilitated Transit Document', i.e. a kind of regionalised visa for a particular border) and agreeing to a number of issues being talked over and looked into in a longer term such as visa-free travel between the EU and Russia, a solution emerged and could be installed. Notably, by raising the stakes by bringing the issue up to the highest level of EU–Russian relations, by treating it as a litmus test and by drawing on the EU's own principles, Russia has been able to gain a legitimate position as an actor capable of influencing the Union's internal strategies. It has achieved the position of a 'semi-insider' at least in the context of the Kaliningrad 'puzzle'. More generally, it has not just been the EU having a compulsory impact (in the form of a Readmission Agreement, the border treaty with Lithuania being signed, passports complying to international standards and facilitation of consulates) by influencing Russia's stand; the EU has also had to compromise. It has been compelled to soften its categorical position regarding visas always being needed once crossing a Schengen border.

Overall, the core factor preventing the EU from having a forceful compulsory impact in Europe's North consists of Russia not opting, or being regarded as ineligible, for membership. Hence, the prospect for establishing a positive linkage between a resolution of pending border issues and Russia moving closer to the EU is limited. In fact, initially the EU ranked rather low in terms of Russia's foreign policy priorities, albeit the situation has more recently changed with the EU now ranking among the top priorities. Initially, the prospects of the EU having leverage as to a compulsory impact have thus been limited. The changes have been further aggravated as the logics of the EU and Russia as to devising political space do not fully overlap. Instead of being narrowed down to subject positions concerning single issues, disputes easily spill over to identity conflicts – with the EU's identity also being challenged, as in the case of the Kaliningrad 'puzzle' – or are interpreted by Russia as efforts to marginalise and subordinate it within the increasingly EU-influenced order emerging in northern Europe. This tends to deprive the EU of the use of the compulsory pathway, or at least downgrade its impact. Consequently, the Union has to search for other forms of influence more related to inductive and persuasive approaches.

Enabling impact

Clearly, a major strategy employed by the EU has been that of deproblem-atisation and, in that context, framing issues differently by taking them out of the security-related context. This has most obviously been the approach applied in the case of the Karelian 'question' with the EU framing the Finnish–Russian border as a normal EU–Russian border void of open border problems or 'hard' security issues. The Euregio Karelia project, which institutionalises the existing forms of EU–Russian cooperation in the Republic of Karelia, best exemplifies the enabling impact of the EU, i.e. a logic of border deproblematisation in the context of the transforma-tion of the Finnish–Russian border. The Euregio serves as a new institu-tional platform, within which questions of cross-border cooperation can be addressed in a depoliticised manner by local and regional actors rather than state governments. The enabling pathway of the EU has thus succeeded in increasing the density of small-scale local cooperation pro-jects across the border. Moreover, it has enhanced their coherence and synergy. But still, this pathway of perturbation is weakened by the overall context of EU–Russian relations, most notably by the problem-atic of the Schengen regime and the increased stringency and uniformity of visa procedures for Russians to enter the EU. Such a strict visa regime is the primary obstacle to the further development of cross-border coop-eration within the framework of the Euregio. The insistence of the EU on the uniformity of the application of the Schengen rules contradicts the Union's own logic of fostering cooperative trans-boundary regimes across contested borderlands. Cronberg's (2003) study explicitly demon-strates the paradox, whereby the EU is simultaneously the 'condition of possibility' of the transformation of the Finnish–Russian border into an integrated borderland of the Euregio, and the main structural constraint to this very transformation. Similarly, in Russian societal dis-course, the issue of visa procedures has assumed paramount significance for EU–Russian relations. Thus, the enabling impact of the EU logic of border deproblematisation is considerably weakened by the EU's own problematisation of the EU–Russian border as a line of exclusion.

An enabling impact has also stood out as a key pathway of perturbation in the case of the Estonian–Russian and Latvian–Russian borders, once going down the compulsory path has largely been blocked. Although having yielded some results, particularly in the case of the Estonian–Russian border, the approach has nonetheless been hampered for a variety of reasons. Framing border questions as practical challenges void of linkages to other issues such as those pertaining to security and identities has, in the first place, been far more difficult along the Estonian–Russian and the Latvian–Russian borders than on the Finnish–Russian border. The latter is also more established in the sense that there has been a recognised and well-functioning border for quite some time already, with the parties having signed a treaty on cooperation in the border areas in 1992. Whereas a Euregio exists in the Karelian case, those on the Estonian–Russian and Latvian–Russian borders either are still being planned and discussed or are not yet fully operational.[16] In the Finnish–Russian case the capitals accept, favour and financially support various forms of cross-border cooperation, whereas in the two other cases, despite some evidence of cooperative initiatives,[17] one may trace the wish to establish, in the first place, firm and divisive borders with less emphasis on the prospects of cooperation. Moreover, the regional and local actors located across the Finnish–Russian border seem to have more experience, knowledge and competence for them to be able to make use of the existing options than is the case across the Estonian–Russian and Latvian–Russian borders.

Kaliningrad stands out as a region providing the EU with considerable enabling impact. This is the case since the Oblast's borders have turned into EU borders with the membership of Lithuania and Poland (this also raising the question of which regime is applied at the border concerning transit in the case of Russian citizens travelling from one part of Russia to another). The socialising effect has been considerable in the case of Kaliningrad itself, although it has also radiated to mainland Russia as Russia has been compelled – with Kaliningrad exposing the country very concretely to the fact that Russia is one of the EU's neighbours – to get

---

[16] E.g. Pskov-Livonia Euregio between Latvia, Estonia and Russia, see www.aluksne.lv/cbc/EN/padome.htm.

[17] There have been several cooperation projects over the years, launched by the Estonian Development Aid Agency (with the funds administered by the Estonian Ministry of Foreign Affairs) and the Estonian Ministries of Interior and Education, in the Pskov region of Russia (e.g. training for tourism-sector leaders conducted by the Estonian Foreign Policy Institute (EVI), see www.evi.ee).

acquainted with the essence of the Union. The EU itself has been inclined actively to use various inductive and persuasive measures (and to avoid categorical enforcement of its rules and regulations) in order to make it clear that vicinity to the Union is benign in its consequences by offering Kaliningrad a considerable range of positive options. Hence special means have been devoted to counteract various social ills and improve border management etc. Kaliningrad itself has more recently become active in using the various options on offer and has demonstrated increased competence in linking up to various parts of the EU. The Oblast endeavours to be part of three different Euregios, out of which one has already been working for a while whereas two others are in the process of being established.

Connective impact

The impact of the increased presence of the EU in Europe's North in the form of a changing discursive context along the Union's new northern borders has – due to a variety of reasons – been limited, although the joint EU–Russian border has been the locus of a considerable number of new, cooperative practices. In fact, Europe's North has during a quite short period of time developed into a rich patchwork of various trans-border and cross-border projects. In the case of the Kaliningrad 'puzzle' a major underlying cause has consisted of the terms of exchange (with transit being the crux of the issue) rather than the connective impact reducing tensions.

The mentalities have been slow to change as the regions in question have, for the most part, a history of being militarised and framed by distinctly security-oriented approaches. This goes for the Finnish–Russian border, Kaliningrad in particular (with the region having been closed to access from Poland and Lithuania during the Cold War) and also, to some extent, the Estonian–Russian and Latvian–Russian border areas in the sense that they were largely seen as being within the purview of the defensive parameters even if not strictly part of the East–West border as such. For example Tartu hosted a huge Soviet military airport and was closed to foreigners, and the Pskov region stood out as a first line of defence with considerable militarisation. This is to say that switching from a kind of defence-oriented, quite militarised mentality to one calling for open and cooperative borders has been somewhat demanding. It hardly takes place overnight as it entails a profound change in self-understanding not merely at the national, but also at the regional and local levels. The fact that Estonia's, Latvia's, Lithuania's and Poland's borders with Russia have also become borders between Russia and NATO has not been particularly conducive to such a change, although in all cases cooperative endeavours have seen the light of the day.

Yet another obstacle to the introduction and implementation of a 'European' discourse and frame of reference is presented by the fact that Europeanisation is understood in quite different terms within the EU and in Russia, and sometimes even in opposite ways. Europe and a European identity constitute, as such, a common ideal, but the Russian reading of what Europe entails is quite distinct from the EU-related one. The Russian reading in some cases appears to stand for a classical, sovereignty-related Europe. It is one premised on clearly delineated borders, whereas the EU harbours a more pluralist and less sovereignty-geared reading. The increased encounter that has occurred with the Union's enlargement in Europe's North between these two actors thus also amounts to a contest between two to some extent different comprehensions as to what 'Europeanisation' entails, with the regional and local levels being drawn into the cross-fire, which severely restricts the options for the EU to approach various social actors directly in the disputed border areas.

Overall, the tensions appear to have been quite mild, although not totally lacking, in the case of the Finnish–Russian border and the Karelian Euregio with the absence of any overt border dispute. The connective impact of the Euregio project consists in its involvement of a wider array of actors, both local and regional politicians and non-governmental organisations, and resides in the coordination of cooperative activities. Moreover, the specific projects – undertaken by the Euregio – are themselves targeted at strengthening the local civil society as a means of preventing the emergence of border conflicts. Yet, the involvement of local civil society actors need not have a conflict-tempering effect, and may well consist of the opposite: the intensification of the conflict issue due to its articulation with identity-related disaccord. In the case of Euregio Karelia, this negative impact is exemplified by the increasing problematisation in the regional and local media of the Republic of Karelia of restitutionist discourse in parts of Finnish society, and the continuing negative perception of Russia and Russians that sustains it. The pluralisation of the space of conflict discourse therefore has entirely contingent consequences, which need not automatically lead to the reduction of conflict intensity (as the broader space may also be used to intensify the conflict). Furthermore, in the case of EU–Russian relations, the border deproblematisation project of the Euregio unfolds in an unfavourable political context in Russia, marked by the increasing societal disillusionment with the state of affairs in EU–Russian relations and the abandonment of ambitious integrationist designs. The project of the Euregio therefore may not have the anticipated societal support and its functioning may well be complicated by the very civil society to whose development it seeks to contribute.

As to Kaliningrad, the pattern is basically the same with the EU having a considerable socialising impact. There has been extensive engagement but also grievances as to the way the border works after having been influenced by the rules and regulations of the EU's border regime. Being framed in the context of a cooperative and integrated vision, Europe has stimulated an exchange of views as to the essence of Kaliningrad with some defensive and restitutionist voices also present. In general, the preparedness to link up with a European type of discourse seems to have increased, however, as also indicated by Kaliningrad's 750 years' jubilee in the summer of 2005.

Engaging the regional and local levels has proved to be rather cumbersome in the case of both the Estonian–Russian and Latvian–Russian borderlands, although the former seems to be more advanced than the latter. In the case of the Latvian–Russian border region, one major obstacle appears to be that there is insufficient knowledge available as to the options offered by the EU in terms of cross-border cooperation, as well as a lack of competent local actors to make use of the possibilities that are potentially there. The societal forces interested in making a try have also faced, it seems, far more reluctant political leaderships both locally and on a national level.

Constructive impact

Despite having views of their own as to what 'Europeanisation' entails, various interpretations might lead to a deproblematisation of borders. The reading should hence not necessarily be that it is the increasing impact of the EU's interpretation that has led the remaining border disputes in northern Europe to being settled, with some residual issues still pending. With Russia being suspicious that the imposition of an EU-related order actually stands for efforts of subordination and aims at pushing Russia to the edges of an increasingly concentric European order (as indicated above all by the introduction of the ENP with its emphasis on bilateral rather than multilateral relations), it is important that Russia has the option to explain normalisation and deproblematisation within the context of its own logic. If that space were not there, one could assume that the border disputes would remain unsettled if not turn increasingly conflictual.

As in the case of Kaliningrad, it appears – if viewed against this background – that progress could be achieved by refraining from efforts of changing the underlying identity-scripts and by recognising that there are various ways of being 'European', with Russia legitimately representing one version, and thereby also defining its interests in a manner of its own.

Importantly, the EU did not aim at projecting itself as the sole model but recognised openly that the EU version of integration might also have adverse effects. This plurality and the option opening up for Russia to show itself as a champion of a 'good' Europe then allowed the parties to negotiate solutions by narrowing down the issues at hand to those of transit. The outcome does not point in the direction of one discursive framework being replaced and taken over by another one, with peaceful transformation then flowing from the increased compatibility of the subject positions. It rather appears that the subject positions became compatible to compromises reached in a dialogue across two identity-scripts that both perceived themselves as standing for a 'good' Europe, albeit in ways of their own.

In the case of the Karelian 'question', there appears to be space for a constructive impact and the application of a logic of border deproblematisation, which already exists in the context of the bilateral Finnish–Russian framework as indicated by the Neighbourhood Agreement signed in 1992. The zero-sum logic of restitution was rejected to start with and the border itself became thoroughly desecuritised due to the dominance of a functionalist and cooperative logic. As the most far-reaching path of perturbation, the constructive impact remains contingent on a multiplicity of factors, related to the overall development of EU–Russian relations. At present, the more ambitious 'change of scripts' scenario, i.e. the emergence of Euregio Karelia as a transnational macro-regional political subject, is made impossible both by EU procedures, which preclude a greater role for the Russian party in budgetary and decision-making matters, and by the wariness of Russian political actors in the north-western region to submit to an externally designed development project in the subordinate capacity of an 'object' of policy rather than its sovereign subject. Thus, the potential for a far-reaching constructive impact in the Euregio Karelia project is both conditioned by the EU's recognition of Russia's demand for greater intersubjectivity in designing and implementing cooperation programmes, and ultimately dependent on the compatibility of the policies of the Euregio with the more general strategic development design for the Russian Northwest.[18]

In the case of the Estonian–Russian and Latvian–Russian border disputes much progress has been discernible, with the state parties having achieved progress in the context of their bilateral contacts, although the treaty approved is still on hold in the Estonian–Russian case. One may assume that as to their respective conceptualisations pertaining to

---

[18] For analyses of strategic policy designs on the macro-regional level of the Russian Northwest see Prozorov (2004d) and Prozorov (2005b).

'Europeanisation', the parties have not been that far apart from each other. Both Estonia and Latvia have been quite security-conscious and sovereignty-geared, and so has Russia. The parties could thus talk with each other without the identity-scripts underlying the discourse being too much at loggerheads. The discourse has, no doubt, remained conflict-related, albeit the interests have been sufficiently common for the prospects of an Estonian–Russian border treaty to be negotiated and perhaps also approved in the near future. Again, the outcome is perhaps not to be interpreted as the EU bringing about – due to enlargement and Estonia's and Latvia's membership – a change in the underlying identity-scripts.

By way of conclusion

In all, the various issues pertaining to the borders located in the northern part of Europe have drawn the EU and Russia into, if not a dialogue, at least an extensive set of negotiations (Tables 5.1, 5.2, 5.3). Russia has recognised the Union's expanding subjectivity in northern Europe and has in this sense gained a posture and voice in the process of constructing political space and drawing borders. Instead of just being allotted with the position of a permanent outsider, Russia has been able to aspire – largely by the use of Kaliningrad's position increasingly inside the Union – after a position of a semi-insider rather than just being pushed into the position of a (close) outsider. It could be argued that there has been a game of recognition (cf. Ringmar 2002), in which the Union has achieved a more established position if seen from the perspective of Russia. However, Russia has also stood to gain from the emerging constellation, with the Union granting Russia recognition as a 'partner' and reacting positively to at least some of the Russian proposals regarding the organisation of political space and border-drawing in northern Europe.

Still, the exchange of views that has emerged does not stand out as one between equal partners basically sharing a joint framework of thinking. A disaccord may still unfold as to Kaliningrad, and the pending issues relating to border practices may drag on as well once the EU enhances its subjectivity in the outer circles of an overall concentric configuration. This takes place, above all, through the new Neighbourhood Policy, and although Russia is not part of that policy which aims at the establishment of a post-enlargement border regime, the increasingly coordinated and coherent policies underpinning the ENP appear to be relevant also in the context of the EU–Russian relationship. The problem is that although premised on the idea of borders as something fluid and mobile, the ENP inevitably brings about asymmetric neighbourhood relations in representing an attempt to gain control over policy developments in the

Table 5.1: (prepared by Andrey Makarychev): Overview of EU influence on the Kaliningrad dispute

Pathway	Impact	Main EU institution	Main addressee	Nature of influence	Facilitating conditions
Compulsory	Partial and fragmented	European Commission (through its Moscow office)	The Kremlin	Conditionality	Russia's WTO accession, the Kyoto protocol ratification, the EU investments in Russia's North-west
Enabling	Partial	European Commission	Wider political elites in Moscow and Kaliningrad	Engagement via the spread of policy ideas and their formalisation through organisational procedures	Permeability (communicative and learning abilities of political elites) and mutability (their readiness to reshape the domestic procedures according to international norms)
Connective	Meaningful	European Commission	Local and regional authorities	Collaborative project-based activity	The attractiveness of *ideas*, economic, political, educational and managerial *practices* and social *norms* promoted by EU
Constructive	Rather significant	European Commission in conjunction with other European institutions	NGOs and 'epistemic communities'	Identity changes	The proliferation of networking practices

Table 5.2: (prepared by Sergei Prozorov): Overview of EU influence on the Karelian issue

Pathway	Impact	Main EU institution	Main addressee	Nature of influence	Facilitating conditions
Compulsory	–	–	–	–	–
Enabling	Present in both positive and negative aspects	European Commission	Government officials at municipal and regional levels	Deproblematisation of the border vs maintenance of visa regime	Existence of regular structures of interaction (Euregio)
Connective	Highly significant	European Commission	Local authorities; civil society actors, including media	TACIS and Interreg funding	Gradual displacement of cultural stereotypes; delegitimation of 'bordering' discourses
Constructive	Potential	(European Commission)	Local and regional-level NGOs	Support for multilevel social networks	Formation of a transnational macro-regional entity

Table 5.3: *Overview of EU influence on the Estonia–Russia and Latvia–Russia border disputes*

Pathway	Impact	Main EU institution	Main addressee	Nature of influence	Facilitating conditions
Compulsury	Absent or modest	–	–	–	–
Enabling	Both positive and negative	European Commission	Wider political elites in Russia and Estonia/Latvia	Reframing issues, keeping them separate from each other, desecuritisation	Existence of regular structures of interaction
Connective	Significant	European Commission	Local and regional authorities	Euroregions facilitating cross-border cooperation; ENP, ENPI	Local and regional interests, lingering suspicions regarding the 'other'
Constructive	Significant	European Commission	'Epistemic communities'	'Europeanisation' of disputes	Demise of cultural stereotypes, the image of the Baltic Sea region as a cooperative one

Union's immediate neighbourhood. In essence, the EU provides the norms and it is up to the neighbours to adopt them if they are to hope for closer relations with the Union.

Notably, the core issue within such a setting is not borders *per se*, but the emergence of structures in which power resides with the core and fades towards the edges. The pursuance of such a policy emphasising inequalities may potentially bring about more serious tensions than the efforts of applying a Schengen-type logic which presupposes clearly delineated entities and brings about rather distinct divisions into the 'ins' and the 'outs'.

In general, Russia appears to have reacted more critically to border-drawing premised on a Schengen type of logic than to the more recent efforts of introducing an ENP-related regime, although the latter has not been wholly problem-free either. At large, the Union's Russia policies do not seem to be very developed, and the EU has – for its part – only recently been compelled to encounter more concretely the various needs of Russia. As to the Union's border policies, the universalising tendencies increasingly appear to have gained in prominence with the recent round of enlargement, and this seems to impact on the border policies pursued as well. Consequently, there is less space for the articulation of policies from bottom-up in the societies at the 'edge' of the EU. As such, the ENP mentions the option of regional policies, but the stress has, until recently, been predominantly on bilateralism, with the edges being targeted individually instead of being encouraged to coalesce as a group. There is also some space, it seems, for region-specific measures in the context of the ENP but, if taken too far, they are seen as endangering the EU's credibility and ability to design and implement more general, all-encompassing policies. Moreover, deviations from general norms and an approval of fuzziness at the outer edges would challenge the Union's rather stiff structure of pillars and the pursuance of quite vertical policies. Hence also, the policies pursued in northern Europe tend to boil down to a redrawing of unambiguous lines, and this despite often preaching the opposite in terms of fuzzy borders. An open Union with ambiguous borders is not taken to be equal to a secure one. The integration project has thus gained considerable aspects – if seen from a Russian perspective – of exclusion. It provides features of a Self–Other hierarchy. Being pressed, the Union is prepared to negotiate to correct such impressions and accept compromises, albeit within limits set by the aim of aspiring after a concentric Europe. The rules of the game are, in fact, rarely open for discussion, with the Union aspiring after the position of a unified and coherent actor.

Once different logics and conceptualisations collide, the EU does not opt for a discussion between equal partners, but basically insists on the application of its own existing policies and principles – understood as the only conceivable basis for an agreement. There is almost no seeking (except in the context of the Northern Dimension and Euregios such as the Karelian one) for the views of outsiders, nor is there any forwarding from the EU's core of proposals and ideas designed to meet the needs of the specific issues or regional concerns at hand. Russia is, for its part, not that well equipped to comprehend the EU's logic in the first place and hence clashes and misinterpretations may occur even in the future.

As to Russia, deviations from the modern, realist and geopolitical logic, calling for fairly strict, statist borders, have often been viewed with suspicion. Deviations are interpreted as bringing about fragmentation, thus spelling danger. Yet it appears that it has, for the most part, been Russia that has occasionally experimented with some specific postmodern, regionalised ideas, being thus able to appeal to the Union's own rhetoric about openness, freedoms, debordering, as well as region-building. The various proposals pertaining to the Kaliningrad puzzle demonstrate this quite clearly, as does the idea of skipping visas in the EU–Russian relationship, although it also becomes obvious that the strategy has so far been met with relatively modest success. Reaching out and appealing to the EU's rhetoric on inclusiveness, openness and horizontal approaches have not carried very far either. The construction of fuzzy borderlands in regard to Russia has not appealed to the EU and the offensive play to utilise the margins in an innovative and spontaneous, rather than strictly rule-bound and administrative manner, has not paid off in any decisive manner.

The lack of success could reside in Russia's own uncertainty about whether the postmodern approaches are really warranted. Russia has by and large been able to launch proposals without fearing that the seriousness of the suggested ideas will eventually be put to the test as the EU has quite rarely been willing to capitalise on these proposals. This inability is partly due to what Browning (2003) labels the EU's 'internal/external security paradox', i.e. a constellation which calls for the reproduction of modernist understandings of subjectivity, central to which is the notion that subjects require clearly demarcated territorial spaces and borders over which they exercise sovereign control. The conflation of identity, territory and sovereignty embedded in the paradox also tends to lead to the reification of selfhood and to the negative characterisation of those outside the borders of the EU as potential threats to the Union's security. The subjectivity and recognition of actors such as Russia as legitimate partners – in the form of semi-insiders – is thus undermined.

Borders are, in this context, comprehended as lines of differentiation and exclusion. Such an approach becomes problematic if applied in a rather regionalised context furnished with networks and a variety of over-lapping spaces, and that is what the essence of northern Europe is increasingly about. Russia is by no means a champion of such a trend but has at least occasionally been able to tune in to such a development as indicated by the negotiations that emerged in the context of Kaliningrad. The postmodern views pertaining to debordering and region-specific solutions offered a bridge to talks with the Union, thereby also bolstering the subjectivity of Russia, as the proposals have qualities that resonate with the Union's own rhetoric.

This achievement – which also implies that Russia is basically able to live with the position it is offered in the context of the EU-based, con-centric Europe and operate in that context in order to bolster its position in the margins – has, however, not undermined the rather hierarchical nature of the discourse. The outcome in the case of Kaliningrad, although in general bringing about results in terms of recognition and subjectivity, does not imply that all the hurdles in the EU–Russian relationship regard-ing northern Europe have been overcome. Quite to the contrary, as one may on good grounds assume that Russia's ambitions to aspire after the position of a semi-insider are bound to continue. Still, the crucial ques-tion remains whether this will take place on traditional grounds, or whether Russia has the narrative resources, historical experiences and political imagination to shift course. It would have more to gain by constituting itself as a link into the new, more postmodern framework. Russia could, in this sense, play a more prominent role in the making of Europe's North and Europe more generally instead of just concentrating on building its 'own' Europe on the ruins of the USSR and trying to protect such a shrinking political space from external and 'hostile' influences.

6 The EU and the Israel–Palestine conflict

Haim Yacobi and David Newman

Introduction

The case study discussed in this chapter departs from the other case studies in this book as neither of the two conflict parties, Israel and Palestine, is geographically or, at least in the near future, politically part of the EU. Yet, while there is no immediate integration perspective for the two conflict parties, both Israel and Palestine have close linkages to the EU, both bilaterally and in the context of the multilateral Euro-Mediterranean Partnership (EMP), in which a framework of association between both countries and the EU has been established. This association dimension renders the Israel–Palestine case study central to the analysis in this book and allows us to test whether association provides for similar mechanisms in the transformation of border conflicts as integration does in the other case studies. Having said this, it is important to remember that there has been European involvement in the Middle Eastern region for centuries and in the Israeli–Arab conflict from the early twentieth century through to the present era and the formation of a common EU foreign policy (Sachar 1999; Heller 2004). As has become a commonplace among European policy-makers, developments in the Israeli–Palestinian conflict have a significant influence on developments in the EU. Consequently, the EC/EU already in the 1970s defined the solution of the Israeli–Palestinian conflict as a key European interest and has since then been constantly involved in many attempts to intervene and mediate in the region, in order to help the two sides arrive at conflict resolution (Hollis 1997; Peters 1999; Dieckhoff 2002; Asseburg 2003).

This chapter examines the role of the EU in the Israeli–Palestinian conflict and focuses in particular on the impact of association on conflict resolution. The main argument put forward here is that the overall impact of the EU on the Israeli–Palestinian conflict has been hampered by several factors. Thus, pathways of EU involvement operate in an uneven manner in the Israeli–Palestinian conflict and there has been little synergy between them. Moreover, the impact of the EU is further circumscribed by the specific way through which each of the conflict parties views the EU. This chapter stresses in particular the ambivalent identity relationship of Israel with the EU, which limits the undistorted operation of pathways in the entire Israeli–Palestinian conflict. Overall, the impact of association is constrained. Rather than gradually becoming part of the domestic political settings in Israel and Palestine, the EU resembles in this conflict on most dimensions a classical third party. In the specific case at hand, the impact of the EU is further limited by the fact that the major external actor involved in the Israeli–Palestinian conflict is the USA. Due to sometimes opposing interests of the USA and the EU, the strong involvement of the USA in the Israeli–Palestinian conflict limits the EU's space of manoeuvring. The EU influence is therefore limited, since it has, in the absence of an integration perspective for Israel and Palestine, relatively few 'carrots and sticks' at its disposal which it can exercise vis-à-vis the two conflict parties. This chapter discusses these various limitations to EU impact that, while effective in other conflicts, is of less influence in the Israeli–Palestinian conflict. However, it will also refer to those areas and avenues of intervention through which the EU has occasionally been able to exercise its influence.

History of the conflict

The dispute over land and borders lies at the heart of the Israeli–Palestinian conflict. Notions of political homeland and mythical territory, which constitute a central part of national identity, are central to the way in which Israelis and Palestinians formulate their respective border and territorial discourses (Newman 2002). The Israeli–Palestinian conflict is a supreme example of the significance of territorial and border conflicts in an era of globalisation, countering many of the 'borderless world' and 'deterritorialisation' narratives of recent years (Newman 2006).

The Israeli–Palestinian 'territorial arena' has witnessed continuous transformations during the twentieth century, involving the break-up of the Ottoman Empire, the first partition of the region and the creation of the Kingdom of Trans-Jordan by the British Mandate in 1921, the partition of Palestine and the creation of Israel and the West Bank/Gaza Strip in 1947–9, territorial expansion by Israel as a result of the Six Days War of June 1967 and territorial contraction as a result of the Israel/Egypt peace agreement of 1979 (Newman 2002). The Oslo Peace Accords of 1993 and the transfer of territory by Israel to the Palestinian Authority (PA), as well as the ongoing attempts to reach a final peace agreement between the two sides, intended to result in the establishment of an independent Palestinian state, will most likely bring about further territorial change.

The history of the Israeli–Palestinian conflict has been discussed in great detail in the literature (for details see: Yacobi and Newman 2004a). In this section, we will instead briefly examine the main periods of territorial change, focusing on the way in which the nature of the conflict has changed over time.

The history of pre-state Palestine is replete with border and territorial changes, the most significant of which were brought about by the replacement of the Ottoman Empire with the British and French Mandates. The basic territorial configuration of Palestine as a modern political entity underwent its initial formulation during this period. The northern border of what are today Israel, Lebanon and Syria was demarcated between the two respective mandate powers. The eastern boundary of Palestine was determined following the British decision to create the State of Trans-Jordan in 1921, resulting in the *de facto* demarcation of the border along the Jordan Valley, while the southern boundary between Palestine and the Sinai Peninsula was also determined at this time, laying the basis for the territorial negotiations which took place between Israel and Egypt over sixty years later. The second major territorial event in this period was the emerging discussion concerning the partition of Palestine west of the River Jordan into two political entities – one Jewish and one Arab. Various British Royal Commissions (such as the Peel and Woodhead Commissions of the 1930s) recommended maps of territorial partition, as did further commissions which were set up following the end of World War II (Galnoor 1994). These proposals reflected the changing demographic and settlement realities which had occurred during this period, resulting eventually in the decision by the British government to relinquish their mandate for Palestine and to return the problem to the United Nations which, in turn, set up its own commission of enquiry. The United Nations Special Committee on Palestine (UNSCOP) partition proposal, favouring a Jewish state, an Arab state and an internationalised Jerusalem, was approved by the UN General Assembly in November 1947.

However, the territorial configuration of the State of Israel, following the signing of the armistice agreements in 1949, was significantly different to that proposed by the UNSCOP Commission and approved by the UN General Assembly. The UN Partition Proposal gave more territory to the proposed Arab state, including many of the Arab population centres which were eventually incorporated inside Israel following the war of 1948–9 (remembered as the War of Independence in Israel and Al-Nakba, the catastrophe, in Palestine). The 'green line', the boundary separating Israel from the West Bank, was drawn up in negotiations

which took place between representatives of Israel and Jordan on the isle
of Rhodes and was then implemented, with minor changes, as the border
between Israeli and Jordanian administered territories. The line functioned as a sealed and armed boundary of confrontation for a period
of nineteen years. While its barrier effects were initially removed in
1967 following Israel's conquest of the West Bank, East Jerusalem and
the Gaza Strip in the Six Days War, the line remained in place as an
effective administrative boundary throughout the period of Israeli occupation. This was largely due to Israel's non-annexation of the Occupied
Territories (except East Jerusalem), thus retaining a clear distinction
between the legal status of Israel vis-à-vis the West Bank/Gaza Strip and
their respective populations. Despite political statements to the contrary,
the 'green line' has remained in situ as a powerful administrative boundary throughout the period of Israeli occupation of the region. Since the
year 2000, as a result of increasing violence in the Israeli–Palestinian
conflict, the border has, once again, taken on the characteristics of a
closed boundary, culminating in the construction of the Separation
Fence/Wall in 2003–5 (see below).

The 1967 Six Days War led to significant territorial changes. The
new territorial configurations provided for an expanded security *cordon
sanitaire* for Israel, while at the same time tripling the length of its land
boundaries, which now had to be patrolled and defended. The capture
of the Sinai Peninsula provided Israel with its most significant security
advantage, both as a security buffer in relation to Egypt and as an area
in which to establish army bases and airfields and in which to undertake
army manoeuvres. Unlike the territory within the 1949 boundaries, the
territories captured by Israel in 1967 do not constitute part of the State
of Israel. Under international law, 'occupied territories' are subject to
the Hague and Geneva Conventions. However, Israel views East
Jerusalem and the Golan Heights as constituting part of the State of
Israel by virtue of the decisions taken by the Israeli Parliament to annex
these territories (or what was termed the 'extension of civilian law to
replace the military administration'), in 1967 and 1981 respectively, but
this interpretation is rejected by the entire international community.
Following the conquest of the West Bank and Gaza Strip, successive
Israeli governments have promoted a policy of settlement construction,
consolidation and expansion within these areas. As of 2005, the settler
population of the West Bank and Gaza Strip had reached 250,000 (not
including settlements in East Jerusalem), creating territorial obstacles
for all future attempts of conflict resolution which would enable the
establishment of a Palestinian state within the pre-1967 Palestinian
territories.

Further territorial change took place as a result of conflict resolution between Israel and its neighbours. Commencing with the implementation of the Camp David Peace Agreements between Israel and Egypt in the 1980s, the gradual implementation of the Oslo Accords between Israel and the Palestinian Authority, the peace agreement between Israel and Jordan in 1995 and, in 2005, the Israeli disengagement from the Gaza Strip, the political map of the region has undergone considerable reconfigurations. Unlike previous territorial modifications, these changes took place as part of a process of conflict resolution. The boundaries that have been determined between Israel, Egypt and Jordan have now taken on international status. In the case of both Israeli–Egyptian negotiations and the ongoing negotiations between Israel and the PA, the intended result of the conflict resolution process involves territorial contraction by Israel, namely to withdraw from all, or part, of the land previously controlled. The peace treaty with Jordan has not resulted in any significant territorial change. Israel's eastern boundary along the Jordan and Aravah Valleys has been ratified, with some minor transfers of parcels of land from Israel to Jordan. The Oslo I Agreement resulted in an Israeli withdrawal from the Gaza Strip and the town of Jericho, while this was extended to include further towns and some Palestinian villages under the terms of the Oslo II Agreement. From a Palestinian perspective, the transition from initial autonomy to full statehood was to be accompanied by further territorial changes, including the transfer of the whole of the West Bank and Gaza Strip to Palestinian control. The two Oslo Accords of 1993 and 1995 effectively carved up the Palestinian territories into exclaves of differentiated autonomy. Thus, approximately a third of the West Bank and almost the entire Gaza Strip were transferred, to varying degrees, to the PA and designated as Area 'A' (full Palestinian control) and 'B' (Palestinian political and Israeli security control), while the remainder of the region was left under full Israeli control (Area 'C'). The long-term status of the West Bank and Gaza Strip was meant to be determined under the future negotiations over a final peace agreement.

Following the breakdown of the Camp David talks in September 2000, the Israeli–Palestinian conflict again increased in intensity and reached high levels of violence. This period was characterised by the second *Intifada*, a sharp increase of Palestinian suicide bombings against Israelis and heavy Israeli military operations in the West Bank and Gaza Strip. In Israel, a right-wing government under the leadership of Ariel Sharon was elected. Under this government, Israel re-entered parts of the PA-controlled areas and retook control in much of the West Bank and Gaza Strip. Despite the significant increase in mutual violence to a degree which had not previously been experienced in over thirty years of occupation, a number of new peace plans were proposed, ranging from the Road Map (the official government plan sponsored by the Quartet – the US, the EU, Russia and the UN) to the Geneva Agreement (negotiated between leading Israeli and Palestinian politicians). Despite the differences in the details of these plans, the major territorial and border configurations were very similar – a two-state solution with a return to the green-line border with minor territorial changes to be negotiated between the two sides. The debate about borders and their deeper significance re-emerged as a result of the construction of the Separation Fence/Wall in 2003, which *inter alia* functions as a barrier against further suicide attacks inside Israel (Makovsky 2004a; 2004b). The construction of the fence/ wall resulted in unilateral territorial changes in favour of Israel. It was constructed in such a way as to include some Israeli settlements which were in close proximity to the green line, although this also resulted in the inclusion of Palestinian villages which now found themselves as 'spatial hostages', located to the west of the fence/wall, but to the east of the green line itself. The construction of this fence/wall thus takes on many of the classic boundary barrier functions, exacerbating and reflecting a situation of extreme conflict on the one hand, while possibly laying the foundations for territorial demarcation of separate political entities, on the other. But the fence/wall is different to previous border proposals in that it has really been implemented and thus become a geographic and political fact.

In 2004, the Israeli Prime Minister Ariel Sharon suggested a unilateral disengagement plan from the Gaza Strip, including the withdrawal of Israeli troops and the evacuation of all Israeli settlements in this region (Makovsky 2005a; 2005b). In the run-up to the presentation of the plan to the Israeli public, Sharon received the backing of the US Administration, including letters from President Bush affirming Israel's long-term right to adjust boundaries in the West Bank and to retain control over some of the major settlement blocks under a future comprehensive peace agreement. Gaza disengagement was implemented in the summer of 2005, despite large-scale opposition from right-wing and settler groups within Israel. The 7,000-strong settler community of the Gaza Strip was evacuated from their houses and relocated to new homes inside Israel. The border contours of the Gaza Strip remained virtually unchanged.

In all of its history as outlined above, the Israeli–Palestinian conflict has been characterised by a strong identity dimension. Territorial claims were always couched in the terminology of Jewish/Palestinian homeland and historical/religious rights, with borders (tangible issues) being no more than a spatial and geographical expression of the core identity issues underlying the conflictive aspirations between Zionism as a national movement and Palestinian nationalism.

The 1948–9 war and the subsequent period – statehood for the Jewish people, statelessness and refugee status for the Palestinians – ultimately turned the conflict into a subordination conflict, characterised by high levels of violence and mutually exclusive territorial claims. Physical force has in most of this period been an acceptable means of dealing with the other side – be it through the military power of the state on the one hand, or the violent activities of guerrilla movements, on the other.

The 1967 war resulted in significant changes in Israeli social, political and cultural reality. For many Israeli Jews, besotted with the military victory, issues of subordination and identity became inherently linked with each other. This was true of Israeli society as a whole, but was particularly intense among the right-wing religious nationalists who attributed the victory to Divine providence and saw this as a sign that the 'liberated' (in their terms not 'occupied' or 'administered') territories of 'Judea and Samaria' should be settled and remain, forever, under Jewish sovereignty. The establishment of the West Bank and Gaza settlement network became a major cause of subsequent territorial change, making the return to pre-existing border configurations ever more difficult even in periods of political negotiations (such as the Oslo Accords of the 1990s or the Camp David and Taba Summits in 2000/1). The power of Israel vis-à-vis the Palestinians became intricately linked with the irredentist and ethno-exclusive identity constructions of larger parts of the Israeli population. For many, identity became transformed into a politics of territory, with notions of homeland and ancestral rights determining the nature of the conflict.

The second *Intifada* (after 2000) and the increase in violence and retaliation practised by both parties in this period reflect, even more strongly than any period in the past, the dynamics of subordination in this conflict from both sides, with the construction of the fence/wall being the most tangible expression of this; the fence/wall demarcates and implements borders on the ground, focusing on the core territorial and demographic issues and the way in which different territorial configurations affect the demographic ratio between Israelis and Palestinians. The unilateral determination and imposed implementation of the new border is a clear expression of raw power. And all of these together reflect the basic identity dimensions of the conflict which underlay the whole *raison d'être* of Jewish statehood, on the one hand, and the desire for Palestinian independence, on the other. The mutual desires for independence, safety and security are intertwined and subsumed with each other, with the struggle for identity by the one side (through agencies of power) giving rise to similar identity struggles by the other. In this sense, territorial change may appear to be no more than a technical border modification on the ground. But in reality it gives rise to intensified forms of identity struggle, as each side continues to perceive itself as existentially threatened by the existence of the other.

As we shall discuss in the following sections of this chapter, the EU has always been keen to influence precisely this subordination dimension of the Israeli–Palestinian conflict through addressing the core political and territorial issues. The EU thus takes the identity dimensions as given, namely that both Israelis and Palestinians are entitled to self-determination, security and sovereignty in separate and independent, ethnically exclusive entities. The fact that power and issue modification, by definition, will affect the way in which both peoples perceive their respective identity concerns is, perhaps, one of the deeper reasons why the EU is unable to have more than a marginal impact on the process of conflict resolution in this region.

EU involvement and change over time

The tension between Israeli ambivalence towards Europe, on the one hand, and Palestinian calls for greater European involvement in the conflict, on the other, has been a key factor that has shaped the role of the EC/EU in the Israeli–Palestinian conflict since the inception of a single European policy on this region in the 1970s (Greilshammer and Weiler 1987; 1988). For Israelis, Europe is the place in which the Holocaust occurred; at the same time, however, the founding generation of Israel was European, perceiving European culture and tradition as constituting the cornerstones on which a modern State of Israel should be founded. For Palestinians, Europe has at least since the late 1960s been seen as a possible counterweight to the USA, which is perceived as an ardent supporter of Israel; yet, Palestinians also have a painful memory of European colonialism in the region, which relates to the experiences with the British Mandate and which continues to affect Palestinian relations with Europe. Following the break-up of the Ottoman Empire, the area of Palestine was administered through the British Mandate, with the creation of the Kingdom of Trans-Jordan to the east of the River Jordan. The State of Israel and the area known as the West Bank, under the direct administration of Jordan, were established in the immediate aftermath of the British withdrawal from the region and the subsequent Israeli War of Independence, Palestinian Al-Nakba. After the establishment of Israel in 1948–9 and the parallel creation of the Palestinian refugee problem, Europe attempted to maintain its influence as a power broker and mediator in the region. In this early period, there was not a single European policy, with different European countries changing their stances contingent upon specific political and time contexts.

Following the establishment of Israel, it was Germany and Britain which were the *bêtes noires* for most Israelis, the former because of the Holocaust, the latter because of Britain's attempts to prevent the establishment of Israel and refuse entry to Jewish refugees and immigrants in the period between 1945 and 1948. During the first decade of statehood, France was an important ally of Israel and was seen by foreign policy-makers as constituting Israel's closest ally in Europe. This was reflected by French assistance in the construction of Israel's nuclear reactor in Dimona during the 1950s. By the time of the 1956 Sinai campaign, France and Britain were then fighting together with Israel against the Egyptian nationalisation of the Suez Canal, while West Germany remained beyond the pale of normal diplomatic relations (Aridan 1994). This situation changed by the 1960s, when West Germany had begun to develop relations with Israel, partly through the leadership of Chancellor Konrad Adenauer and the implementation of a major reparations package to Holocaust victims and their families. Since then, (West) Germany has become one of Israel's closest European supporters, although Israeli leaders never lose the opportunity of exerting the guilt complex on German governments when their leaders utter statements which may be interpreted as being too pro-Palestinian and not sufficiently pro-Israel.

The 1967 war constituted a major turning point not only in the Israeli–Palestinian conflict, but also in the European approach to the region. European support for Israel became more tenuous, while the continuation of the occupation and the building of settlements have switched much European support for the allegedly pre-1967 underdogs (Israel) to the allegedly post-1967 underdogs (the Palestinians). In particular, Israeli–French relations have undertaken a significant turn for the worse, while Israeli–British relations continue to experience ups and downs. The tension between Israel and the European states continued throughout the 1970s. This was expressed mainly after the 1973 war and the Arab oil embargo, which was partially used as a tool to put pressure on the Europeans to actively intervene in the Israeli–Palestinian conflict. Moreover, in the course of the 1960s and 1970s, the Palestinian Liberation Organisation (PLO) under the leadership of Yasser Arafat emerged as the main political voice of Palestinians. Despite several terror attacks which were linked to the PLO, such as the assassination of Israeli participants at the 1972 Olympic Games in Munich, the PLO not only managed to become firmly established on the international political scene, but was also increasingly accepted by Western European countries, such as France, Britain, Sweden, Austria and, with a more cautious approach, West Germany, as the legitimate political representative of the Palestinian people.

This gradual change of tides in European relations with Israel and Palestine also affected the emerging single European policy on the Middle East. Thus, in the course of the 1970s, as a result of an increasing antagonism between Israel and the EC and a parallel rapprochement between the EC and Arab countries, Europe became one of the leading international supporters of Palestinian self-determination. This culminated in the Venice Declaration of the European Council of 1981, in which the heads of state and government declared that they support the right of Palestinians to self-determination. Ever since, the Venice Declaration has become a symbol of European policies on the Middle East, being rejected by many Israelis as one-sided and referred to by Palestinians as a quasi-legal confirmation of their political claims.

In this context of a strong politicisation of the Venice Declaration, subsequent Israeli governments in the 1980s rejected any formal involvement of the EC in the regulation of the Israeli–Palestinian conflict. This only changed, gradually, as a result of the Madrid Peace Conference in 1991, which was convened after the end of the second Gulf War. While the Madrid Conference was sponsored by the USA and the then Soviet Union, the EC/EU managed to become a junior partner in the context of Madrid's multilateral peace framework (Peters 1996a). Thus, the EC/EU successfully threw in its economic weight and was handed over the responsibility for the Regional Economic Development Working Group (REDWG). REDWG was the most active working group in the multilateral track of the peace process and while it produced little effect on the ground, it nevertheless brought together Palestinians, Israelis, Jordanians and Egyptians who jointly developed ideas for several economic cooperation projects in the region (Peters 1996b). The significance of the Madrid Conference, which preceded the Oslo Agreement between Israel and the PLO of 1993, with regard to greater EU involvement in the region thus relates mainly to the economic dimension. However, it also had a political significance since REDWG formally marked the end of the absence of a direct European involvement in the Israeli–Palestinian conflict.

The economic emphasis of the EU's new role in the Middle East in the context of REDWG also set an important precedent for future developments. Thus, throughout most of the 1990s, the EU's role in the Israeli–Palestinian conflict was characterised by a strong emphasis on the economic dimension, as reflected by the steady increase in trade relations between Israel and the EU and the fact that the EU became by far the main external donor to the PA. Moreover, this emphasis on economic relations also shaped the association of both countries with the EU in the EMP framework. Thus, with both Israel and the PLO, the EU has concluded Association Agreements, which contain a strong economic and a relatively small political dimension (Stetter 2007). This emphasis on the economic dimension of EU involvement in the Israeli–Palestinian conflict has led many observers to argue that the EU is a 'payer' but not a 'player' in the Israeli–Palestinian conflict (Perthes 2004).

However, building on the Venice Declaration, the EU also developed in this period its political stance on the conflict. This process arguably culminated in the 1999 Berlin Declaration of the European Council (Alpher 2000). This document directly calls for the establishment of an independent Palestinian state and thus predates similar calls by the Bush Administration. Following the failure of the bilateral negotiations in the Oslo years, the Berlin Declaration opened the possibility of European recognition of an independent Palestinian state, even if this state was to be declared unilaterally. As the British General Consul in Jerusalem stated, 'the EU is ready to recognise the Palestinian State if it is declared' (*Al-Hayat Al-Jadida*, 4 April 1999, in: www.memri.org/bin/articles). The Berlin Declaration also signalled a stronger political involvement of the EU in the Israeli–Palestinian conflict. Thus, while in the Oslo years the EU only had a minor role in the political track – as for example during the signing ceremony of the Wye River Memorandum, at which the EU Special Representative to the Middle East Peace Process, Miguel Angel Moratinos, was one of the co-signers of the agreement – the EU's political role gradually increased since the year 2000 and the outbreak of the second *Intifada*. This is reflected by the participation of the High Representative for the Common Foreign and Security Policy, Javier Solana, in the Mitchell Commission and, more importantly, the EU's formal role as a member of the Quartet.

The EU's position on the main issues in the Israeli–Palestinian conflict has not dramatically changed since the beginning of the formulation of its single foreign policy position on this matter in the 1970s. On many issues, the EC/EU has issued statements that were some years later adopted in a similar way by other countries in the international community, most notably the USA. Unlike in the case of the internal differences relating to the war in Iraq, the EU has been fairly unified over what it sees as the only way forward to conflict resolution in Israel and Palestine. It continues to call on Israel to withdraw its military forces from the Occupied Territories, to freeze all settlement activities leading to their eventual evacuation, the establishment of an independent Palestinian state and, at the same time, the cessation of all violent and terror activities on the part of the Palestinians and the recognition by Palestine and Arab states of a secure Israel in internationally recognised boundaries.

However, behind this issue dimension looms the aforementioned complex identity relation between both Israelis and Palestinians with Europe. And it is this ambivalent identity relationship, in particular in EU–Israeli relations, which until today limits the impact of the EU on the Israeli–Palestinian conflict. Thus, the commonly held perception in Israel that 'Europe' is pro-Palestinian is reflected in the way that both Israeli policy-makers and the Israeli media seize on every European statement which is construed as allegedly favouring the Palestinians. This is supplemented by a dominant perspective among large parts of the Israeli public that despite the ongoing integration in EU foreign and security policies, what really matters in Europe are the policy positions of specific European countries, notably Britain, Germany and France. Moreover, Muslim fundamentalist attacks in the EU, such as in Madrid, Amsterdam or London, are often compared in Israel with Palestinian suicide bombings in Israel. The growth of the Muslim population in Europe and the rise of anti-Semitic attacks in some European countries in 2002 and 2003 as well as attempts from European civil society to impose an academic boycott on Israeli universities, have all contributed to this general feeling inside Israel that Europe cannot be trusted (Dachs and Peters 2004). Single events, such as the attempt by Belgian judicial authorities to put Ariel Sharon on trial as a war criminal, or a Norwegian discussion on a boycott of Israeli goods, are in this context seen as part of a wider anti-Israeli European policy which, it is assumed, underlies the overall EU policy to the region.

Pathways of EU involvement

In this section we examine the extent to which each of the four pathways of EU involvement is relevant for understanding the role of the EU in the Israeli–Palestinian conflict. Our discussion of pathways shows that two of them – the connective and the enabling – are of greater significance in this conflict than are the compulsory or the constructive. However, a key characteristic of EU involvement in the Israeli–Palestinian conflict is that the application of pathways differs with regard to both conflict parties. While the connective pathway has had some limited impact with respect to both parties, the enabling pathway is of greater significance with respect to the PA.

Compulsory

While in some cases of intervention in conflict situations the EU is able to exercise a carrot and stick policy, most notably holding out the benefits of future membership in case of non-resolution, this is not the case with respect to both Israel and Palestine – although the possibility of Israel's accession to the EU has occasionally been raised by European and Israeli politicians, such as Finance Minister (and former Prime Minister) Benjamin Netanyahu's statement to the effect that 'Israel will be interested in full integration' (*Maariv* newspaper, 20 June 2003), or some policy papers which examine the potential for full EU membership on the part of Israel (Veit 2003). Overall, membership of Israel in the EU is not considered by most observers a likely scenario (Tovias 2003).

One of the reasons for this is that in Israel the membership issue becomes intermingled with identity discourses. According to Avi Primor, a former Israeli ambassador to the EU, the potential for collaboration with the EU is mainly economic. Yet, as he argues, if Israel were to become a full member of the EU, it would be required to 'give' to the EU in proportion to the benefits it receives. For example, Israel would have to agree to the freedom of movement, capital, goods and services with all other EU member states. Membership would enable the entrance of European migrants and European capital to Israel (*Maariv* newspaper, 20 June 2003). A similar argument was put forward by the foreign news editor of *Haaretz* daily newspaper, who notes that Israel is either unable or uninterested in meeting as much as 60 per cent of the commitments required before joining the EU. It has even been argued that free access to European migration would require the annulment of the law granting Jews the automatic and exclusive Right of Return to the Jewish nation state (www.haaretz.co.il, 23 July 2003). While this argument seems untenable from a legal perspective, given that many EU countries have specific citizenship provisions for those people they consider compatriots, it nevertheless reflects the underlying identity tensions between Israel and the EU to which we shall return further below.

The EU's policy regarding Israel in the context of the EMP is formally based on 'partnership and cooperation, and not exclusion' (http://europa. eu.int/comm/external_relations). The main pillar of bilateral relations between both sides is thereby the economy. Thus, since the 1960s, the EC/EU has become Israel's main trading partner. Based on figures for 2001, Israeli exports to the EU represented 31 per cent ($6.9 billion) of total Israeli exports, and Israeli imports from the EU 41 per cent ($11.4 billion) of total Israeli imports. Economic collaboration between the EU and Israel is also expressed by the policy of the European Investment Bank to grant loans for Israeli projects in the context of the EMP, including infrastructure and environmental projects.

Against the background of intensifying economic ties between Israel and the EU, what has been the compulsory impact of the EU on Israeli policymakers with regard to the Israeli–Palestinian conflict? A major point of contention in this respect concerns the marketing of goods that have been produced by Israeli manufacturers located in the Occupied Territories. Israel refused until November 2003 to distinguish between goods manufactured in Israel and goods produced in the Occupied Territories. The formal Israeli opposition to such a distinction is based on the EU's recognition of the Paris Agreement that created a Customs Union between Israel and the PA. Israel argues that recognition of the Paris Agreement does not allow for goods manufactured in the Occupied Territories to be treated differently from goods produced in Israel. However, due to the continuous pressure from the EU, Israel subsequently agreed to adopt a compromise solution of including the city of origin on the label. Yet, Ehud Olmert, the Industry Minister at the time, stressed that the agreement in no way implied a change in Israel's political position on the Occupied Territories or a willingness to concede those parts of the territories that the government insisted must remain part of Israel under any future agreement (*Haaretz* newspaper, 25 November 2003, www.haaretz.co.il).

In this context it is also important to mention the ENP, launched in 2003, in which the linkage between economic cooperation and conflict resolution has become an explicit objective. Thus, the ENP policy involves 'a significant degree of economic integration and a deepening of political cooperation, with the aim of preventing the emergence of new dividing lines between the enlarged EU and its neighbours'.[1] In the framework of the ENP, the EU concluded Action Plans with both Israel and Palestine.

But beyond the often declaratory political statements by the EU in the context of the EMP and the ENP, there are also more stringent European positions which seek to exercise a more compulsory influence on Israel in order to resolve the conflict, including the call for economic sanctions and an arms ban against Israel as a means of breaking the impasse. Such statements, emphasising the 'stick dimension', are subject to strong criticism within Israel, as reflected in the writings of one of Europe's main critics in Israel:

Europeans have only a few sticks to operate against Israel ... There are no military sanctions, neither is there significant financial support similar to that of

---

[1] Euromed Reports Nos. 77, 78 and 79 in www.eu-del.org.il.

the USA ... Of course they can hurt the economic relations between Israel and the EU but this raises questions which go beyond the economic, and touch upon the ethical and the political.[2]

A more cynical statement concerning the ineffectiveness of European pressure on Israel was published in *Nekudah*, a popular journal among Israeli settlers, reflecting the anti-European and anti-external interventionist positions of large parts of the Israeli public:

International pressure – if it at all occurs – will be expressed in two dimensions: the denial of American financial support, and an economic embargo from European countries and some others ... Apparently, a European economic embargo is more problematic ... but economic interests will always be stronger than political interests. Belgium has already called for a decrease in commercial relations with Israel. France, on the other hand, avoids calling for an embargo on Israel ... What is the difference between the two? The French like us more? – Definitely not. They just sell us more; Israelis like driving Peugeot, Renault, Citroën, and the French people will not give up such a serious market. On the other hand, our commercial relations with Belgium are negligible (Belgian chocolate is good, but 'Elite' chocolate [an Israeli chocolate firm] is not bad), and hence the Belgians can make such declarations. Israel imports from the EU twice as much as it exports, and economically speaking Europe has no interest in cancelling its agreements with Israel. (Feiglin 2003: 34–5)

That does not mean to say that relevant Israeli interest groups ignore the importance of economic cooperation between Israel and the EU. This is expressed, for example, in the case of a group of Israeli industrialists who went on a mission to the EU to counter attempts to minimise economic relations with Israel or boycott its goods. As one of the Israeli participants said: 'In all the meetings we had we explained Israel's position and that business with us should continue ... people in Europe are brainwashed by the media.' Another member of the industrialist delegation acknowledged the power of the EU, stating that, 'the power of the EU is not always expressed. But when we were there we felt it. Europe and the EU have power that we must consider' (*Maariv* newspaper, 28 May 2002).

To sum up this section, let us suggest that the political logic that stands behind the compulsory pathway is doubtful in relation to the Israeli–Palestinian conflict. The membership of Israel or Palestine in the EU is in the near future not a realistic option, despite some European and Israeli voices to the contrary who see such a possibility as constituting a carrot for Israel to more actively bring an end to the conflict. The compulsory impact of the EU in the Israeli–Palestinian conflict is limited to the association of both parties with the EU in the EMP framework. However,

---

[2] Interview with Gerald Steinberg, Bar Ilan University, 26 February 2004.

this association does not contain a strong compulsory dimension and, therefore, has had only a minor effect on the conflict. But one cannot ignore the future effects of Israel's close association with the EU, which is expressed for example in a classified report of the Israeli Ministry of Foreign Affairs. This report warns that a deterioration of EU–Israeli relations would cause serious economic and political damage to Israel (*Haaretz* newspaper, 13 October 2004, www.haaretz.co.il). As economic and cultural relations between the EU and Israel become stronger, so too the expected impact of losing these ties as a result of EU compulsory actions would make it more difficult, albeit by no means impossible, for Israel to deal with (Tocci 2005c).

Enabling

The type of impact that the EU has on Palestine is different to that which can relate to Israel. As we have shown above, with respect to Israel, the EU has tried to use economic incentives to apply a compulsory impact on Israel, albeit with limited effect. Due to the significantly less developed relations between Palestine and the EU, the compulsory pathway of economic carrots and sticks operates less in this context. However, with regard to Palestine, the EU has had a much greater impact on the wider political level, since the PA depends on substantial EU assistance for its daily existence and management of its fledgling institutional structure. This financial dependence has become even more acute since the outbreak of the second *Intifada*, as the social and economic conditions within the PA have deteriorated to the worst situation since the beginning of Israeli occupation in 1967.

This European approach to directly affect societal developments in Palestine can already be traced in the Venice Declaration of 1980.

The European Union's strategic objective in its relations with the West Bank and Gaza Strip is to contribute to the creation of an independent, democratic and viable Palestinian state living side by side in peace and security with Israel. At the same time, ongoing efforts to alleviate the humanitarian situation and the hardship of the Palestinian population should continue. (http://europa.eu.int/comm/external_relations)

This statement brings to the fore the differences in the EU's relations with Israel and the PA. While EU relations with Israel are based on trade cooperation between two highly developed Western economies (Ahiram and Tovias 1995), the EU's relations with the PA are mainly based on the provision of significant financial assistance and aid packages that aim at a more structural impact on Palestinian society, thereby contributing to a transformation of the Israeli–Palestinian conflict. This constitutes an attempt to stabilise the weak economic and political structures of this nascent state (Stetter 2003). This approach is expressed by the fact that the EU has been the biggest donor to the PA, and that there is no other country in the world that has received as large an amount of assistance from the EU as Palestine (Stetter 2003: 157).

In addition to €2 billion aid in the period 1994–9, the EU provided between June 2001 and 2002 €10 million per month in direct budgetary assistance to the PA. The support was directed towards the budget of the PA, helping to secure expenditures such as public service salaries, social, educational and health. An additional €10 million was allocated by the EU to the World Bank Emergency Services Support Programme to cover operational costs in the health sector in Palestine, and a further €10 million was donated by the EU in a special programme to support services at the level of municipalities (Yacobi and Newman 2004a; 2004b). The EU also transferred €29 million to the PA for humanitarian reasons (*Haaretz* newspaper, 28 October 2002, www.haaretz.co.il). In the run-up to the Israeli disengagement from the Gaza Strip in the summer of 2005, the G8 countries, of which four are EU members, committed themselves to a further $3 billion of direct assistance and aid to the PA.

The extent to which EU aid had an enabling impact on the conflict can in particular be seen with regard to the EU's support for democratic reforms on the political level in Palestine. Thus, the EU in cooperation with other Western states has been active in exerting pressure on the PA to undertake significant governmental and administrative reforms (http://europa.eu.int/comm/external_relations/gaza/intro). In June 2002, the PA, in response to domestic and international pressure, adopted a wide-ranging programme of reform. A number of important measures were taken, such as the adoption and entry into force of the Basic Law, or legislation on the independence of the judiciary. In February 2003, the Palestinian Legislative Council (PLC) adopted the 2003 budget, which was for the first time made public. Significant progress was made with regard to the management of the PA's public finances (following major international criticism of the way in which previous aid and assistance packages had been managed by the Palestinian leadership, and particularly President Yasser Arafat).

During the second *Intifada*, EU assistance was aimed at maintaining the daily existence of the PA and, at the same time, these aid packages were linked to demands for internal economic and democratic reform on the part of the Palestinian leadership. In this period, the EU supported the PA with direct budgetary assistance at a time when customs revenues were withheld by the government of Israel. According to Chris Patten, a former External Relations Commissioner of the EU, without the EU assistance 'there would have been no Palestinian interlocutor for the negotiations now under way' and he also added that 'at every step, the EU's help was made conditional on reforms that would make a viable Palestinian state a reality one day and in the short term make the Palestinian territories a better, safer neighbour for Israel' (*The Financial Times*, 17 July 2003).

Through the agency of its financial assistance, the EU thus supported reforms in Palestine and pushed for the establishment of a democratically elected and accountable Palestinian leadership. This enabling process was meant to indirectly support favourable conditions for a rapprochement between the PA and Israel. At an Ad Hoc Liaison Committee in Rome in December 2003, the international community argued that 'EU budgetary support and its conditions as well as US support, has over the past years been successful in advancing key reform measures such as financial accountability' (europa.eu.int/comm/external_relations/gaza/intro). According to a report by the International Monetary Fund, the conditionality attached to EU assistance to the PA has contributed to a transformation of 'the Palestinian Authority to a level of fiscal responsibility, control, and transparency which rivals the most fiscally advanced countries in the region' (europa.eu.int/comm/external_relations/gaza/intro).

In order to strengthen the rule of law in Palestine, the European Commission also supported the modernisation of the Palestinian judicial system with a programme launched at the end of 2003. The €7 million judiciary reform programme seeks to reinforce the judicial institutions created in the Basic Law, provide training for judges and prosecutors, and fund the refurbishment of courts. The EU also provides extensive support for the preparation of Palestinian elections as it did for the first time in the Presidential elections of 1996, and was thus also actively involved in the Presidential elections which took place in January 2005, following the death of Yasser Arafat. In addition to these programmes specifically addressing democratic reform issues, the Commission aims to ensure that part of the financial assistance programmes of the EU is devoted to capacity building on the wider societal level (e.g. private sector institutions, NGOs, municipalities).

How is this enabling function perceived on the Palestinian side? Samih Shbeib, an academic at a Palestinian university, highlights the importance of this pathway by stating that 'the stronger we are [in good governance reform] the better European support we'll get'.[3] Other Palestinians share this point of view, as the following quote exemplifies:

---

[3] Interview with Samih Shbeib, Birzeit University, 22 May 2004.

The EU intervention in this conflict is always needed and always good. It is wanted and positive. Europe is a historical partner of the Arab world and we share with Europe the Mediterranean Sea, so we have with Europe much more in common than we do with the USA. There are also commercial and economic relationships with Europe, and this supports our relationship with it ... Europe has an effective role; it has been the main partner for the PA as well as the main 'fund supporter' for the Palestinians, so it can play a more effective role when there is will.[4]

However, not all Palestinians agree with this position. Samir Hazboun, a Palestinian academic at Al-Quds University and the Executive Director at DATA, a Research and Consulting Institution in Bethlehem,[5] criticises this heavy reliance of the PA on the EU. He argues that 'what we want from the EU is to be more Palestinian than we are, to resist the occupation and get us a state! We should recognise that the EU is an ally of the PA, not a replacement.' Thus, many Palestinian activists would prefer the EU to take on a more direct political interventionist role, supporting the establishment of a Palestinian state and exerting pressure on Israel to end occupation rather than betting on the indirect effects of the enabling pathway. But this, in turn, fails to take into account the limited compulsory influence that the EU has on Israel. For its part, the EU is aware that it can assist the PA through a variety of economic programmes, help create better management practices through an enabling policy and, thereby, 'persuade' the Israeli authorities that there is a 'partner' on the other side to whom political power can gradually be transferred in a process of conflict resolution.

Thus the enabling pathway, in the form of supporting democratic and administrative reforms in Palestine, constitutes a central form of intervention in the Israeli–Palestinian conflict, and probably has a greater impact than does any form of direct political intervention.

Connective

The EU has a connective influence on the Israeli–Palestinian conflict through its support of non-governmental agencies (NGOs) in Israel and Palestine that engage in the promotion on the wider societal level of peace and cooperation between both sides. The rationale of the connective impact of the EU in the Israeli–Palestinian conflict has been summarised by a former EU Ambassador to Israel as follows:

[4] Interview with Ahmed Majdalani, Birzeit University, 15 May 2004.
[5] Interview, 19 July 2004.

What we are trying to achieve is basically two things. To keep alive some sort of dialogue, a variation of exchanges ... Israeli–Palestinian civil society ... people-to-people ... And secondly, what we are trying to achieve is a peace camp in Israel which supports a non-military solution ... So we support the groups which are the NGOs ... we are talking about centre and left ... even though there are some religious groups and some that we support, basically, most of the NGOs are situated on the centre left.[6]

This financial or organisational support of peace-oriented non-governmental organisations on both sides, which has become known by critics as the 'peace industry' – perhaps the most flourishing and growing industry in the region – is largely financed by European and EU-related institutions (although there is also significant American support for many of these initiatives through governmental and non-governmental funding agencies). In addition to promoting grass-roots activities, the support of Israeli and Palestinian NGOs, Track II dialogue-networks and joint Israeli–Palestinian research (particularly in the area of health) has helped create an important network of contacts and backdoor negotiations, which take on added importance in periods when Track I negotiations (direct contacts between senior government officials) are not taking place, such as during the second *Intifada*. Many of these networks continued to operate in this period, thus providing one of the last anchors of regular and cooperative contact between both conflict parties.

Yet, some Israeli critics of the EU have argued that EU money has been used to promote 'offensive' political pamphlets that reflect an extremist 'post-Zionist agenda', an expression which is used in a derogatory sense to describe any pro-peace groups of the left as well as 'radical NGOs in the Israeli–Arab sector, which disseminate false allegations of discrimination and Israeli human rights abuses' (Steinberg 2004: 8–9). The fact that the EU sponsors these pro-peace initiatives, be they located on the grass-roots level such as the people-to-people programmes, or the Partnership for Peace Programme, is seen by some representatives in both the Israeli government and the media as an expression of European pro-Palestinian sentiment. A former EU Representative in East Jerusalem has rejected these arguments:

I would accept this critique if we were financing NGOs in Israel who are fighting against the government. We are supporting NGOs that are trying to find a solution for peace. That's it. These NGOs should be free to develop some ideas. I don't see anything bad in it ... It is not a political tool; it is intended mainly to support associations which are trying to cope with problems on the

---

[6] Interview with former EU Ambassador Chevallard, 24 April 2004.

ground. I don't think it's bad for the government in Israel to have some people who are supporting peace.[7]

For different reasons, EU funding for joint Palestinian–Israeli projects on the civil society level also has its critics among those organisations that directly benefit from such funding. They point to the unclear agenda of the EU, which brings to the fore manifold implementation problems that hamper the effectiveness of these policies:

> From my contact with the EU I can say that 90 per cent is a passive financial resource – they did not have a specific coherent agenda that reflects their interests ... We maintain technical contact with them and they do not even use our reports.[8]

The EU Partnership for Peace Programme was set up in 2004 as a replacement for the people-to-people programmes, which had been in operation in the previous decade. Despite its name, the Partnership for Peace Programme did not demand that funded projects have both an Israeli and Palestinian partner, not least because the limited number of Palestinian partners – in comparison to a larger number of Israelis – had suffered an immense overload of work during the previous years and had therefore not always been able to deliver the final product. It was also felt that some projects – those aimed at promoting peace-related activities and understanding of the other – needed to take place within specific communities and that the meeting at grass-roots level in each community, if not adequately prepared in advance, could bring about tensions and animosity instead of the desired spirit of reconciliation and cooperation.

One such project concerns the Ben Gurion University project, which is operated through its Centre for the Study of European Politics and Society. It aims to create a training programme for teachers in the religious school system – a school system which has generally adopted right-wing hardline political attitudes towards the conflict in general and the Palestinians in particular – in order to develop a greater understanding of the Muslim and Palestinian 'other' and, at a second stage, to impart these understandings to the pupils and students at their educational institutes. Because of the sensitivities involved among the respective Jewish and Muslim religious populations, such a project needs to be undertaken within the separate communities, rather than as a joint Jewish–Muslim project, where the initial chances of success would be even more limited.

To sum up, in this section we have shown that the EU is the central contributor to the support for peace-oriented NGOs in the

---

[7] Interview with former EU Representative in East Jerusalem, 28 April 2004.
[8] Interview with Dr Jeff Halper, Director of ICAHD, 4 March 2004.

Israeli–Palestinian conflict. However, this path of intervention created tension mainly in Israel, where it provoked anti-European sentiments which limited the possibility to enhance the societal reach of alternative agendas to the predominance of the securitisation discourse in the Israeli–Palestinian conflict. It is also important to point out that the sum total of people affected by the connective network is relatively small when compared to the total number of people affected by the conflict. However, even with these caveats it must be emphasised that EU programmes have brought together thousands of Israelis and Palestinians, most of them linked to academic, diplomatic or political elites. This connective network, supported by the EU, has no overall power to end the conflict but it provides a stable context for those advocating greater Israeli–Palestinian cooperation and must therefore be seen as an element in conflict containment.

However, the vast majority of Israelis and Palestinians have never had any meaningful contact with the 'other side', beyond the role of the other as a soldier looking through the barrel of his gun/tank, or the role of the other as a worker subject to the constraints of the separation barrier and limited freedom of movement. Most of the NGO-related activities do not touch upon the daily lives of the millions of Israelis and Palestinians who continue to fear each other and who prefer the construction of walls and borders as barriers, rather than the creation of bridges and spaces of interaction.

Constructive

To what extent is the constructive pathway, which is the most indirect but – if successful – also the most persuasive mode of transformation, relevant to the Israeli–Palestinian conflict? In other words, does the EU and the association of Israel and Palestine with the EU provide a context for a gradual transformation of identities in Israel and Palestine that would be conducive to conflict resolution? In our perspective, due to the limited reach of association, this pathway – namely the attempt to trigger a recon-struction of identities on both sides that is conducive to peace – encounters many limitations.

This is because of two reasons. The first is the fact that this pathway depends on a long-term process that requires at least some economic and political stability, which is lacking in the Israeli–Palestinian conflict due to the consistently high levels of violence since both countries became associated with the EU. The second reason has to do with the sensitive notion of identity on both sides, which is so central to the escalation of the conflict. Attempts by the EU to change the underlying identity-scripts in

Israel and Palestine have been limited despite the stated objective to do so. Thus, as Breteche, a former EU Representative in East Jerusalem stated:

It's very clear. You have a policy, which may be simplistic, but it is very clear for us. We consider that what we want in this region, or what we would like to see in this region, which is neighbouring Europe, is peace. Not only between Israel and Palestine, but also with Lebanon and Syria, and it is done more or less with Jordan, Egypt . . . Without this state of Palestine, side by side with Israel, without that peace couldn't be achieved. So if we want to do that . . . we need a state. So if we need a state, we need a strong, transparent, well-managed, peaceful state.[9]

Notwithstanding this objective, the overall constructive impact of the EU on the Israeli–Palestinian conflict is restricted mainly because of the weak form of integration of both parties with the EU. In addition, as we have outlined above, the constructive impact of the EU is hampered by the specific way in which the EU addresses Israeli and Palestinian identities in the conflict. Thus, while the establishment and expansion of the EU is a peace project that focuses on the removal of ethnic and national barriers as part of a transformation to a wider, diluted, regional pan-European identity, the EU's approach to the Israeli–Palestinian conflict rests on a different logic. Thus, the resolution of the Israeli–Palestinian conflict is, by contrast, constructed in a way in which ethnic and national identities are afforded their ultimate expression through the establishment (not dissolution) of borders through territorial separation and exclusivity. What happens in the aftermath of successful conflict resolution is another matter. In the perspective of the EU, it is at this later stage where borders may be removed and where notions of integration and cooperation may become relevant to Israelis and Palestinians. There is thus a basic dissonance between the European project and the main developments in the Israeli–Palestinian conflict with regard to core issues such as national identity, sovereignty and self-determination. This dissonance has from the outset negatively affected the power of the constructive pathway in the Israeli–Palestinian conflict.

Comparing pathways and conditions of EU impact

As we have argued in the previous section, the compulsory impact has been of little relevance in the Israeli–Palestinian conflict given the lack of 'carrots and sticks' which the EU can effectively apply to both conflict parties, in particular Israel. This weakness of the compulsory impact

---

[9] Interview with Jean Breteche, former EU Representative in East Jerusalem, 28 April 2004.

results primarily from the absence of a membership perspective for Israel and Palestine in the near future, but also reflects the limited potential of the association setting for effective conflict transformation. As we have pointed out, the effects of the enabling impact on the Palestinian side have been greater. However, the effect of the EU assistance programmes in Palestine on the overall conflict remain limited, not least because reference to the EU is used in both Israel and Palestine to mark difference (and thus antagonism) rather than cooperation. The connective pathway has also had an impact. Through the support of peace-oriented NGOs and grass-roots community development, it appears that the connective level is the only sphere in which dialogue between both parties is actually taking place. However, the number of people directly affected is limited and these projects focus almost exclusively on small groups within an elite sector of society. Finally, we have shown that the constructive impact, which depends on a high degree of integration and internalisation of European norms of conflict resolution on a wider societal level, has been almost absent in the case of the Israeli–Palestinian conflict, which continues to be characterised by ethnocentric and exclusive notions of national identity and affiliations.

The effects of the different pathways are also conditioned by the groups at which they are targeted. Both the compulsory and the enabling pathways are aimed at governments and administrations, which tend to view EU involvement, through the prism of conflict, as an external intervention. Thus, notwithstanding the lukewarm approach by the EU to establish a shared sense of belonging in the framework of the EMP, the EU is perceived in both Israel and Palestine as a third party that meets with suspicion, in particular in Israel. Thus, the EU is judged – and used – by both parties on the basis of whether it is 'biased towards me' or 'against me'. In the case of the connective impact, the targeted activities are aimed at groups which, by definition, promote conflict resolution and dialogue, and, as such, the chances of bringing people together are far greater than on the wider societal level. As far as the constructive pathway is concerned, this relates more to a post-conflict scenario, a situation that has not been reached in the Israeli–Palestinian context (Table 6.1).

According to Jeff Halper, director of a left-wing NGO that receives EU funding, it would be preferable if the EU was to ask the different organisations funded by it 'to have a better dialogue between Israelis and Palestinians'. Moreover, EU funding should reach beyond the specific Israeli–Palestinian context and more seriously address regional cooperation in the entire Middle East. Halper further argues that in EU funding a sharper definition of objectives is required:

Table 6.1: *Overview of EU influence on Israel–Palestine*

Pathway	Main EU institution	Main addressee	Nature of influence	Conditions
Compulsory	European Parliament; elected and appointed officials	Governments, particularly Israel political leadership	Economic pressure (EMP)	Conflict antagonism
Enabling	Aid agencies; European Commission	Governments; particular Palestine officials; local authorities	Political culture; democratisation	Conflict; fiscal dependency
Connective	European Commission	NGOs; grass-roots	Local communities; grass-roots/civil society	Conflict resolution; peace industry; social and economic elites
Constructive	All	Political leadership and conflict societies	Identity-scripts	Post-conflict; peace/ cooperation; integration

I would propose the following: to focus on human rights and to use language which is 'neutral'. To strengthen the civil society on both sides as well as in the Middle East. To use the tools they have and not to try and intervene directly in peace issues.[10]

In a similar vein, Adar Primor, the foreign policy editor of *Haaretz* newspaper, sees the connective dimension as the most relevant dimension where the EU can impact on the conflict. He argues that a massive investment in civil society and the organisation of conferences 'is important despite its minor channel for change ... [but] at the end of the day it will have an effect'. Furthermore he suggests that 'on the Palestinian side it is more significant than here [in Israel], and it can play a central role to help in establishing a Palestinian state'.[11] Interestingly enough, a similar position is put forward by Mahdi Abdel Hadi, the head of Passia, a Palestinian NGO. Abdel Hadi criticises the results of EU funding and argues that

---

[10] Interview with Jeff Halper, Director of ICAHD, 4 March 2004.
[11] Interview with Adar Primor, 9 March 2004.

there have been trials of the implementation of people-to-people projects between Palestinians and Israelis which ended disastrously! They [the EU] tried to make links between the two people on different levels but, after the project finished, or most times ended incomplete, nobody would know anybody.[12]

The effectiveness of the four pathways is, most importantly, contingent upon the attitudes of the two conflict parties to Europe, in general, and the EU, in particular. Despite the differences between Israel and Palestine, they both have critical opinions on the role of the EU in the conflict, although direct political criticism is far greater in Israel than in Palestine. As far as Palestinians are concerned, criticism mainly relates to the perspective that the EU should take tougher action against Israel, and not fall into what many Palestinians perceive as the pro-Israel bias of the USA.

While the PA welcomes direct EU intervention as a means of balancing the allegedly pro-Israeli bias of the USA, Israel has developed an ambivalent relationship towards the EU and, in recent years, has become quite antagonistic towards Europe. The perception of the EU as a pro-Palestinian and anti-Israeli entity has been the main condition that limited the impact of the EU in the Israeli–Palestinian conflict. The ambivalence of this relationship is reflected by the fact that, on the one hand, 80 per cent of Israelis support in some way or another an Israeli membership in the EU – with more than 10 per cent of Israelis holding an EU passport[13] – while at the same time the EU, as a political body, encounters huge scepticism and distrust in Israel. This suspicion in Israel is reflected in anti-European statements from political leaders and opinion-makers in the media. Leading the way has been an English-language right-wing newspaper, the *Jerusalem Post*. Its editorial and opinion columns demonstrate a consistently strong anti-European bias (Stephens 2004).

The major issue to arouse the feelings of anti-Europeanism in Israel has been the accusation that some of the EU assistance to the PA was used for the purchase of arms, which were then used in terrorist attacks against Israeli citizens. The EU denied this, although it did admit that not all the funds were used in the way intended and that there had not been an adequate system of control or management of the way in which these funds were used.

The matter could have been resolved had the EU Commission agreed to set up a Committee to examine the accusations but this was initially

---

[12] Interview, 17 August 2004, Jerusalem.
[13] The poll, which included common core questions, was taken in February and December 2003 by Dr Mina Zemach of the Dahaf Polling Institute for the Delegation of the EU Commission in Israel.

turned down by the then EU Commissioner for External Affairs, Chris Patten. It took a formal request on the part of a large group of members of the European Parliament for this Committee to be eventually set up. Patten himself did not succeed in endearing himself to the Israeli public because of his continuous refusal to visit Israel, despite invitations on the part of the Foreign Ministry and a number of Israeli universities which would have provided him with a stage for delivering a statement on EU–Israel relations and ironing out some of the tensions in EU–Israeli relations which have developed over the past few years. The fact that many Israelis viewed Patten as the most anti-Israel EU Commissioner contributed to the poor relations between the two (Pardo 2004).

Thus it has been the intense funding by the EU for the benefit of the PA, while to some extent effective on the enabling level, which has brought about increased antagonism on the part of many Israelis, thus reflecting the way in which the Israeli–Palestinian conflict and EU policies on this conflict have become intermingled. This attitude in Israel, namely that aid and assistance by the international community to the PA reflects a pro-Palestinian bias, was highlighted again following the G8 decision of July 2005 to allocate $3 billion for Palestinian reconstruction. Given the fact that this decision was taken only one day after the London terrorist bombings, and given the fact that this attack was regarded almost automatically by most Israelis as being comparable to Palestinian terrorism, many Israelis perceived this as constituting a 'reward for terrorists', promoted primarily by the European members of the G8.

In this context Steinberg (2004: 1) argues that EU policies towards Israel have produced few, if any, successes. Thus, 'the evidence demonstrates that Europe's approaches and initiatives have been highly unrealistic, and relations with Israel are marked by sharp confrontation, including politically and ideologically motivated boycotts'. While the 'evidence' for such a pronounced statement is debatable, this quote is highly intriguing since it brings to the fore the deep alienation that exists between parts of Israeli society and the EU. This sharpened tension between both sides has also been referred to by Rosemary Hollis who argues that relations between Israel and Europe have been deteriorating due to these identity issues. Thus, the perception of a rising anti-Semitism in Europe as well as a European desire to achieve conflict resolution while focusing almost exclusively on the need of Israel to change its policy have increased the psychological gap between the sides. 'Little thought has been devoted on how to reframe Israeli thinking by inducements rather than pressure, and certainly not as an incentive to detach from the region' (Hollis 2004: 192).

The negative Israeli attitude towards the EU and the more positive approach towards the USA become, however, surprising when we consider that EU policies on conflict resolution often do not differ greatly from those of the USA (Freedman 2002; Clawson 2003). Thus, both the EU and the USA have stated categorically their demand for a two-state solution, a complete freeze on all settlement activity, the cessation of violence and terror, and the cessation of the construction of the Separation Fence/Wall, as well as the need for internal economic and democratic reforms of the PA. The EU and the USA are equal partners in the Quartet, which drew up the Road Map. While the Bush Administration partially stepped back from the Road Map during 2004–5, the EU has reinstated this as the main policy option, to be resumed immediately following the implementation of the Gaza Disengagement Plan, which is endorsed by both the USA and the EU.

Oded Eran, Israeli Ambassador to the EU, points out the differences in the assessment of the USA and the EU in Israel:

What happened to Europe's image in Israel is amazing. If we compare the positions of the EU and the USA in the central three issues of the conflict: territories, refugees, Jerusalem – their positions are almost similar ... However, we refer to the USA as a friend and to Europe as an enemy, or at least a dormant enemy. (*Maariv* newspaper, 17 July 2003)

Realising that the government had taken its anti-European sentiments too far, Israeli Foreign Minister Silvan Shalom stated, in his first public statement on assuming office in February 2003, that he would make an effort to improve relations between Israel and the EU. Israeli Prime Minister Ariel Sharon made a number of pro-European remarks, for example on his visit to the British Prime Minister Tony Blair in July 2003, although at the same time castigating European leaders for continuing to make official visits to the Palestinian President Yasser Arafat thus undermining the position of then Prime Minister Mahmud Abbas (Abu Mazen). Sharon warned the European leaders that by continuing to visit Arafat they were undermining the status of Abu Mazen and, by association, the continuation of the peace process.

However, the death of Arafat in November 2004 and the orderly transfer of power to a new President meant that Israel has become unable to use the 'no partner' justification for the implementation of unilateral policies. The invitation of Abu Mazen to both the White House and Downing Street within the first few weeks of his election as Palestinian President means that it has become more difficult for Israel to play out the USA against the EU in this respect.

Conclusions

As noted in the introduction of this book and in some case studies, both academic analyses as well as the public discourse see integration as a crucial element in maintaining peace. However, in the Israeli–Palestinian context, which lacks such an integration perspective, the dynamics of pathways have only unfolded in an insufficient manner.

Because of its historical involvement in the region, as well as its geographical proximity, the EU will, however, continue in its attempt to be a major political player in the Israeli–Palestinian conflict. This attitude is reflected in huge aid and assistance packages on the one hand, and attempts to influence politics in Israel and Palestine, on the other. For its part, Israel readily accepts the vast amounts of assistance that it receives – especially from the USA – but is adamant in its determination that its foreign and defence policies must be independently decided and implemented without any external pressure or influence. Israel also views third-party active intervention in the conflict with great suspicion, arguing that it must determine its own policies and that it cannot rely on third-party presence. And, as noted above, Israel rejects European active intervention, perceiving the EU as 'non-honest' brokers – much in the same way that the Palestinians perceive the USA.

A public opinion survey carried out by the Steinmetz Centre for Peace Research analysed Israeli attitudes towards the role of third-party intervention in the conflict. Surprisingly, over 30 per cent of the Israeli Jewish population (the Arab-Palestinian citizens of the country, who make up 20 per cent of the population, have always favoured greater international intervention) expressed some support for third-party intervention. This ranged from direct peacekeeping activities, aimed at keeping Israelis and Palestinians apart from each other, preventing acts of violence and terrorism, and acting as a physical buffer between the two sides, to a more active monitoring role which would oversee the implementation of a peace process and ensure that each side is fulfilling its signed commitments (Hermann and Yuchtman-Yaar 2002). When, as part of the same survey, the respondents were asked who they would like to see as active peace-keepers, the USA ranked first, followed by Britain – but a long way behind. France was positioned at the bottom of the list of countries.

Opinions are divided in Israel as to whether and how the EU should change its approach if it is to attract more sympathy for its attempts to be actively involved in, and accepted as part of, the political process. Dominique Moïsi argues that the primary responsibility of the international community and, in particular, the Europeans is to re-establish trust between Europe, Israel and Palestine (*The Financial Times*, 2 July 2001). More specifically, Moïsi details what must be demanded from both sides. On the Palestinian side, he proposes, beyond the calculated manipulation of violence, that what is unacceptable is the absence of the rule of law, the corruption, if not stopped, and the continuing use of educational texts filled with hatred. As for the Israeli side, he stresses that 'continued building of settlements on disputed land is unacceptable and should lead to trade sanctions, implemented by the EU'.

However, for the time being, it appears that the main third-party role is reserved for the USA, a US-led group of international monitors/peace-keepers or representatives from third-party countries which are not perceived by either Israel or the Palestinians as being biased one way or another. At the most, from an Israeli perspective the EU role in a third-party set-up would be more limited, focusing on the development of governmental, military and civil society institutions as part of the new Palestinian State, as an advisory body or even as a transition administration filling the vacuum between Israeli withdrawal and full Palestinian statehood (Newman and Peters 2002; Indyk 2003). Given the fact that the EU would most likely be the main donor to a new Palestinian state, this would also be more acceptable to the Palestinians, particularly given the criticism on the part of some EU leaders concerning the way in which past assistance has been used. Thus, the USA is perceived more in the role of a peacekeeper and implementer, while the EU is seen more in the role of an institution and government builder in the new State of Palestine. This would follow well the active participation of EU-funded projects during the past decade in which the EU has focused on Track II negotiations, people-to-people activities, and the funding of bilateral and trilateral research projects between Israelis, Palestinians and Europeans aimed at creating new models of cooperation and other peace-related activities that blur the boundary between classical third-party intervention and a deeper association of Israel and Palestine with the EU.

7   The EU as a 'force for good' in border conflict cases?

Michelle Pace

Introduction

This chapter takes a look at how EU actors conceptualise their role and that of the EU in border conflict transformation.[1] It does this as a mirror image of the five case studies presented in this volume so as to add a more critical and reflective account of the formulation and impetus of EU policy. The chapter's core argument is that what drives EU actors is *their* self-representation of the EU as a 'force for good' and that they see themselves as 'forces for good' in the transformation of border conflicts. It cautions that these representations of the EU as a 'force for good' very effectively mask the power inherent in EU involvement in conflicts. The pathways of EU involvement developed by Albert, Diez and Stetter (this volume) are taken as the essential ways in which this EU power operates. In developing my argument about the construction of the EU as a 'force for good' I take as my empirical basis the self-positioning of EU policy-makers – interviewed in two rounds of interviews carried out in Brussels in January 2004 and February 2005 – vis-à-vis the five conflict cases covered in this edited collection, as well as a thorough analysis of EU documentation regarding the five border conflicts. I argue that EU actors are part of and their practices replicate an epistemic community. Policy-makers working in Brussels accept an optimistic version of the narrative of the EU as a 'force for good', which they continuously validate, produce and reproduce. This understanding of the EU is in line with what Michel Foucault (1970) referred more elaborately to as a *mathesis* – a rigorous episteme suitable for enabling cohesion of a discourse and thus uniting a community of its followers. I refer to this process of forming a self-maintaining EU epistemic community (based on the narrative of the EU as a 'force for good') as an EU mindset. This chapter thus highlights a

[1] Special thanks go to all project partners and to my interviewees in Brussels for their time and frankness. I would like to dedicate this chapter in memory of Alessandro Missir di Lusignano, for his enthusiasm and great thirst for knowledge.

203

triple *problematique* with this mindset. Firstly, the fact that EU actors see themselves as 'forces for good'; secondly, they represent the EU as a 'force for good'; and thirdly, academic constructions of the EU's 'normative or transformative power' as necessarily a 'good' thing (Duchêne 1973; Nicolaïdis and Howse 2002; Smith 2005; Grabbe 2006; Manners 2006) are in the main problematic, as they are part rather than a critical analysis of the epistemic community. I therefore argue that as analysts we need to distance ourselves from the very subjects of our investigations, their self-descriptions and the discursive practices they hold of the EU's role.

Having said this, however, in seeking explanations of why EU actors act the way they do in cases of border conflict transformations through integration and association, I maintain that the self-description of EU actors as 'forces for good' offers a perspective which helps us as analysts understand why for instance Commissioners relate more to the 'connecting impact' of the EU in border conflicts (see below) or why Council officials are more likely to try to apply pressure to achieve dialogue (compulsory impact) between conflict parties in their rhetoric. This perspective may also help us examine further why Commissioners are much more into the discourse of the EU as a 'force for good' and why their stance, to slightly overstate the point, regularly portrays the EU as the 'best thing' that ever happened for peace in the world. I also maintain that the construction of the EU as a 'force for good', to the extent that it is shared by conflict parties, is in itself a conflict resolution device. The pathways of EU impact thus rely on the continuous production and reproduction by EU actors of the EU as a 'force for good' without any questioning of such constructions.

The first section outlines the conditions that facilitate constructions of the EU as a 'force for good'. The second elaborates on how EU actors' self-representation of the EU as a 'force for good' relates to the four pathways introduced in chapter 1 of this volume. The third section briefly highlights some of the limitations of narratives of the EU as a 'force for good'. The chapter concludes by suggesting that the 'force for good' discourse captures the workings of this narrative, which in turn sets the conditions for and connections between different forms of EU impact through integration or association on border conflict transformation. The examples used in this chapter inevitably overlap with some of those in preceding chapters; however, these can only add emphasis to the points raised in this as well as the rest of the chapters in this volume.

Conditions

This section will explore the conditions that enable EU actors to project an image of the EU as a facilitator in the transformation of border conflicts through projections of its 'force for good' and will serve as a good backdrop for the ensuing section.

The representation and continuous reproduction of the EU – by EU actors – as a 'force for good' creates a sense of a self-fulfilling prophecy. This has been the case in the opening of negotiations with Turkey (and some of the Balkan states), as one member of the European Parliament emphasised:

The Netherlands, one of Turkey's traditional allies within Europe, has played a key role in European debates on Turkish EU accession. It was under a Dutch Presidency in December 2004 that the EU agreed to open accession talks with Turkey. You have to remember that the Dutch debate on Turkish accession has been taking place against a difficult background. The country's economic growth ground to a virtual halt in 2002. Recent years have brought rising unemployment and painful cuts in public spending. As the self-confidence of the 1990s gave way to uncertainty, there have been heated debates on immigration and the preservation of cultural values. The populist politician Pim Fortuyn rose to rapid prominence on an anti-immigration and anti-Islam platform, shattering many taboos before being assassinated in 2002. In November 2004, Dutch film-maker Theo van Gogh was murdered in the streets of Amsterdam by an Islamist militant. In June 2005, the Dutch public rejected the proposed European Constitution by a large margin, despite the support of the country's political elite. However, despite the political turmoil and the rise of anti-immigration sentiment, a political consensus in favour of Turkish membership has been developed and maintained. Across the political spectrum, politicians went to considerable lengths to inform themselves about the changes underway in Turkey and to make a serious assessment of the costs and benefits of accession. In anticipation of the EU's decision to open negotiations in December 2004, a series of studies were undertaken by Dutch institutes to examine different facets of the issue. These studies led to a debate that was remarkably well informed. According to Eurobarometer polls, a majority of the Dutch population is opposed to Turkish accession. *Yet despite the polls, Dutch politicians in both government and opposition have endorsed a 'strict but fair' approach, actively making a case to the electorate in favour of Turkish accession once the country meets all European criteria.* They have by and large rejected arguments based on religious or cultural identity, while stressing the importance of fair dealings and the positive signal which Turkish accession would send to the Islamic world.[2]

In these cases, the EU had to open negotiation talks as otherwise it would have undermined the very *raison d'être* on which it stands – what it is bound with – which in turn empowers the Other to make claims on what they have been promised (Diez 2005). The framing of the EU as a 'force for good' makes it very difficult for EU member states to reject enlargement to include Turkey on legitimate grounds. Although Turkey's

---

[2] Interview, European Parliament (Brussels, 22 February 2005); emphasis added.

reward of membership at the end of its reform process is much less certain than for other candidates (especially after the EU's partial freezing of negotiations with Ankara announced in December 2006), it has the possibility to turn to rhetorical action (Schimmelfennig 2001). Basing its claims on the collective identity and constitutive liberal values and norms of the EU, it could shame reticent EU member states into complying with community rules and honouring past commitments.[3] EU member states are aware that Turkey will add greater economic weight and geographical reach to an enlarged EU and thus the EU can gain greater geopolitical clout on the international stage with Turkey's accession. Thus, through Turkey's supporters within EU organisations (UK, Greece and the European Commission, among others), Turkey was able to commit EU institutions to granting the opening of membership talks to successfully democratise Turkey (Turkish discourses echoing EU discourses). The imposition of EU norms on conflict parties through integration and association also conditions the power of projections of the EU as a 'force for good'. In turn the projection of the EU as a 'force for good' in this case enabled a transformation in Greek–Turkish relations (Rumelili, this volume, chapter 4).

In the case of Northern Ireland, member states consented to EU involvement in the conflict: Britain and Ireland in a way agreed to the conditions under which constructions of the EU as a 'force for good' work. As Fernando Criado-Alonso stated:

> The EU sought to internationalise the Northern Ireland issue building on the fact that both governments decided to work together: no other two EU member states ever agreed to use the EU to solve their conflict – this did not happen in the case of the Basque issue, for example.[4]

The discourse of peaceful resolution through the EU context (through the construction of the EU as a 'force for good') translated itself into a framework of structural funds which shields many organisations in the conflict from politicisation, and a PEACE programme aimed at reconciliation between the two conflict parties. The PEACE programme in particular created the impetus and encouraged people in the conflict areas to start thinking of their identity in ways other than their nationality. Their attention was instead diverted to project work with communities that they previously would not have dreamt of working with.[5]

---

[3] In fact, in mid-February 2007, ties between the EU and Turkey appear to be 'cooling', with Turkish Foreign Minister Abdullah Gul cancelling a key meeting in Brussels, in what analysts consider as a political move by the Turkish authorities (Beunderman 2007).

[4] Intervention at the EUBorderConf final project conference. Brussels (November 2005).

[5] Interview, European Commission, DG Regional Policy (Brussels, 22 January 2004).

Thus, the power of EU actors' self-description of the EU as a 'force for good' is based on an assumption that through international socialisation – a process driven by the logics of appropriateness and arguing – conflict parties can be induced to accept the internalisation of international norms. In this way, conflict parties are led to adopt the constitutive rules of the EU. The cases of Cyprus and Israel/Palestine defy such narratives (Demetriou, Yacobi and Newman, this volume, chapters 3 and 6). The following section will elaborate on the points raised here by looking at how the discourse of the EU as a 'force for good' relates to the four pathways of EU impact.

The discourse of the EU as a 'force for good' and the four pathways of EU impact

Having reviewed the circumstances that enable constructions of the EU as a 'force for good' in this section, I outline how EU actors' self-representation relates to the four pathways introduced in chapter 1 of this volume.

Compulsory pathway

Before elaborating on the actors involved in the projection of the EU as a 'force for good' in border conflicts, it is important to recall the distinction between internal and external conflicts, conflicts at the EU's borders and mixed/internal conflicts, as the type of conflict has consequences for which actor can be involved. As outlined in the Introduction to this volume, our cases can be found on the 'inside' of the EU (Northern Ireland), 'outside' the EU (Israel/Palestine) or at the EU's borders, where we have the case of Europe's North, Cyprus and the Greek/Turkish case as examples of mixed/internal conflicts. When conflicts are internal or mixed/internal, decisions taken under the Common Foreign and Security Policy (CFSP) pillar influence EU actors' involvement in these disputes. For external conflicts, the EU's foreign policy is the main policy area that affects EU actors in border disputes.

The EU has progressively tightened its instruments for foreign policy in this regard. Once a consensus is built in the Council, it is channelled into action through a specific actor: the Special Representative (SR). The role of the SR is, on the one hand, one of a facilitator and a consensus builder and, on the other hand, of a focal point and the EU's interface with the parties in conflict through almost permanent presence on the ground (or what can be termed 'interaction density' for the amelioration of identification/identity processes on all sides of a conflict). In the case of a subordination conflict (the Israeli–Palestinian example in this volume), the EUSR's mandate is to provide active support to actions and initiatives leading to a final settlement of the conflict; to contribute to the implementation of international agreements reached between the parties and engage with them in the event of non-compliance with these agreements; and to report on possibilities for EU engagement and on the best way of pursuing EU initiatives and ongoing Middle East Peace Process (MEPP)-related EU efforts. In this case, the Council of the European Union, General Secretariat division, has a Policy Unit, with a task force on the Middle East.[6] According to one of his close aides, efforts by Marc Otte, the EU Special Representative for the MEPP, have been aimed at precisely trying to persuade both parties to the conflict to change the ways in which they perceive the other (that is, to lead to a change of identity-scripts).[7] His indirect, informal discussions with representatives from both the Israeli and the Palestinian sides serve as the basis for effectively carrying out his responsibilities and role on behalf of the EU as a 'force for good'. The SR is an example of a specific EU actor working to reproduce what the EU stands for in its role as an external actor in border conflict situations.

Moreover, in terms of EU actors involved in the reiteration of the EU's narrative as a 'force for good', when Finland joined the EU, Finland's eastern border became the only land border between the EU and the Russian Federation. Thus Finland has been quite vocal vis-à-vis EU relations with Russia in the case of Europe's North. Due to historical reasons, Germany is regularly engaged in the Israeli–Palestinian conflict.

Each EU member state also has the opportunity to leave its own imprint on EU policy towards border conflicts when it holds the Presidency. The way border conflict issues are dealt with in the EU depends on the particular member state Presidency's priorities – which may in turn shift (albeit slightly) the priorities of the Council for those six months.[8] The active role of the Finnish Presidency in the second half of 2006 in issues involving Russia is a case in point.

The Common Strategy on the Mediterranean *acquis* places the Council and the High Representative for Common Foreign and Security Policy in the position of a strategic player in constructing the EU's role as a 'force for good' in conflict situations in the Mediterranean region (Attiná 2001: 282). This contrasts with the institutional structure designed in Barcelona in November 1995 (when the Euro-Mediterranean Partnership or EMP was launched) and other official documents of the EMP through which

---

[6] Interview, Council of the European Union (Brussels, 24 January 2004).
[7] Interview, Council of the European Union (Brussels, 21 February 2005).
[8] Interview, Council of the European Union (Brussels, 24 February 2005).

the Commission was given a stronger strategic role in producing and reproducing the narrative of the EU as a 'force for good'. As the guardian of the integration and association processes, the Commission emerges as endorsing the discourse of the EU as a 'force for good' more forcefully than perhaps any other EU actor in the context of border conflicts.

Within the Commission, the role of the Euro-Mediterranean Committee for the Barcelona Process is a central forum for providing the impetus, monitoring and follow-up, and evaluation of actions and initiatives in the Barcelona Process as a whole (European Commission 1999).

Other important mechanisms for the Commission's weight in representations of the EU as a 'force for good' in the context of the compulsory pathway include regular reports on candidate states' progress towards accession. This is evident in the case of the Greek/Turkish dispute. The concerns raised by the Commission in its 2003 regular report on Turkey's progress towards accession, pertaining to international law issues (see below on the substance of 'force for good' discourse), echoed the Greek position which leads us to the conclusion that there is substantial input from one conflict party in this case in the EU's actors' thinking and policy-making process (European Commission 2003b).[9] This is an example of how the craftsmanship of a particular individual member state adopts the Commission's discourse of the EU as a 'force for good' to gain domestic political benefit. There are also cases to the contrary, for example with the Commission's first recommendation on Cyprus (see Demetriou in this volume, chapter 3).

The Commission's endorsement of the discourse about the EU as a 'force for good' may further be understood through the presence of over 120 of its delegations and offices around the world which act:

not only as the eyes and ears of the Commission in their host countries but also as its mouthpiece vis-à-vis the authorities and the general population. This is particularly important in cases of conflict on the ground. There is a huge potential for the future EU delegations to represent EU external policy in bilateral relations with third countries. This depends on the signature of the new Constitutional Treaty.[10]

For instance the Commission Delegation in Russia offers EU actors possibilities for the projection of the EU as a 'force for good' in the case of Europe's North. The question of how far these delegations and their representatives are effective in constructing the EU's image as a 'force for

[9] See especially part B.3 of this report: *Ability to Assume the Obligations of Membership* and part D: *Accession Partnership: Global Assessment* pp. 57–127 and 138–41 respectively. This influence is even stronger in the Council.
[10] Interview, European Commission, DG External Relations (Brussels, 23 January 2004).

good' is dealt with in the case study chapters of this volume where the Commission's authority in the reproduction of this discourse depends on how it is received by the conflict parties.

From an analysis of the parliamentary debates dealing with the regions covered in this volume, it emerges that the members of the European Parliament (MEPs) do not easily buy into the discourse of the EU as a 'force for good'. For instance, in a report on the European Neighbourhood Policy, MEPs emphasise that this policy – which is aimed at avoiding the emergence of new, dividing borders after the EU's enlargement of May 2004 – should not be an instrument of 'settling for the status quo but of committing the European Union to support the aspirations of the peoples of our neighbouring countries to full political freedom, with democracy and justice' including the stricter use of political conditionality (European Parliament 2005). This does not mean that MEPs do not play a role in producing a self-understanding of the EU as a 'force for good' – witness the reference to political freedom etc. in the preceding quotation. A thorough analysis of parliamentary debates reveals the positive role MEPs played in the Northern Ireland case and shows that they pushed for change.[11] Finnish MEPs also reproduce the construction of the EU as a 'force for good' in Europe's North case.

The EU has come to symbolise prosperity, security, ideals of tolerance and freedom and thereby attracts peoples and politicians all over the East and South who want to associate with these ideals and therefore want to become part of the EU. We have witnessed this very recently in the case of Ukraine. For many people, the EU represents a special area of human hope, the originator of the idea of human rights. The EU's belief system is embedded in Enlightenment values stressing the possibility of the growth of democracy and of liberal societies.[12]

In the case of association, EU actors resort to emphasising to conflict parties the importance of implementing association and cooperation agreements signed by the conflict parties with the EU, as these processes bring conflict parties closer to the EU's image as a 'force for good'. As Demetriou and Rumelili highlight in their chapters above, relations with Cyprus before it joined the EU on 1 May 2004 and with Turkey include navigating conflict parties through association and cooperation agreements in order to direct them closer to the EU's model of cooperation. These relations are also managed by the Enlargement DG and are based on first-generation association agreements.

[11] For the Northern Ireland case, European Parliament debates were analysed from 1973 to date.
[12] Interview, European Parliament (Brussels, 22 February 2005).

Enabling pathway

As mentioned in the previous section, part of the description of the EU's active role in the transformation of border conflicts is constructed through providing carrots for integration or association as ways forward for conflict parties to emulate. Integration means eventual membership, but through association EU actors endeavour to create a discursive framework that generates similar dynamics to integration, yet falls short of sharing the EU institutions and involvement in decision-making. Creating a discursive framework that brings about change in conflict transformation ultimately operates through the enabling as well as the constructive pathways. This discursive framework turns the projection of the EU as a 'force for good' into a self-fulfilling prophecy (as mentioned in the previous section), allowing conflict parties to claim what they have been promised as carrots (in cases of EU membership) or to take the opportunities offered through association to negotiate better terms for their relation with the EU. Through the *acquis communautaire* (membership), as well as the *acquis* of association (through the Barcelona Process or Euro-Mediterranean Partnership for Mediterranean partners and Partnership and Cooperation Agreements in the case of Europe's North), conflict parties are encouraged to either join the 'club' or participate as close outsiders through association. These mechanisms enable EU actors to further their ideals of the EU as a 'force for good'. This they can do either through collective action or through the engagement of individual member states with conflict parties.

Thus, the 'force for good' discursive framework offers political leaders opportunities to legitimise domestic policies aimed at diminishing conflicts, from which the constructive impact of redefining political identities may follow. Moreover, EU actors' self-description of the EU as a 'force for good' produces a platform for activists, civil society organisations and NGOs to use rhetorical and symbolic tools, including shaming tactics, to get their political leaders to comply with the values, norms and ideals that EU actors advance (Demetriou, this volume, chapter 3). The European Coal and Steel Community (ECSC) and thereafter the European Community (EC) and the EU explicitly refer to the constitutive norms of the Western community in their basic treaties and define the promotion and protection of liberal democracy, democratic peace and multilateralist collaboration as their basic purpose (Schimmelfennig *et al.* 2006). Representations of the United States for instance, as a military minded, unilateralist, external actor in border conflict cases, are asserted in Brussels through rhetorical moves as an Other against which the EU's mindset is set (see also Diez 2005). Such

'Mars vs Venus' representations (Kagan 2003) by EU actors of the USA in turn allow conflict parties to refer to the EU's epistemic community to validate domestic moves.

The pillars or substance/s of the narrative of the EU as a 'force for good' are based on the ideals of liberal democracy, multilateral collaboration, cooperation, interaction, international law, peace, human rights, social and economic development, etc. – a discourse that unites EU actors as a community of its followers and which is to be emulated by conflict parties. The potential for the sharing of these ideals through their adoption by conflict parties is manifested in the case study chapters of this volume and does not require further elaboration here. However, the study of political discourses in the volume's case studies has also brought to light the possibilities of *negative* effects in domestic contexts when conflict parties abuse references to the EU's mindset.

Connective pathway

The construction of the EU as a 'force for good' is also made possible through the creation of specific programmes aimed at reiterating a positive image of the EU. Coercive measures are unlikely options for EU actors, as they do not tally with the narrative of the EU as a 'force for good'. Thus, in the Israeli–Palestinian case EU actors adopt the EU's connective impact through establishing contact between conflict parties; working towards mutual understanding from each party to the conflict about the Other's grievances; and analysing, together with conflict parties, the reasons for the eruption of violence.

Standard practices of the production and reproduction of the EU as a 'force for good' include soft diplomatic efforts such as dialogue which reiterate the EU *not* as an actor that reverts to coercion in cases of conflict within or at its borders but as one that believes in normative measures. For example, while within track-one diplomatic efforts EU actors often have to work around the constraints of *realpolitik*, in the domain of track-two diplomacy, non-official dialogue initiatives are placed centre-stage where communication, negotiation, mutual understanding and direct encounters are the main instruments at hand for forging a positive role for the EU in border conflict cases such as the Israeli–Palestinian case.[13] Within this

---

[13] Track-one diplomatic activities include informal consultations, 'good offices', special envoys, mediation, negotiations, international condemnations, fact-finding missions, diplomatic and economic sanctions (Nan 2003). Joseph Montville, who coined the term 'track two' in 1982, defined track-two diplomacy as: 'an unofficial, informal interaction between members of adversary groups or nations that aims to develop

thinking, dialogue between EU actors (especially Council Representatives using association mechanisms) and conflict parties plays an important role in allowing EU actors the opportunity to learn more about the conflict, the concerns and needs of conflict parties while at the same time building a valuable bridge between conflict parties themselves. These possibilities offer the direct application of EU actors' self-understanding of the EU's role in conflict cases.

What makes the Commission's discourse of the EU as a 'force for good' particularly relevant is the Commission's responsibility for the EU budget's second biggest external relations programme, the Mediterranean Development Assistance (MEDA), and other regional budget lines which go towards the EU's role in forging people-to-people linkages. On their part, the Council – together with the EP – comprises the budgetary authority, and decides the annual EU budget allocation for MEDA and other regional budget lines for the Mediterranean and the Middle East. DG Relex (External Relations) represents the EU in, and manages EU financial support of, the MEPP, in particular through assistance to the Palestinian Authority. This DG is also responsible for preparing Commission contributions to key foreign policy activities relating to countries of the region as well as to the MEPP.

EU actors have sought to influence the MEPP by constructing the EU as a positive force and as a result the EU was, up until January 2006, by far the largest donor of aid to the Palestinian Authority.[14] Roy Ginsberg (2001) rates this impact as significant because, without it, the Palestinian economy would have collapsed and the Authority would not have been able to finance even the basic functions of governance. The conflict might have escalated further had the EU not supported the PA financially. Aid to refugees from conflict zones as in the Gaza Strip is also

strategies, influence public opinion, and organize human and material resources in ways that might help to resolve their conflict … [It] is a process designed to assist official leaders to resolve or, in the first instance, to manage conflicts by exploring possible solutions out of public view and without the requirements to formally negotiate or bargain for advantage' (quoted in Hottinger 2005: 13). Track-two activities involve dialogue with and training of influential elites, advocacy, empowerment, development and social and economic activities (Hottinger 2005). Put simply, track-one activities involve official government-to-government diplomatic interaction; track-two activities engage conflict resolution professionals, that is, unofficial, non-governmental, analytical, policy-orientated, problem-solving efforts by skilled, educated, experienced and informed private citizens interacting with other private citizens.

[14] According to a senior official in the Hamas government, Iran has, as at January 2007, outweighed the EU in this respect, becoming the single biggest donor to the Palestinian Authority. Analysts argue that the international boycott of the Hamas-led authority imposed in 2006 (see main text for more on this) has given Iran an opportunity to increase its influence in the Middle East (Urquhart and MacAskill 2007: 15).

characteristic of EU foreign assistance programmes that reiterate and reproduce EU actors' self-description (see Nabulsi 2006). However, this self-understanding of the EU as a 'force for good' has faced some serious challenges since the Hamas victory in the Palestinian vote of 25 January 2006 when Hamas won 74 out of the 132 seats in the Palestinian Legislative Council or PLC, the Palestinian Authority's Parliament (International Crisis Group 2006; Malki 2006; Shikaki 2006). Although the EU sent its own mission to observe the elections – which were declared as fair, free and transparent – it reacted by freezing direct aid to the PA, thus ignoring the democratic expression of the Palestinian people (even though it had made democracy one of the conditions for its help) and depriving many Palestinians of their live-lihood. In Palestine, and in the wider Arab world, this was interpreted as an imposition of a severe and inhumane regime of sanctions by the EU against Palestinians under occupation. In the words of the UN Special Rapporteur, Professor John Dugard, sanctions were imposed on the occupied rather than the occupier: the first time an occupied people has been so treated (Plate-forme Euromed 2007).

Therefore, although Palestinians appeared to take their first steps towards a process of democratisation, the EU's reactions to the electoral win by Hamas stand in stark contrast to EU discursive practices regarding the importance of fair, free and transparent elections as crucial dimensions of the much needed 'democratisation' momentum on the Palestinian side for a possible resolution to the Israeli–Palestinian conflict. So, while full democratisation requires both competitiveness and inclusion, in line with projections of what the EU stands for, the success of Islamist parties does not seem to feature on the EU's 'force for good' radar.

On a more positive note, in the case of Europe's North, as Joenniemi points out in this volume (chapter 5), the Euregio Karelia exemplifies constructions of the EU as a 'force for good' logic through a trans-boundary regional integration programme that sidelines the issue of territorial restitution. This echoes the ethos of collaboration and cooper-ation embedded in the substance of the EU as a 'force for good' narrative. In a similar vein, the EU's contribution to the International Fund for Ireland and the PEACE I and PEACE II programmes have been highly supported by MEPs who in this case help reproduce the narrative of the EU as a 'force for good' (Hayward and Wiener in this volume, chapter 2). DG Regional Policy has also been highly involved in Northern Ireland through, for example, the Interreg programmes and in the case of Europe's North through the PHARE programmes.

In the case of Russia, the DG Relex and DG Justice and Home Affairs (migration policy/people crossing borders, financial support for border crossings) are also involved in the self-perpetuation of the EU as a 'force for good' discourse[15] as the Commission plays a leading role in implementing the Action Plan of the Northern Dimension. It is responsible for programming projects and presenting appropriate follow-up proposals. These projects are aimed at reiterating the positive impact of the EU in that they bring people together to collaborate on a mutually beneficial theme. EU actors emphasise that these collaborations in turn bring about peaceful coexistence between neighbours.

Constructive pathway

Constructions of the EU as a 'force for good' highlight how EU discursive practices contingently produce and reproduce particular kinds of EU actors. In turn, through their own self-understandings, EU actors hope to change the identity-scripts of conflict parties. The EMP, a process-oriented EU instrument, aims at improving communication, interaction and relations between Mediterranean partner countries, including conflict parties (Israel, Palestine, Syria, Lebanon, Jordan and Egypt; and between Mediterranean partners and EU actors), with the objective of creating an appreciation of each other's identities. The overall aim of the Barcelona Process is thus to build a Euro-Mediterranean regional identity where all partners experience respect for different collective identities.

In the case of the Middle East conflict, by projecting the EU as a 'force for good', EU actors seek to set the ground for pre-negotiations and to leave parties to the conflict to establish the actual negotiation terms.[16] As one EU official who works on the Middle East put it:

We know that one of the issues in the MEPP is identity-related and therefore a very sensitive point ... for the Jewish majority to dissociate their sense of identity from the unitary Jewish state, they need to connect more to the European sense of

---

[15] In 'The Hague Programme', the new Justice and Home Affairs multi-annual programme adopted in November 2004, the European Council considered the development of a coherent external dimension of the Union's policy of freedom, security and justice as a 'growing priority'. The Justice and Home Affairs unit of external relations covers a broad range of themes including border management and a broad geographical area including Russia, candidate countries, the Caucasus and Central Asia (European Council 2004).

[16] These stages of resolution are adapted from a model conceptualising progress from a series of dialogue events originally developed by McCartney (1986). The author focuses especially on the relationship between the conflict parties and the success of joint efforts through contact and confidence building, empathy for the other side, joint analysis of conflict issues, explorative problem solving and joint activities with the possibility that the dialogue might feed into official negotiations or pre-negotiations.

identification ... which in turn makes Palestinian independence a less threat-ening prospect.[17]

Thus, through a double move, the EU brings conflict parties together (connective pathway) in a context which allows them to dissociate them-selves from particular identities – in this case that of a unified Jewish state (constructive pathway).

As can be concluded from the section above, the workings, productions and reproductions of the EU as a 'force for good' narrative are more apparent in the compulsory and connective (direct) pathways than in the enabling and constructive (indirect) pathways. This observation leads us to the limits of this discourse as developed in the next section.

Limits of EU actors' narratives

As the conflict case chapters of this volume highlight, and in line with chapter 1, the model of EU perturbation includes possibilities where the EU's impact can lead to the *intensification* of existing conflicts or to the creation of new ones especially at the EU's own external borders. This observation links to the limits of EU actors' self-description of the EU as a 'force for good', which will be the main focus of this section.

During episodes of violence (subordination conflicts) as in the Israeli–Palestinian case, given EU actors' self-understanding as forces for good,

the EU often opts to do nothing, staying in the shadow and leaving the USA to act ... Because of the lack of power parity, the stronger party (Israel) often influences the EU's involvement for its own benefit, leaving the fundamental issues unaddressed.[18]

Thus the projection of the EU as a 'force for good' is open to abuse by conflict parties, as is well documented in the preceding chapters of this volume, which in turn sets limits to the effects of such projections. There is also a further danger that the pathways of EU involvement in border conflict transformation lead to the EU becoming part of the problem, rather than part of the solution, as in the case of Europe's North (Joenniemi, this volume, chapter 5) and the Middle East (Plate-forme Euromed 2007).

Thus, through an EU pathway of influence, asymmetries between conflict parties are widened rather than narrowed. In a similar vein, the EMP has not yet had any visible indirect effect on the major unresolved

[17] Interview, European Commission, DG External Relations (Brussels, 23 February 2005).
[18] Interview, European Commission, DG External Relations (Brussels, 22 January 2004).

conflicts in the Mediterranean area – Israel–Palestine and Cyprus, to mention just a few (Pace 2006); on the contrary, the persistence of these conflicts has had a negative effect on the Barcelona Process (European Commission 2005: 19) which in turn weakens the narrative of the EU as a 'force for good'.

Moreover, continual EU actors' oscillations between normative and strategic priorities further limit projections of this discourse (Lavenex and Schimmelfennig 2006). For example, an arms-exporting EU member state may keep silent on a conflict case that involves a key importer of its arms. Business (in particular where energy security is concerned) usually dominates the EU's approach to Russia rather than human rights norms embedded in constructions of the EU as a 'force for good' (MacAskill 2006).

Debates about the EU's military capabilities (especially following the Hizbollah–Israeli war of summer 2006) for peacekeeping severely challenge EU actors' self-understanding of the EU as a moral force based on principles, norms and values but not coercion or any form of military might.

As one interviewee put it:

In the Foreign Affairs Committee we are unable to exercise leadership because we do not have armies, therefore we have no prestige … Europe has set itself the objective of creating a rapid reaction force – a force of 60,000 men that can be put in place within sixty days' notice. You ask yourself why can't Europe do this already, seeing that it's got about one and a half million troops. The answer is it simply can't and it's going to require a serious effort to change this situation. The rapid reaction force, I hope, is a beginning. I hope that we will go further. In any case, it will be a good thing if at the end of this process we have more flexible and more mobile forces.[19]

In a slightly converted interpretation of the narrative of the EU as a 'force for good', Robert Cooper argues that the EU as an enlightened 'post-modern' entity should intervene militarily and take a pre-emptive approach when necessary to contain threats and '*defend the world*' (own emphasis) – thus still masking the EU's role in normative terminology. Cooper further urges EU members to increase their military capability to better measure up to the status and power of the American military forces, thus calling for a more aggressive diplomatic strategy (Cooper 2004) – which moves the discourse of the EU as a 'force for good' on to new grounds.

In a way one can argue that narratives of the EU as a 'force for good' get caught up in their own trap:

Sadly, there is a deterioration of the quality of life for Palestinians and also for Israelis. People's day-to-day occupation is immoral. Freedom for Israelis from

---

[19] Interview, Council of the European Union (Brussels, 23 January 2004).

fear and for Palestinians from occupation is urgently needed. They feel this every day. On the one hand, terrorists use their instruments because they know they are effective. On the other hand, Israel knows they cannot occupy the Territories for ever: in this sense we support the occupation clause under the Geneva Convention. Israel as an occupier has responsibilities which, following the second *Intifada*, it cannot afford to maintain, so we fill that gap.[20]

In the case of Europe's North, the high status offered to Russia through regular EU–Russia summits is surely difficult to justify in light of the 'force for good' discursive practice, given Russia's deficient democratic and/or human rights performance (Makarychev 2005b). Because of Russia's strategic importance, the EU puts aside its projection as a 'good' power and adopts an inconsistent strategy towards its neighbour to the north. As Timothy Garton Ash argues:

So long as we remain dependent on their energy and raw-material supplies, our political leverage over such states will be limited. Russia is a major worry, especially for us in Europe, and we need a more coordinated EU policy towards our Eurasian neighbour ... but we also need to keep articulating our own values, not parroting theirs. (Garton Ash 2006: 27)

Thus, in practice, EU–Russian relations challenge EU actors' constructions of the EU's episteme: EU policy towards Russia is still framed within a normative power discourse wherein, through their rhetoric, EU actors argue that they do take into account human rights (to defend why they do business with Russia). This they continue to annunciate, despite recent research which highlights Russian peoples' concerns about the state of democracy and human rights in their societies (EU-Russia Centre 2007):

At the same time, those in power elsewhere in Europe continue to communicate with their Russian counterparts, continue to consume information from official Russian sources and media, continue to observe alarming Russia-related events – and continue trying to understand why Russians do not defend their democratic freedoms. Europe assumes that Russian beliefs, ambitions, preferences and values are the same as in the rest of Europe, and finds it difficult to understand the underlying reasons for such passive political behaviour by a majority of Russians, running alongside unsurpassed popularity of the ruling regime.

The limits of EU actors' self-description of the EU were further tested in this case. The importance of minority rights was underscored by the 'Pact on Stability in Europe' launched in May 1994 at the initiative of the French Prime Minister Edouard Balladur (Schimmelfennig *et al.* 2006). This pact called upon all EU membership candidates to settle their border and minority conflicts and provide for minority protection in a series of

---

[20] Interview, Council of the European Union (Brussels, 20 January 2004).

bilateral negotiations and treaties. As Joenniemi clearly highlights in his contribution to this volume, 'the lack of a border treaty did not stand out as an obstacle to prevent Estonia from joining the EU ... although [the EU has] a policy which stipulates that countries joining should be devoid of open border disputes with their neighbours' (p. 141).

Conclusion

This chapter has argued that self-representations of the EU as a 'force for good' by EU actors restrain conflict parties through normative influences including the normative authority of EU institutions, the legitimacy (and domestic resonance) of EU norms and identification of conflict parties with the EU. In the context of this volume, the EU's constructed 'goodness' as a signifier with institutionalised content has been powerful in *some* of the cases of border conflict through *some* pathways as analysed here but not in others. Thus, we can speak of the power of the construction of EU 'goodness' as a matter of degree. Some individual elites and civil society representatives from conflict areas buy into the representation of the EU as a 'force for good' and in turn influence others in their conflict area. Successful constructions of the EU as a positive force in conflict cases (through their transformation) would secure a role for the EU globally (however masked) and deliver ensuing gains in legitimacy for its continuously reiterated liberal values and norms through the integration or association equals peace argument (Schimmelfennig *et al.* 2006). While successful constructions of such EU narratives enable EU actors to *facilitate* border conflict transformation, it is important to bear in mind that the EU's role and power in border conflict transformation rely on the continuous discursive production and reproduction of itself by EU actors as a 'force for good'.

In mapping out *how* the EU is constructed as a 'force for good' in the transformation of border conflicts through the self-description of EU actors, this chapter has shed light on how EU actors do not merely reproduce a positive image of the EU episteme: this epistemic community works these discourses out, or animates them, using narrative technique and historical and exploratory attitudes (Said 1993). Through this thorough picture of the EU's role in border conflict transformation by means of integration and association, this chapter has highlighted EU actors' perceptions of their role while the five conflict case chapters have examined the perception of conflict parties of the EU and of how it plays its role. It is the contention of this chapter that the two sides of this coin point to the need for further theorisation, building on the contribution of this present volume, on the power of the discourse of the EU as a 'force for good' as projected by EU actors.

Conclusion

Stephan Stetter, Mathias Albert and Thomas Diez

Recalibrating the integration–peace nexus

This book began by referring to the impact of European integration on the Franco-German border conflict. This example was the historical nucleus from which the belief in the major 'post-World War II promise', namely that European integration has the power to substantially transform borders from lines of conflict into lines of cooperation, originally departs (Miard-Delacroix and Hudemann 2005). This assumption does indeed often nurture the belief system(s) of EU decision-makers and the image of the EU in conflict societies, as the previous chapters, and in particular chapter 7, have shown. We have not argued in this book that the assumption of such a nexus between integration and peace is entirely misguided (Tavares 2004). Indeed, there are plenty of examples that show integration has had a positive effect on border conflicts in Europe. What we have, however, attempted to show from both a theoretical and an empirical perspective is that any linear and one-dimensional conceptualisation of a catalytic function of integration and association on border conflicts does not stand the test of rigorous empirical research. Thus, the case studies in this book on border conflicts in Northern Ireland, Greece and Turkey, Cyprus, Russia and Europe's North as well as Israel and Palestine have shown that alongside the manifold instances of catalytic effects of integration (and to a lesser extent association) on border conflicts, there always looms the potential of integration and association leading to an intensification of border conflict dynamics.

Such an ambivalent impact of integration and association on border conflicts has been evident in all of our five case studies. Thus, while in Northern Ireland the funding of peace-related cross-community activities significantly contributed to a desecuritisation of cross-border relations, the study of political discourses in Northern Ireland shows that reference to the EU often is a rather divisive factor in domestic politics, with Republicans broadly supporting European integration, which they regard as a way to bypass British sovereignty in Northern Ireland, and unionists – to different degrees – being anxious that European integration might have precisely this effect. In a similar way, the manifold conflicts between Greece and Turkey have for a long time intensified *despite* increasing institutional ties of both countries with the EC/EU. In many ways, EC/EU membership of Greece has thereby contributed to the securitisation of Greek–Turkish relations. However, developments in the Aegean region since 1999 also point to the conflict-diminishing effects of integration on Greek–Turkish relations.

This effect of integration also operated in Cyprus, where the years prior to the accession of the Republic of Cyprus to the EU were characterised by an almost mystical belief in the power of integration to overcome the conflict on the island, with the opening of the Green Line being the most visible result of such a desecuritisation. However, the failed referendum on the Annan Plan in southern Cyprus in May 2004 made clear that such a link between integration and peace is far from automatic. Rather, it has affected the Turkish-Cypriots more than their Greek-Cypriot neighbours, who have used the integration framework instead more to enhance their own position in the conflict.

The situation in Europe's North, where the EU member states of Estonia, Finland, Latvia, Lithuania and Poland have a common border with Russia, brings to the fore a similarly complex picture regarding the impact of integration on (old and new) border conflicts in this region. Thus, dynamics of increased cross-border cooperation, which are directly related to European integration, go hand in hand with many examples in which the integration of north-eastern European states into the EU has led to an intensification of conflicts with Russia.

Our case study on the Israeli–Palestinian conflict has, finally, shown that it is not only integration but, to a lesser degree, association that can impact on border conflicts. Thus, there are some noteworthy examples of how the association of both Israel and Palestine with the EU in the context of the Euro-Mediterranean Partnership (EMP) has helped to establish or at least to sustain cooperation between both sides. However, negative perceptions of the EU in Israel have at the same time hampered this (already limited) effect of association on the overall transformation of the Israeli–Palestinian conflict.

Already such an episodic glance at what is in fact a rather mixed balance-sheet of how integration and association impact on border conflicts elucidates that a recalibration of the linear integration–peace nexus is required if we want to specify the potential *and* obstacles of border conflict transformation in Europe and Europe's periphery induced by the EU. In order to outline the contours of how such a recalibration of the integration–peace nexus could look, we will provide in this conclusion a systematic and comparative analysis of the main conceptual insights of the various theoretical and empirical chapters of this book.

We will proceed in three steps. Firstly, we will briefly outline how the conflict model, which was set out in chapter 1, contributes to the comparative analysis of border conflicts. Our main argument here is that this framework provides a methodological tool that helps us to avoid treating every individual border conflict as a conflict *sui generis*. Moreover, our emphasis on the discursive processes through which conflictive identities become constructed in the first place links our theoretical framework with the literature on securitisation processes, thereby specifying the way in which securitisation relates to broader conflict dynamics (Buzan *et al.* 1998; Wæver 2003). Secondly, we will systematically assess the way in which the four pathways of EU involvement, which were also outlined in chapter 1, affect border conflicts. Here we argue that in the long run the impact of the EU on border conflict transformation is most significant with regard to the indirect pathways of EU involvement, i.e. the enabling and, if successful, the constructive impact, although the compulsory impact can produce significant effects in the short term, in particular when coupled with a clear membership perspective. This does not mean that direct forms of EU involvement are negligible, but rather directs attention to our key argument that the impact of the EU on border conflicts is higher the more there is an interplay between different pathways. However, the ultimate success (or failure) of integration and association in border conflict transformation depends on conditions that are not all within the EU's control. Thus, the third section will specify the precise conditions of positive (i.e. conflict-diminishing) and negative (i.e. conflict-enhancing) forms of EU impact. In a nutshell, we argue here that these conditions of EU impact depend on a complex interplay between conditions on the domestic and the EU levels. While the EU certainly can try to set the structural conditions for border conflict transformation, the actual use made of the 'promise' of integration and association ultimately depends on how the domestic actors interpret this perturbation of the conflict by the EU.

Border conflicts and the identity dimension

As we have argued in chapter 1, any analysis of the role of the EU in border conflicts should start from a general theory of social conflict and only then address the specific ways through which the EU seeks to impact on such conflicts. Otherwise, such analyses would not only risk ignoring the structural features of all types of social conflicts, but would also fail to develop a theoretically compelling approach that allows the study of border conflicts from a comparative perspective (see Dahrendorf 1957; Coser 1964). In this conclusion we do not aim to specify in a comprehensive fashion how the five different case studies in this book have contributed to the fine-tuning of the conflict theoretical model set out in chapter 1. What we do, however, aim for is to highlight those conflict theoretical insights that are of direct relevance to the study of the role of the EU in concrete border conflicts. Thus, a recurring feature of all five case studies is that border conflicts are first and foremost characterised by a type of conflict communication that has become locked in at the stage of an identity or subordination conflict. In other words, the conflict nurtures and sustains the construction of two opposing identities on the basis of which territorial claims become mutually exclusive. The more these adversary identity constructions permeate into wider political and societal practice, the more they also form the basis for the justification of (physical) separation between the two communities – and ultimately also serve as a justification for recourse to violence. In such conflicts, in which the identities of the conflict parties become the core of conflict communication, responsibility for the conflict is usually attributed to the other side, while one's own policies are justified as a mere reaction. It is this communicative device which ultimately problematises and securitises the (physical and social) borders that separate two conflict parties.

It is precisely such a lock-in effect of conflict communication at the identity level, which has been, from a comparative perspective, the key shared feature of the five border conflicts studied in this book. As opposed to identity and subordination conflicts, conflict episodes and issue conflicts hardly give rise to sharp binary distinctions between two social communities; the social border between both sides is not topical in conflict discourse. In contrast, to varying degrees and with changes over time, all the five conflicts studied in this book are characterised by societal discourses that construct a sharp border between the two main conflict parties on many levels of political and wider societal discourse. Such adversary (and mutually exclusive) identity constructions between 'Unionist' and 'Republicans', 'Greeks' and 'Turks', 'Israelis' and 'Palestinians' or 'Jews' and 'Arabs', 'Europeans' and 'Russians' as well as 'Greek-Cypriots' and 'Turkish-Cypriots' then evolve into social artefacts that turn into almost indisputable control points in political and wider societal discourses within – but also beyond – conflict societies.

These adversary identity constructions are then the prime communicative mechanisms for conflict narratives, not only at the political level but also in many academic analyses of these conflicts. In other words, the conflict becomes mapped on to social borders – and these borders then allow a distinction between two oppositional communities, thereby allowing the conflict to make sense. This is where our model encounters the so-called Copenhagen School of Security Studies, which has focused on securitisation dynamics in political discourses (Wæver 1998b). Seen from that perspective, the securitisation of the individual identity of each social group then problematises the border which separates this community from the other to such an extent that wide parts of political and wider societal relations between both sides become almost automatically framed in conflictive terms. In the border conflicts studied here, such discursive practices have two main effects. Firstly, they legitimise and render rational various degrees of physical segregation between both sides, which either clearly delineate both communities (green lines, state boundaries, EU external borders) or lead to more complex territorial fractures within shared urban and regional spaces (checkpoints, fences, 'invisible' borders within neighbourhoods). Yet, these more complex territorial fractures are also characterised by the typical features of identity and subordination conflicts, including physical segregation between two communities. The intensity of these conflicts might often not be immediately apparent to an uninformed outside observer but nevertheless strongly informs political and wider societal practices in such 'shared conflict spaces', e.g. in Belfast and Jerusalem or in ethnolinguistic relations between 'minority' and 'majority' communities in Karelia, Estonia or in western Thrace.

Secondly, and of direct relevance to the role of the EU in border conflicts, these discursive mechanisms of identity conflicts also shape the way in which outsiders observe the conflict. As far as the EU is concerned, our case studies have on several occasions shown that the EU often tends to adopt and take for granted the identity delineations that emerge as a result of the conflict. Thus, even in those instances in which the EU acts as a catalyst, it often reinforces and stabilises at the same time the binary distinctions between conflict parties, as is, for example, the case in Northern Ireland. This does not, of course, mean that the EU would be unable to contribute to a desecuritisation of identity relations. What it does, however, point to is the observation that the general dynamics of (border) conflicts do not only affect the reading of the conflict by the parties immediately involved, but that third parties such as the EU are also – almost necessarily – drawn into the discursive environment created by the conflict. In more theoretical terms, the EU is perturbated by the conflict before it might (or might not) perturbate the conflict itself.

Assessing the interplay between the four pathways of EU impact

The empirical analysis of our five case studies has confirmed our initial assumption that there are indeed several pathways through which the EU can have an impact on border conflicts. Yet, none of these pathways is as such sufficient to turn conflict into cooperation and we have found that a mix of pathways usually is the most effective way for significant EU impact. Having said that, we have also found that pathways of EU involvement can have a negative impact, which is why we have argued above that the integration–peace nexus does require certain recalibrations. Thus, while it is true that the EU often has a positive impact on border conflicts, this is not always the case and, therefore, the question whether pathways operate in a positive or negative manner cannot be settled from a theoretical perspective but depends on conditions that will be discussed further below.

As far as the compulsory impact (pathway 1) is concerned, the comparative analysis of our different case studies shows that this pathway operates most effectively in those cases in which carrots and sticks by the EU are coupled with accession negotiations with at least one conflict party. It is the combined result of these two factors, rather than the compulsory impact of the EU *per se*, that can force policy-makers to restrain themselves from conflict-enhancing moves. As Bahar Rumelili has argued, such a dynamic has, for example, operated in Greece during the 1970s, when the Karamanlis government softened its stance vis-à-vis Turkey in order not to endanger the accession negotiations of Greece with the EC. A similar development occurred on both sides of the Cypriot border during the accession negotiations of the Republic of Cyprus with the EU in the years 2000 to 2004. The compulsory impact of the EU in Northern Ireland has, according to Katy Hayward and Antje Wiener, always been rather marginal, the prime reason being that when the Republic of Ireland and the United Kingdom sought EC membership in the late 1960s and early 1970s, the EC had not yet developed the institutional and structural capacities to demand from accession countries (one of them also being a permanent member of the United Nations Security Council) that they settle a conflict prior to EC entry. What has been said above about developments in Greece and Cyprus points to other limitations of the compulsory impact, namely that policy-makers in conflict societies might decide to make only instrumental and tactical concessions in the course of accession negotiations. Since such policies do not alter the adversary identity constructions and the securitisation of the border between both conflict parties, the overall impact of the compulsory impact on border conflicts is often only short-term.

In the long run, the EU's compulsory impact might then even have a negative effect on border conflicts since – after accession has been attained – policy-makers might again pursue conflict-enhancing policies in order to silence domestic criticism of them having previously bowed to European pressure. Such a course of events has been observed in Greece during the 1980s and most of the 1990s, as well as in Cyprus after 1 May 2004. Moreover, it has – to a lesser extent – also affected developments in Estonia and Latvia, which have become more assertive towards Russia after both countries entered the EU in 2004 – while the compulsory impact of the EU operated quite well in Europe's North during the accession period, in which the legal status of the Russian-speaking minorities in both countries had been significantly improved as a result of the EU's compulsory impact. In a similar way, the example of Turkey shows that the EU has, following the 1999 Helsinki Summit, been quite successful in the promotion of domestic changes. As Bahar Rumelili has argued in her chapter, the compulsory impact of the EU *in conjunction with* a credible membership perspective has put in motion a reshuffle of domestic political coalitions in Turkey, which then indirectly led to a desecuritisation of Greek–Turkish relations. However, whether these changes will have a long-term effect ultimately depends not only on the success of the accession negotiations with Turkey but, even more importantly, on the degree to which the desecuritisation of Greek–Turkish relations affects political and wider societal discourses in both countries.

In the absence of a credible membership perspective, the direct impact of the EU on border conflicts remains severely circumscribed. This holds true in two different settings. On the one hand, if both conflict parties are already part of the EU (as is, for example, the case in Northern Ireland), the EU – and more specifically the Council – has little direct leverage on the conflict. On the other hand, if both conflict parties are for the time being not considered eligible for membership (as, for example, in the case of Israel and Palestine), the intended compulsory impact of the EU on the governments of these countries can act as a boomerang. Thus, as occasional attempts by the EU to exert compulsory impact on Israel (rules of origin dispute, debates on economic sanctions) and Palestine (investigation on use of EU funds) show, this negative conditionality has not increased the leverage of the EU on the conflict but rather toughened the bilateral relations of the conflict parties with the EU, with the negative side-effect of depriving the EU of more indirect forms of involvement.

All this does, of course, not mean that the compulsory impact of the EU is meaningless. However, our case studies clearly show the limits of the compulsory impact in the absence of a membership perspective, and also after membership has been secured. As Olga Demetriou has argued in her chapter on Cyprus, the failed referendum on the Annan Plan in southern Cyprus clearly shows the limits of the compulsory impact if incentives (granting membership) and disincentives (withdrawing membership) are not at the EU's disposal at all stages of the conflict resolution process.

This also points to the limits of the compulsory impact if political decisions related to the conflict are limited to the governmental level and do
not impact on the wider political and societal discourses in conflict
societies. However, as David Newman and Haim Yacobi have reported
in their chapter on Israel–Palestine, the increasing relevance of the EU as
a foreign policy actor might gradually increase the compulsory impact on
outsiders in the absence of a membership perspective. Thus, a classified
report from the Israeli Foreign Ministry leaked to the press argued that
because of Israel's strong associational ties with the EU, a deterioration of
its relationship with the EU might be too costly for Israel. The report then
stated that Israel would be well advised to acknowledge the growing
political impact of the EU as a foreign policy actor, including the EU's
interest in a lasting settlement of the Israeli–Palestinian conflict. Of
course, strong associational ties are not a one-way street and provide
both sides with political leverage. The opportunities of being such a
'semi-insider' have not only operated in the case of Israel (or Turkey
prior to 1999). As Pertti Joenniemi has argued in his chapter, this position
as a 'semi-insider' has also helped Russia in its negotiations with the EU
on the transit issue between Kaliningrad and mainland Russia.

   While the compulsory impact is most effective during the usually rather
short period of accession negotiations, we have found that the enabling
impact (pathway 2) has a more long-term and often positive effect on
border conflict transformation. The way in which reference to the EU in
domestic political discourses has an impact on border conflicts can take
two main directions. On the one hand, policy-makers can legitimise
conflict-diminishing moves through reference to the EU, in particular
by referring to European integration as a win-win mechanism that also
overcomes hostility between long-time foes. On the other hand, however,
if the image of the EU in conflict societies is negative or ambiguous,
reference to the EU in political discourses has occasionally also been
used in order to justify a further securitisation of the conflict. Bahar
Rumelili has, for example, observed such a negative enabling impact in
her analysis of political debates in Greece prior to 1999. In this period, a
majority of Greek policy-makers regarded Greece's EU membership as a
negotiating leverage vis-à-vis Turkey. This negative effect of the enabling
impact on the ability of moderates in Greece (and Turkey) to legitimise a
desecuritisation of Greek–Turkish relations only changed with the
Helsinki Summit decision to grant candidacy status to Turkey. This
decision brought together a once unlikely coalition in Greece, with hardliners supporting Turkish membership since they believed that this would
increase the EU's (and Greece's) compulsory impact on Turkey, while
moderates could place their hopes on a gradual socialisation of Turkish

policy-makers into EU discourses. In a similar way, the Helsinki Summit decision changed the structure of domestic political coalitions in Turkey. Thus, prior to 1999 desecuritising moves in Greek–Turkish relations were only rarely legitimised by reference to the EU, since this would have almost automatically been framed within the Turkish political elite as an indirect concession to Greece. It was then the credible membership perspective of 1999 that rendered reference to the EU (and the expected gains of EU membership) a legitimising factor that forged a broad coalition of hardliners and moderates who both supported EU membership of Turkey and who, for different reasons, now had a shared interest in pursuing conflict-diminishing policies vis-à-vis Greece.

These developments in south-eastern Europe point to the more general way in which the EU becomes a legitimising model and symbolic inspiration in political discourses in conflict societies, thereby ultimately challenging the entrenched political structures that relate to the individual border conflicts. Such a process has been systematically outlined by Katy Hayward and Antje Wiener, who have referred to the various ways in which reference to the 'win-win model' of the EU has become a discursive frame through which a rather heterogeneous group of political parties in Northern Ireland has, following the Good Friday Agreement, legitimised increasing cross-border cooperation to their respective constituencies. The significance of the enabling impact stems then in particular from its ability to bridge previously adversary identity constructions on both sides, in particular with regard to hardliners and peace-sceptics. While in Northern Ireland political groups such as Sinn Féin and the UUP did not, from a general perspective, give up on their uncompromising political claims with regard to the conflict as such, reference to the EU allowed them nevertheless for the first time to support once-unacceptable cross-border cooperation. This step was justified by the argument that the new cooperation, based on the EU model, threatens nobody and (economically) benefits everybody. The case studies on Greece–Turkey and Northern Ireland thus show that the significance of the EU's enabling impact lies in its subtle power to transform the dynamics of political discourse in conflict societies if reference to the EU becomes a legitimising factor in the desecuritisation of cross-border relations.

If successful, the enabling impact of the EU can thus contribute to a deproblematisation of the border as well as a desecuritisation of the conflict at a much broader scale, as reported by Pertti Joenniemi in his study on cross-border cooperation in the Euregio Karelia. Joenniemi has also pointed to the long-term socialising effects of the enabling impact. Thus, reference to the EU model has been a justification for policies in Russia that contributed to a desecuritisation of cross-border relations, for example governmental reforms in the Russian Republic of Karelia that facilitated cross-border cooperation with Finland as well as efforts of the Kaliningrad Oblast to attain membership in three different Euroregions. These desecuritising dynamics of the EU's enabling impact also operated in northern Cyprus, where the massive peace demonstrations of 2003/4, which originated from non-governmental sectors, were from the outset symbolically linked to and legitimised by reference to the EU model. Yet, as we have argued above, reference to the EU can, under certain conditions, also be used to legitimise an increase in conflict intensity. Another negative enabling impact of the EU on border conflicts is evident in southern Cyprus, where reference by political leaders to EU norms such as the four freedoms and to a 'European solution' enabled a further securitisation of the conflict, while opponents of securitising policies were referred to as 'traitors' collaborating with the EU, now represented as a 'foreign power'.

As far as association with the EU is concerned, the impact of the EU's enabling power is generally more restricted. However, Haim Yacobi and David Newman have argued that reference to the EU model was nevertheless an important factor in Palestine in order to legitimise the governmental reform packages (strengthening the judiciary, creating the post of a prime minister, enacting a basic law) of the Palestinian Authority in the years 2002 and 2003. As Yacobi and Newman argue, through these policies the EU probably had a greater alleviating impact on the conflict than through all its direct interventions in this period.

The EU's connective impact (pathway 3) is also an important tool in the transformation of border conflicts. However, its effectiveness depends on further conditions, in particular a prior desecuritisation of cross-border relations on a wider societal scale. Thus, as long as conflicts remain at a high level of securitisation, the intensity of the conflict is a severe hindrance to the EU's connective impact, since it stands in the way of establishing cross-border cooperation that could potentially be supported by direct EU support measures. Bahar Rumelili has detected such a disconnecting effect in her study of cross-border cooperation between Greeks and Turks prior to 1999, and by Haim Yacobi and David Newman in their study of EU support for NGOs in Israel and Palestine since the outbreak of the second *Intifada* in September 2000. These examples point to a major weakness of the EU's connective impact, namely that this pathway is highly susceptible to more general developments of the conflict, which might disrupt or discourage current or future cross-border cooperation. A second hindrance to the effectiveness of the EU's connective impact on border conflicts then has to do with EU internal issues, namely slow and inefficient administrative procedures that hamper the power of this pathway. For example, Turkey only became eligible for funding of certain cross-border projects after it gained the status of a candidate country. In this and other case studies, such as Cyprus and Israel–Palestine, the complex and cumbersome funding procedures were another hindering factor that limited the overall effectiveness of the connective impact. Moreover, as Olga Demetriou has pointed out, the non-recognition of Turkish as an official language of the EU after the Republic of Cyprus joined the EU has a disconnective effect on possible cross-border cooperation that would be facilitated if funding proposals could be made in Greek and Turkish.

EU membership of both conflict parties is a factor that positively influences the EU's connective impact since it increases the range of cross-border projects that the EU, namely the European Commission, can support in border conflict areas. It is in this context that Katy Hayward and Antje Wiener have highlighted the way in which the PEACE funds administered by the Commission have become a central factor in desecuritising cross-border relations in Northern Ireland and the border region with the Republic of Ireland. In contrast, cross-border cooperation that overlaps with the EU's external borders often meets certain restrictions that prevent the EU from exerting its full connective impact. Thus, strict external border regimes and visa provisions limit the ability of participants in cross-border projects to regularly meet on both sides of the border, which has for example been the case with regard to Greek–Turkish cross-border projects. If new external EU borders are established, as has been the case in Europe's North in 1995 (Finland) and 2004 (Estonia, Latvia, Lithuania, Poland) with Russia, these new borders might even disconnect previous forms of cross-border cooperation. This effect is then only partially outweighed by the overall conflict-diminishing impact of new EU-funded cross-border projects, such as the Euregio Karelia across the Finnish–Russian border.

When looking at the interplay between different pathways, a paradoxical effect has been traced in several of our case studies. Thus, the EU often uses its connective impact to bypass hesitant governments in conflict areas. As was the case in Israel–Palestine and Cyprus, this might increase the EU's connective impact on NGOs committed to cross-border cooperation but might also encourage hardliners in these regions to delegitimise EU measures as an illegitimate interference of a 'foreign power'. This points to the problem that while EU funding might be considerable in terms of funds committed, the EU fails to have an impact on sceptics or hardliners. Thus, while in Northern Ireland the EU successfully convinced hardliners of the benefits associated with cross-border funding, developments in Israel and Palestine went in an opposite direction, with a small number of those already convinced being actually affected by and supportive of EU funding. This is not to dispute that even such a limited connective impact could have a stabilising function since it creates small islands of cooperation in conflict areas, as Haim Yacobi and David Newman have argued with a view to Israel–Palestine. However, it stands in stark contrast with other cross-border projects, such as the Euregio Karelia or the Northern Ireland PEACE funds. In these two projects, the EU was more successful in reaching out to a wider range of actors, thereby increasing its role in the desecuritisation of cross-border relations.

As we have argued in chapter 1, the constructive impact (pathway 4) of the EU is the most powerful but also the most demanding pathway, since it relates to a change of identity constructions in conflict societies, which is in itself already directly related to a change in conflict communication as such. As our case studies document, there are two main ways in which the constructive impact of the EU operates in border conflict areas. Firstly, in those conflicts in which cross-border relations are heavily securitised, the constructive impact of the EU often is a divisive factor, since both sides 'use' the EU in order to underpin the construction of adversary identity patterns rather than overcome these differences. Thus, as Bahar Rumelili has shown, Greece during the 1980s and 1990s referred to its 'European' identity in order to distance itself from an allegedly aggressive 'Asian' Turkish identity. What is interesting to note is that such discursive linkages between the identity dimension and reference to a European identity often go hand in hand with a rather ambivalent identity relationship of such countries with the EU itself. Thus, national identity constructions in both Greece and Turkey – but also in Cyprus and Israel – are ambivalent insofar as 'Europe' becomes at the same time both an aspiration (to be or to become 'European' or 'Western') and a threat (interference by 'Europe' in 'domestic' affairs, negative historical experience with European powers).

It is then a fruitful institutional relationship with the EU, which might over time facilitate its own identification with 'Europe', thereby paving the way for a reconstruction of the adversary identity constructions that underpin the respective conflict. Bahar Rumelili has highlighted such a structural impact of the constructive pathway in her study of domestic political discourses in Greece and Turkey, where the increasing integration of both countries (entry of Greece into the Eurozone, candidacy status of Turkey) relaxed the previous ambivalence of national identity constructions regarding 'Europe'. Olga Demetriou has referred to a similar effect of the constructive pathway, which has according to her study been a major factor that explains identity changes in northern Cyprus that resulted in the rewriting of history books of Turkish-Cypriot high schools in 2004.

Since this pathway relates to changes in conflict-related identity-scripts, the effects of the constructive pathway are usually the result of a long-term process. As our case studies have confirmed, such long-term effects of European integration might not do away with the conflict as such, but nevertheless shatter previously mutually exclusive identity constructions by providing a shared European reference point. As Katy Hayward and Antje Wiener have shown, such changes of identity constructions induced by European integration can, for example, be traced in political and wider societal discourses in Northern Ireland, where reference to a shared European identity dimension provides a bridge for at least parts of the Catholic and Protestant population. This is not to argue that the constructive pathway has triggered a wholesale reshuffling of identity constructions in Northern Ireland or Greece–Turkey away from conflict identities. Yet, in our case studies we have collected evidence that long-term effects stemming from European integration have the power to limit the societal reach of conflict communication by putting in place alternative reference points for (shared) identity constructions.

However, as long as the borders between the EU and one or two of the conflict parties are visibly upheld, the cooperative logic of the constructive impact can gain little ground in conflict societies. This is, firstly, the case in the context of association, where the power of the EU to affect domestic identity constructions is severely limited by the lack of linkages of associated countries with the EU. This is probably the deeper reason why attempts to project the 'European logic' to the Middle East have so far not proved successful in fundamentally transforming identity constructions in Israel and Palestine. Secondly, as the cases of Greece–Turkey prior to 1999 and Europe's North indicate, a strict EU external border regime tends to undermine the ability of the EU's constructive impact to transform identity-scripts in conflict areas. Building on this comparative reading of the EU's impact on the five border conflicts studied in this book and drawing from the substantive analysis in the various empirical chapters, Table 8.1 provides a systematic summary of the main dynamics which shape the way in which the four pathways operate.

Addressing the conditions of positive and negative EU impact

In the previous section we have already referred to the argument that whether pathways of EU impact operate in a positive or in a negative manner depends on certain conditions that require further specification. There is thus no linear positive impact of the EU on border conflicts, and the integration–peace nexus is far from automatic. As the various

Table 8.1: *Comparative overview of main EU influence on border conflicts*

Pathway	Impact	Main EU institution	Main addressee	Nature of impact	Facilitating conditions
Compulsory	Short term: Strongest when coupled with membership perspective; mixed results, often loses grip after membership has been attained	Council (Commission) (Parliament: voicing threats)	Governments; political leadership	Membership negotiations; economic dependence	Intense negotiation process; credibility of membership perspective; status as semi-insider with considerable gains
Enabling	Long term: Crucial for successful overall impact	Council (Commission) (Parliament)	Policy-makers at national and sub-national levels; governments	Forming of 'unlikely' coalitions; socialisation; legitimisation of practical (socio-economic) gains traded for concessions	Positive image of EU; political willingness; contours of European identity on both sides
Connective	Long term: Depends on continuous desecuritisation of border; often limited to areas within EU borders	Commission (Council)	Cross-border communities; local authorities; NGOs	Structural funding, programmes; often bypassing unwilling governments	Desecuritisation of border; effective procedures; reach to wide range of actors
Constructive	Long term: Most powerful and demanding pathway; change of identity-scripts	EU as 'idea', 'value'; Commission; Council; Parliament	Political elite and opinion-makers; policy-makers at all levels; NGOs; public opinion	Shared European identity as reference point; emergence / consolidation of multiple identities cross-cutting conflict borders	Shared reference to EU on both sides; firm institutional embedding into EU structures; devisibilisation of border

empirical chapters in this book have emphasised, the power to transform border conflicts depends on a complex interplay between EU-related and domestic conditions. Moreover, a significant change in border conflict patterns usually requires a mix of pathways, with the indirect pathways being in most cases more effective than the direct interventions by the EU. However, we do not wish to conceal that there is evidence that, through its increasing relevance as a foreign policy actor, the EU might in the future significantly increase its compulsory and connective power beyond its internal borders.

As far as the factors facilitating the impact of the EU on border conflicts are concerned, we have identified several positive conditions of EU impact, which can broadly be separated into EU-related and conflict society-related conditions. As far as the latter dimension is concerned, the effectiveness of pathways crucially depends on the existence of domestic constituencies that support cross-border cooperation. The willingness and ability of local actors to use the EU as a symbol and legitimate reference in the domestic context, of course, depends on the condition that the EU itself ensures that its involvement in conflict areas is not perceived as biased, since otherwise EU involvement is likely to become drawn into the binary logic of conflict communication. It is thus the credibility of the EU on both sides of the conflict that allows local actors to emphasise the win-win setting of EU impact. While it is true that domestic actors in border conflict regions tend to read into 'Europe' their own interpretation of the conflict, the impact of the four pathways on border conflicts is positively conditioned by such an undistorted interplay between EU-related and domestic conditions. As our case studies have demonstrated, such a positive condition of EU impact relates either to a credible membership perspective or to the long-term effects stemming from integration into the EU. Thus, we want to highlight in particular that EU impact across the four pathways is strongest when coupled with a credible membership perspective. This not only increases the EU's compulsory impact but can spur a positive and reenforcing cycle of EU impact on several dimensions. This re-enforcing cycle comprises a substantive strengthening of the EU's bargaining power (compulsory impact), an empowering and legitimisation of moderate political forces as well as the emergence of new domestic coalitions between moderates and former hardliners (enabling impact), an increase of scope and support for cross-border cooperation and cross-border contacts (connective impact) and, finally, an emergence and consolidation of a 'deep' transformation of (national) identity-scripts and the emergence of a (parallel) shared European identity on both sides (constructive impact).

However, cautioning against too high expectations with regard to the impact of the EU on border conflict transformation, our case studies have referred to several factors that hamper the overall impact of the EU. These negative conditions of EU impact relate to four main dimensions. Firstly, the absence of a credible membership perspective significantly diminishes the impact of the EU on border conflict societies. This has been the case in Turkey prior to 1999 but also relates to the limited effect of the EU on wider societal developments in the context of association as has been discussed in this book with regard to our case study on Israel–Palestine. Secondly, the strictness of the EU's external border regime negatively affects the power of individual pathways. Thus, in Europe's North, Cyprus and Greece–Turkey prior to 1999 the conflict is characterised by one side being part of the EU (central and eastern European member states, Republic of Cyprus, Greece) while the other side is subject to a relatively strict exclusion (Russia, TRNC, Turkey). Strict provisions at the EU's external border not only limit the range of people-to-people contacts across the border, but also establish a self–other hierarchy between 'insiders' and 'outsiders' that tends to reproduce conflictive identity patterns in border conflict areas rather than undermine them. Thirdly, (perceived) biases of the EU in conflict societies are another important factor that prevents the EU from making full use of the pathways. Such perceptions of the EU being biased in favour of the other conflict party have been documented here with regard to political discourses in Israel, among Unionists in Northern Ireland, Turkey prior to 1999 and Russia. Finally, several of our case studies on individual border conflicts as well as Michelle Pace's chapter on the EU dimensions have referred to the way in which institutional shortcomings on the side of the EU constitute another negative condition. This relates to both negative effects stemming from the institutional fragmentation of EU decision-making structures in Brussels, and cumbersome decision-making structures on the ground, for example with regard to funding procedures for cross-border cooperation in conflict areas.

Conclusion: the EU between normative power and powerful mediator

In this concluding chapter we have attempted to outline in a systematic manner how the comparative insights from five different case studies contribute to a better understanding of the various ways with which the EU – for better or for worse – has, through the mechanisms of integration or association, an impact on border conflicts in Europe and Europe's periphery. While there might be disagreement with regard to the overall assessment of the EU's impact on individual border conflicts, whether studied in this book or not, our discussion has provided ample evidence that integration and to a lesser extent association are an important perturbation for border conflicts, both directly and, even more important, indirectly. As Michelle Pace has outlined in her chapter, this role of the EU in border conflicts has also a considerable feedback on identity constructions and policies at the EU level, and it is in that sense also that the EU gets inevitably perturbated by border conflicts the more it encounters them. Yet, notwithstanding our key argument that the EU has – on a theoretical and empirical level – a positive impact on many border conflicts, we caution against an all too optimistic image of the EU as a normative power and a force for good, as it often appears in official EU rhetoric and, occasionally, academic writings. While it is true that the post-World War II model of peaceful cooperation between former long-time foes is indeed a powerful recipe for securing cooperation, peace and, ultimately, a reconstruction of identities, this should not divert attention from those instances in which the EU has contributed to an increasing securitisation of cross-border relations. Having said this, the unique nature of the EU impact is still the attraction that the aforementioned 'European promise' holds for conflict-ridden societies. As much as institutional reforms, a streamlining of decision-making structures at the EU level, a growing global political and military role as well as debates about the ultimate borders of the EU are needed, the EU is thus well advised not to lose this subtle power of integration and association on the way.

References

Aall, P. R., Miltenberger D. T. and Weiss, T. G. 2000. *IGOs, NGOs and the Military in Peace and Relief Operations*. Washington, DC: United States Institute of Peace Press.

Aalto, P. 2002. 'The European Geopolitical Subject in the Making? EU, Russia and the Kaliningrad Question', *Geopolitics* 7 (3): 143–74.

2003a. 'Post-Soviet Geo-politics in the North of Europe', in Lehti, M. and Smith, D. J. (eds.), *Post-Cold War Identity Politics: Northern and Baltic Experiences*. London: Frank Cass, pp. 253–74.

2003b. 'Semi-Outsiders or Close Outsiders? Russia and Its Kaliningrad Region in European Integration'. Paper presented at a 'New World Politics' Conference, Hämeenlinna, 12–13 December.

2003c. *Constructing Post-Soviet Geopolitics in Estonia*. London: Frank Cass.

Adamson, F. 2002. 'Democratization in Turkey, European Union Enlargement and the Regional Dynamics of the Cyprus Conflict: Past Lessons and Future Prospects', in Diez, T. (ed.), *The EU and the Cyprus Conflict: Modern Conflict, Postmodern Union*. Manchester University Press, pp. 163–80.

Adler, E. and Barnett, M. (eds.) 1998. *Security Communities*. Cambridge University Press.

Agathangelou, A. M. 2005. *The Global Political Economy of Sex: Desire, Violence, Insecurity in Mediterranean Nation States*. London: Palgrave Macmillan.

Agathangelou, A. M. and Ling, L. H. M. 1997. 'Postcolonial Dissidence within Dissident IR: Transforming Master Narratives of Sovereignty in Greco-Turkish Cyprus', *Studies in Political Economy* 54: 7–38.

Ahiram, A. and Tovias, A. 1995. *Whither EU–Israeli Relations? Common and Divergent Interests*. Frankfurt: Peter Lang.

Ahtiainen, I. 2000. 'The Never-Ending Karelia Question', *Helsingin Sanomat International Edition*. www.helsinki-hs.net/news.asp?id=20000718xx17.

Aksu, F. 2001. 'Turkish–Greek Relations', *Turkish Review of Balkan Studies* 6: 167–201.

Albert, M. and Brock, L. 1996. 'De-bordering the State: New Spaces in International Relations', *New Political Science* 35 (1): 69–107.

2000. 'De-bordering the World of States: New Spaces in International Relations', in Albert, M., Brock, L. and Wolf, K.-D. (eds.), *Civilizing World Politics: Society and Community Beyond the State*. Lanham: Rowman and Littlefield, pp. 19–44.

2001. 'What Keeps Westphalia Together? Normative Differentiation in the Modern Systems of States', in Albert *et al.* (eds.), pp. 29–49.

Albert, M., Jacobson, D. and Lapid, Y. (eds.) 2001. *Identities, Borders, Orders: Rethinking International Relations Theory*. Minneapolis: University of Minnesota Press.

Aleksandrov, O. 2001. 'The Role of the Republic of Karelia in Russia's Foreign and Security Policy'. *Working Paper* 5. Zurich: Eidgenössische Technische Hochschule Zürich.

Alpher, J. 2000. 'The Political Role of the EU in the Middle East: Israeli Aspirations', in Behrendt, S. and Hanelt, C.-P. (eds.), *Bound to Cooperate: Europe and the Middle East*. Gütersloh: Bertelsmann Foundation, pp. 193–208.

Anderson, B. 1991. *Imagined Communities: Reflections on the Origin and Spread of Nationalism*. London: Verso.

Anderson, D. M. 1993. 'Policing and Communal Conflict: The Cyprus Emergency, 1954–60', *Journal of Imperial and Commonwealth History* 21 (3): 177–207.

Anderson, E. 1990. 'How Narva, Petseri, and Abrene Came to Be in the RSFSR', *Journal of Baltic Studies* 19 (2–4): 395–412.

Anderson, J. 1998. 'Integrating Europe, Integrating Ireland: The Socio-economic Dynamics', in Anderson, J. and Goodman, J. (eds.), *Dis/Agreeing Ireland: Contexts, Obstacles, Hopes*. London: Pluto Press, pp. 73–88.

Anderson, J. and O'Dowd, L. 1999. 'Ethno-Political Conflict, Globalisation and the Irish Border', *Regional Studies* 33: 681–96.

Anderson, M. 1996. *Frontiers: Territory and State Formation in the Modern World*. Cambridge: Polity Press.

Anderson, M. and Bort, E. 2001. *The Frontiers of the European Union*. London: Palgrave.

Andreas, P. and Snyder, T. (eds.) 2000. *The Wall around the West: State, Borders and Immigration Controls in North America and Europe*. Lanham: Rowman and Littlefield.

Archer, C. 2005. 'Regional Security, the War on Terrorism and the Dual Enlargements', in Browning (ed.), pp. 13–30.

Area Development Management/Combat Poverty Agency (ADM/CPA) 1999. *Programme for Peace and Reconciliation*. Briefing Paper on Socio-Economic Development, Reconciliation and Cross Border Work in the Southern Border Counties of Ireland. Monaghan: ADM/CPA.

Aridan, N. 1994. 'The British Reaction to the Gaza Raid of 1955', in Golani, Moti (ed.), HaHetz, Hashachor: *The Gaza Raid and the Israeli Policy of Retaliation During the Fifties*. University of Haifa (Hebrew), pp. 47–57.

Armbruster, H., Rollo, C. and Meinhof, U. 2003. 'Imagining Europe: Everyday Narratives in European Border Communities', *Journal of Ethnic and Migration Studies* 29: 885–99.

Arthur, P. 1983. 'Anglo-Irish Relations since 1968: A "Fever Chart" Interpretation', *Government and Opposition* 18 (2): 157–74.

   2000. *Special Relationships: Britain, Ireland and the Northern Ireland Problem*. Belfast: Blackstaff Press.

Arvanitopoulos, C. 1994. 'The Belief System of Constantine Karamanlis', *Mediterranean Quarterly* 14 (1): 61–83.

Ashley, R. K. 1988. 'Untying the Sovereign State: A Double Reading of the Anarchy Problematique', *Millennium: Journal of International Studies* 17 (2): 227–62.

Asseburg, M. 2003. 'The EU and the Middle East Conflict: Tackling the Main Obstacle to Euro-Mediterranean Partnership', *Mediterranean Politics* 8 (2/3): 174–95.

Athanassopoulou, E. 1997. 'Blessing in Disguise? The Imia Crisis and Turkish–Greek Relations', *Mediterranean Politics* 2 (3): 76–101.

Attalides, M. 1979. *Cyprus, Nationalism and International Politics*. London: Macmillan Press.

2004. 'The Political Process in Cyprus and the Day After the Referendum', *The Cyprus Review* 16: 137–48.

Attiná, F. 2001. 'Conclusions: Partnership Building', in Attiná, F. and Stavridis, S. (eds.), *The Barcelona Process and Euro-Mediterranean Issues from Stuttgart to Marseille*. Milan: Dott. A Giuffrè Editore.

Ayres, R. 1996. 'European Integration: The Case of Cyprus', *The Cyprus Review* 8: 39–62.

Azar, E. E. 1990. *The Management of Protracted Social Conflict*. Dartmouth: Aldershot.

Bardon, J. 1995. 'Ireland's Partition: A Brief History', in D'Arcy and Dickson (eds.), pp. 21–37.

Barnett, M. and Duvall, R. (eds.) 2003. *Power in Global Governance*. Cambridge University Press.

2005. 'Power in International Politics', *International Organization* 59 (1): 39–75.

Batt, J. 2003. 'Introduction', in *Kaliningrad in Europe* (A study commissioned by the Council of Europe, edited by Bartosz Cichocki). Strasbourg: Council of Europe.

Baxendale, J., Dewar, S. and Gowan, D. (eds.) 2000. *The EU and Kaliningrad: Kaliningrad and the Impact of EU Enlargement*. London: The Federal Trust.

Belge, M. 2004. 'Observations on Civil Society', in Belge, T. (ed.), pp. 27–32.

Belge, T. (ed.) 2004. *Voices for the Future: Civic Dialogue Between Turks and Greeks*. Istanbul: Bilgi University Press.

Bendiek, A. 2004. *Der Konflikt im ehemaligen Jugoslawien und die europäische Integration. Eine Analyse ausgewählter Politikfelder*. Opladen: Leske und Budrich.

Berg, E. and Ehin, P. 2006. 'What Kind of Border Regime is in the Making? Towards a Differentiated and Uneven Border Strategy', *Cooperation and Conflict* 41 (1): 53–71.

Berg, E. and Oras, S. 2003. 'Kümme Aastat Eesti-Vene Piiriläbirääkimisi', in Kasekamp, A. (ed.), *The Estonian Foreign Policy Yearbook 2003*. Tartu: The Estonian Foreign Policy Institute, pp. 45–75.

Bertrand, G. 2004. *Turkish Cypriot's Exit, Voice and Loyalty*, www.weltpolitik.net/print/931.html.

Beunderman, M. 2007. 'EU–Turkey Ties Cooling Further', *EUObserver*, 16 February, available at: http://euobserver.com/9/23514.

Bew, P. and Meehan, E. 1994. 'Regions and Borders: Controversies in Northern Ireland about the European Union', *Journal of European Public Policy* 1 (1): 95–113.

Bicchi, F. 2006. '"Our Size Fits All"': Normative Power Europe and the Mediterranean', *Journal of European Public Policy* 13 (2): 286–303.

Bilge, A. S. 2000. *Buyuk Dus, Turk–Yunan Siyasi Iliskileri [Great Idea: Turkish–Greek Political Relations]*. Ankara: 21. Yuzyil Yayinlari.

Birand, M. A. 1991. 'Turkey and the "Davos Process": Experiences and Prospects', in Constas (ed.), pp. 27–39.

2000. *Turkiye'nin Avrupa Macerasi 1959–1999 [Turkey's European Venture]*. Istanbul: Dogan Kitapcilik.

Birckenbach, H.-M. and Wellmann, C. (eds.) 2003. *The Kaliningrad Challenge: Options and Recommendations*. Münster: Lit Verlag.

Bleiere, D. and Henins, R. 2004. *The Eastern Latvian Border: Potential for Trans-Frontier Co-operation with Russia*. Riga: Latvian Institute for International Affairs. January.

Boal, F. W., Murray, R. C. and Poole, M. A. 1976. 'Belfast: The Urban Encapsulation of a National Conflict', in Clarke, S. C. and Obler, J. L. (eds.), *Urban Ethnic Conflict: A Comparative Perspective*. Chapel Hill, NC: Institute for Research in Social Science, University of North Carolina, pp. 77–131.

Bock, H.-M. (ed.) 1998. *Projekt deutsch-französische Verständigung. Die Rolle der Zivilgesellschaft am Beispiel des Deutsch-Französischen Instituts in Ludwigsburg*. Opladen: Leske + Budrich.

Boer, M. den, 2002. 'To What Extent Can There Be Flexibility on the Application of Schengen in the New Member States?', in Anderson, M. and Apap, J. (eds.), *The New European Borders and Security Cooperation: Promoting Trust in an Enlarged European Union*. Brussels: Centre for European Policy Studies and SITRA, pp. 139–49.

Bourdaras, G. 2004. 'Greece will Shun Veto but May Raise the Bar Higher for Ankara', *Kathimerini* (Athens, English edn), 29 November.

Bradley, J. 1995. 'The Two Economies of Ireland: An Analysis', in D'Arcy and Dickson (eds.), pp. 38–52.

Bradley, J. and Hamilton, D. 1999. 'Making Policy in Northern Ireland: A Critique of Strategy 2010', *Administration* 47: 32–50.

Brennan, P. 1995. 'The European Union: The Island's Common Cause', in D'Arcy and Dickson (eds.), pp. 69–76.

Breuilly, J. 1993. *Nationalism and the State*. Manchester University Press.

Brewin, C. 2000. *The European Union and Cyprus*. Huntingdon: Eothen Press.

Briand, R. J. 2002. 'Bush, Clinton, Irish America and the Irish Peace Process', *Political Quarterly* 73 (2): 172–80.

Bridle, A. 2002. 'The Relevance of the Euro to Northern Ireland'. Paper delivered to the UACES Annual Conference, Belfast, September.

Brown, M. E. and Rosecrance, R. N. (eds.) 1999. *The Costs of Conflict: Prevention and Cure in the Global Arena*. Oxford: Rowman and Littlefield.

Browning, C. S. 2002. 'The Internal/External Security Paradox and the Reconstruction of Boundaries in the Baltic: The Case of Kaliningrad'. *COPRI Working Papers* 21. Copenhagen Peace Research Institute.

Browning, C. 2003. 'The Internal/External Security Paradox and the Reconstruction of Boundaries in the Baltic: The Case of Kaliningrad', *Alternatives* 28 (5): 545–81.

(ed.) 2005. *Remaking Europe in the Margins: Northern Europe after the Enlargements*. Aldershot: Ashgate.

Browning, C. and Joenniemi, P. 2005. 'Conclusion: Europe-Making and the North after Enlargement', in Browning (ed.), pp. 205–24.

Bryant, R. 2004. *Imagining the Modern: The Cultures of Nationalism in Cyprus*. London: I. B. Tauris.

Burton, J. W. 1972. *World Society*. Cambridge University Press.

Buzan, B. and Wæver, O. 2003. *Regions and Power*. Cambridge University Press.

Buzan, B., Wæver, O. and de Wilde, J. 1998. *Security: A New Framework for Analysis*. Boulder, CO: Lynne Rienner.

CAIN. *Conflict Archive on the Internet*, University of Ulster, http://cain.ulst.ac.uk.

Campbell, D. 1998a. *National Deconstruction: Violence, Identity and Justice in Bosnia*. Minneapolis: University of Minnesota Press.

1998b. *Writing Security: United States Foreign Policy and the Politics of Identity*. Minneapolis: University of Minnesota Press.

Chigas, D. and Ganson, B. 1997. 'Grand Visions and Small Projects', in Chayes, A. and Minow, M. L. (eds.), *Imagine Coexistence: Restoring Humanity After Violent Conflict*. San Francisco, CA: Jossey Bass, pp. 59–84.

Christiansen, T. and Jørgensen, K.-E. 2000. 'Transnational Governance Above and Below the State: The Changing Nature of Borders in Europe', *Regional and Federal Studies* 10 (2): 62–77.

Christou, G. 2004. *The European Union and Enlargement: The Case of Cyprus*. London: Palgrave.

Chrysostomides, K. 2000. *The Republic of Cyprus: A Study in International Law*. The Hague: M. Nijhoff.

2001. *Ὑπεράσπιση της Πολιτικής του Αύριο: Κυπριακές Πολιτικές Συνέχειες [In Defence of Tomorrow's Policy: Cypriot Political Continuities]*. Athens: Kastaniotis.

Clawson, P. 2003. 'US and European Priorities in the Middle East', in Lindstrom, G. (ed.), *Shift or Rift: Assessing US–EU Relations after Iraq*, pp. 127–46. Paris: EU Institute for Security Studies.

Cleanthous, N. 2002. Speech Presented at Panel on 'The Cyprus Question after Copenhagen', Association for Social Reform (OPEK), Nicosia, 16 December.

Coakley, J. 1999. 'The Foundations of Statehood', in Coakley, J. and Gallagher, M. (eds.), *Politics in the Republic of Ireland*. Third edition. London: Routledge, pp. 1–31.

2001. 'Ethnic Conflict and its Resolution: The New Northern Ireland Model'. *IBIS Working Paper* 9. Dublin: Institute for British–Irish Studies, University College Dublin.

2003. 'The North–South Institutions: From Blueprint to Reality'. *IBIS Working Paper* 22. Dublin: Institute for British–Irish Studies, University College Dublin.

Cockburn, C. 2004. *The Line: Women, Partition and the Gender Order in Cyprus*. London: Zed Books.

Connolly, W. E. 1991. *Identity/Difference: Democratic Negotiations of Political Paradox*. Ithaca: Cornell University Press.

Constas, D. (ed.) 1991. *The Greek–Turkish Conflict in the 1990s: Domestic and External Influences*. New York: St Martin's Press.

Cook, S., Poole, M. A., Pringle, D. G. and Moore, A. J. 2000. *Comparative Spatial Deprivation in Ireland: A Cross-Border Analysis*. Dublin: Oak Tree Press.

Cooper, R. 2004. *The Breaking of Nations: Order and Chaos in the Twenty-First Century*. New York: Grove Press.

Coser, L. A. 1964. *The Function of Social Conflict*. New York: Free Press.

Couloumbis, T. A. 1994. 'Introduction: The Impact of EC Membership on Greece's Foreign Policy Profile', in Kazakos and Ioakimidis (eds.), pp. 189–98.

Couloumbis, T. A. and Tziampiris, A. 2002. 'The End of Greek History?', *Kathimerini* (English edn), 20 December.

Couloumbis, T. A. and Yannas, P. 1994. 'Greek Foreign Policy Priorities for the 1990s', in Featherstone and Ifantis (eds.), pp. 160–75.

Council of the European Union 1996. *Turkey/Imia Islet*, Common Foreign and Security Policy Statement, 9144/96.

Crocker, C. A., Hampson, F. O. and Aall, P. R. 2003. 'Ready for Prime Time: The When, Who and Why of International Mediation', *Negotiation Journal* 19 (2): 151–67.

Cronberg, T. 2002. 'A Europe Without Divides? The EU–Russian Partnership and the Case of Virtual Borders'. *COPRI Working Papers* 37. Copenhagen Peace Research Institute.

   2003. 'Euregio Karelia: In Search of a Relevant Space for Action', in Hedegaard, L. and Lindström, B. (eds.), *The NEBI Yearbook*. Nordregio: Nordic Centre for Spatial Development, pp. 224–39.

Cross-Border Consortium 2003. *Submission on 'A Shared Future' Consultation Paper*. Monaghan: ADM/CPA, Community Foundation for NI, Co-operation Ireland.

Cunningham, M. 1997. 'The Political Language of John Hume', *Irish Political Studies* 12 (1): 13–22.

   2001. *British Government Policy on Northern Ireland 1969–2000*. Manchester University Press.

Dachs, G. and Peters, J. 2004. 'Israel and Europe, the Troubled Relationship: Between Perceptions and Reality', *Israeli–European Policy Network Papers*, http://hsf.bgu.ac.il/europe/uploadDocs/iepnpgdjp.pdf.

Dahrendorf, R. 1957. 'Towards a Theory of Social Conflict', *Journal of Conflict Resolution* 2 (2): 170–83.

   1961. *Gesellschaft und Freiheit*. Munich: Piper.

D'Arcy, M. and Dickson, T. (eds.) 1995. *Border Crossings: Developing Ireland's Island Economy*. Dublin: Gill and Macmillan.

Dauksts, B. and Puga, A. 1995. 'Abrene', in Forsberg (ed.), pp. 178–87.

Decker, F. 2002. 'Governance Beyond the Nation-state: Reflections on the Democratic Deficit of the European Union', *Journal of European Public Policy* 9 (2): 256–72.

Defrance, C. 2001. 'La création du réseau de centres culturels français en Allemagne dans l'immédiat après-guerre', *Lendemains* 103/4: 83–96.

Demetriou, O. 2004a. 'Cyprus Commentary', *EUBorderConf Newsletter* 7. Birmingham: Department of Political Science and International Studies, University of Birmingham.

2004b. 'The EU and Border Conflicts: The Case of Cyprus'. Paper presented at the Conference 'An Appraisal of Europe: Conflict, Rights and the Environment in Cyprus', Intercollege, Nicosia, September.

2004c. 'The EU and the Cyprus Conflict: A Review of the Literature'. *Working Paper Series in EU Border Conflicts Studies*, Working Paper No. 5. Birmingham: Department of Political Science and International Studies, University of Birmingham.

2004d. 'The EU and the Cyprus Conflict: The View of Political Actors'. *Working Paper Series in EU Border Conflicts Studies*, Working Paper No. 9. Birmingham: Department of Political Science and International Studies, University of Birmingham.

2005. 'The EU and the Cyprus Conflict: Discourses on the Border, the Conflict and the EU'. *Working Paper Series in EU Border Conflicts Studies*, Working Paper No. 18. Birmingham: Department of Political Science and International Studies, University of Birmingham.

Denieul, F. 1997. 'Frontières et territoires', Cahiers No. 2 in *Les nouvelles frontières d'un monde sans frontières*, Plain Sud. Marseilles: Editions de l'Aube.

Deutsch, K. W. *et al.* 1957. *Political Community and the North Atlantic Area*. Princeton University Press.

Deutsch, M. 1991. 'Subjective Features in Conflict Resolution: Psychological, Social and Cultural Influences', in Väyrynen, Raimo (ed.), *New Directions in Conflict Theory*. London: Sage, pp. 26–53.

Dieckhoff, A. 2002. 'The European Union and the Israeli–Palestinian Conflict', in Hanelt *et al.* (eds.), pp. 147–60.

Diez, T. 1997. 'International Ethics and European Integration: Federal State or Network Horizon?', *Alternatives* 22 (3): 301–3.

2000. 'Last Exit to Paradise? The EU, the Cyprus Conflict, and the Problematic "Catalytic Effect"'. *Copenhagen Peace Research Institute Working Papers*, 4/2000.

(ed.) 2002. *The European Union and the Cyprus Conflict: Modern Conflict, Postmodern Union*. Manchester University Press.

2004. 'Europe's Others and the Return of Geopolitics', *Cambridge Review of International Affairs* 17 (2): 319–35.

2005. 'Constructing the Self and Changing Others: Reconsidering "Normative Power Europe"', *Millennium: Journal of International Studies* 33 (3): 613–36.

Diez, T. and Rumelili, B. 2004. 'Open the Door: Turkey and the European Union', *The World Today*, August/September: 18–19.

Diez, T., Stetter, S. and Albert, M. 2006. 'The European Union and Border Conflicts: The Transformative Power of Integration', *International Organization* 60 (3): 563–93.

Diez, T. and Whitman, R. 2002. 'Analysing European Integration: Reflecting on the English School – Scenarios for an Encounter', *Journal of Common Market Studies* 40 (1): 43–67.

Dijk, H. van 1999. 'State Borders in Geography and History', in Knippenberg, H. and Markusse, J. (eds.), *Nationalising and Denationalising European Border Regions, 1800–2000: Views from Geography and History*. Dordrecht: Kluwer, pp. 21–38.

Donnelly, C. 2000. 'Kaliningrad from a Security Perspective', in Baxendale *et al.* (eds.), pp. 215–22.

Dorussen, H. 2001. 'Mixing Carrots with Sticks: Evaluating the Effectiveness of Positive Incentives', *Journal of Peace Research* 38 (2): 251–62.

Dountas, M. 1995. 'Turkey: In Europe or in Asia?', *Ta Nea* (Athens), 1 March.

Doyle, M. W. 1997. *Ways of War and Peace: Realism, Liberalism, and Socialism.* New York: Norton.

Droushiotis, M. 1996. *Η 'Εισβολή' της Χούντας στην Κύπρο [The Junta's 'Invasion' in Cyprus]*. Athens: Stachi.

1998. *EOKA, Η Σκοτεινή Όψη [EOKA, The Dark Side]*. Athens: Stachi.

2002a. *1974, Το Άγνωστο Παρασκήνιο της Τουρκικής Εισβολής [1974, The Unknown Background of the Turkish Invasion]*. Nicosia: Alphadi.

2002b. *EOKA B & CIA [EOKA B and the CIA]*. Nicosia: Alphadi.

Duchêne, F. 1973. 'The European Community and the Uncertainties of Interdependence', in Kohnstamm, M. and Hager, W. (eds.), *A Nation Writ Large? Foreign-Policy Problems before the European Community*. London: Macmillan, pp. 1–21.

Efinger, M., Rittberger, V. and Zürn, M. 1988. *Internationale Regime in den Ost-West-Beziehungen. Ein Beitrag zur Erforschung der friedlichen Behandlung internationaler Konflikte*. Frankfurt am Main: Haag und Herchen.

Ehin, P. and Mikenberg, E. 2003. *The Reasons for the Low Level of Estonian–Russian Cross-Border Activities: Southern-Eastern Estonia*. Tallinn: Estonian Foreign Policy Institute.

Elwert, G. 2001. 'Conflict: Anthropological Aspects', in Smelser, N. J. and Baltes, P. B. (eds.), *International Encyclopedia of the Social and Behavioral Sciences*. Oxford: Elsevier Science, pp. 2542–7.

Emerson, M. 2002. *The Elephant and the Bear: The European Union, Russia and the Near Abroads*. Brussels: Centre for European Policy Studies.

Emerson, M., Aydin, S., Noucheva, G., Tocci, N., Vahl, M. and Young, R. 2005. 'The Reluctant Deputante: The European Union as Promoter of Democracy in its Neighbourhood'. *CEPS Working Document* 223. Brussels: Centre for European Policy Studies.

Ertekün, N. M. 1997. *The Greek Cypriot Eagerness and Agitation for EU Membership – Why?*, www.cypnet.co.uk/ncyprus/history/cyproblem/articles/bolum2.html.

Eskelinen, H., Liikanen, I. and Oksa, J. (eds.) 1999. *Curtains of Iron and Gold. Reconstructing Borders and Scales of Interaction*. Aldershot: Ashgate.

EU Bulletin 1997. *29 April 1997 EC–Turkey Association Council Conclusions*, 4–1997.

EU Programmes Body (SEUPB) n/d [2003]. *INTERREG IIIA Programme 2000–2006 Ireland/Northern Ireland*. Monaghan: Special EU Programmes Body.

Euregio Karelia 2002. *Ekarelia – Euregio Karelia as a Cultural Information Society*. Karelia: Euregio Karelia.

European Commission 1991. *Europe 2000: Outlook for the Development of the Community's Territory: A Preliminary Overview*. Communication from the Commission to the Council and European Parliament. Brussels: European Commission.

1996. *Report on Developments in Relations with Turkey* (COM (96)0491). Brussels: European Commission.

1997a. *General Report on the Activities of the European Union*, http://europa. eu.int/abc/doc/off/rg/en/1997/enm00097.htm.

1997b. *Agenda 2000 – Volume I – Communication: For a Stronger and Wider Union*. Strasbourg, 15 July. DOC/97/6, available at www.infoeuropa.ro/ ieweb/imgupload/1997_Agenda_2000.pdf.

1999. Third Euro-Mediterranean Conference of Foreign Ministers – Barcelona III, Stuttgart, Germany, 15–16 April, 1999. Formal Conclusions.

2003a. 'Continuing Enlargement: Strategy Paper and Report of the European Commission on the Progress Towards Accession by Bulgaria, Romania and Turkey'. http://europa.eu/scadplus/leg/en/lvb/e50014.htm.

2003b. *2003 Regular Report on Turkey's Progress Towards Accession*. Enlargement. European Commission – Directorate General for Enlargement.

2004. 'European Neighborhood Policy Strategy Paper'. COM (2004) 373 final, 12 May, Brussels.

2005. 'Communication from the Commission to the Council and the European Parliament. Tenth Anniversary of the Euro-Mediterranean Partnership: A Work Programme to Meet the Challenges of the Next Five Years', *EuroMed Report* 89, 14 April.

n/d. *Northern Ireland in Europe*. European Commission Representation in the UK, www.cec.org.uk/info/pubs/regional/ni/contents.htm.

European Council 1997. *Luxembourg European Council Conclusions*. Brussels: European Council.

1999. *Helsinki European Council Conclusions*. Brussels: European Council.

2002. *Copenhagen European Council Conclusions*, in Bulletin of the European Union, December issue, http://europa.eu.int/abc/doc/off/bull/en/200212/ i1003.htm.

2004. *Presidency Conclusions. 4/5 November 2004*. Brussels: European Council, 8 December, 14292/1/04 REV 1 CONCL 3.

2005. *Brussels European Council 16–17 December 2004 Presidency Conclusions*, Brussels, 1 February. 16238/1/04 REV 1.

European Parliament 1996a. *Resolution on the Situation in Turkey and the Offer of a Ceasefire Made by the PKK*, 18 January. B4-0060, 0076, 0086 and 0089/1996.

1996b. *Resolution on the Provocative Actions and Contestation of Sovereign Rights by Turkey Against a Member State of the Union*, 15 February. B4-0146, 0154, 0164, 0245, 0249 and 0254/1996.

2005. *Report on the European Neighbourhood Policy*. Foreign Affairs Committee, Rapporteur Charles Tannock, Document A6-0399/2005, 7 December.

EU-Russia Centre 2007. *Voices from Russia: Society, Democracy, Europe*. Brussels: EU-Russia Centre and Moscow: Levada Centre.

Fairlie, L. and Sergounin, A. 2001. *Are Borders Barriers? EU Enlargement and the Russian Region of Kaliningrad.* Helsinki: The Finnish Institute for International Affairs.

Fay, M. T., Morrissey, M. and Smyth, M. 1998. *Mapping Troubles-Related Deaths in Northern Ireland 1969–1998.* Derry/Londonderry: INCORE, University of Ulster.

Featherstone, K. 1994. 'Introduction', in Featherstone and Ifantis (eds.), pp. 3–16.

Featherstone, K. and Ifantis, K. (eds.) 1994. *Greece in a Changing Europe: Between European Integration and Balkan Disintegration?* Manchester University Press.

Feiglin, M. 2003. 'A Different Strategic Policy', *Nekudah* 262: 31–5 (Hebrew).

Ferguson, J. 1990. *The Anti-Politics Machine: 'Development', Depoliticization and Bureaucratic Power in Lesotho.* Cambridge University Press.

FitzGerald, J. D., Quinn, T. P., Whelan, B. J. and Williams, J. A. 1988. *An Analysis of Cross-Border Shopping.* Dublin: Economic and Social Research Institute, paper 137.

Flint, C. 2003. 'Geographies of Inclusion/Exclusion', in Cutter, S. L., Richardson, D. B. and Wilbanks, T. J. (eds.), *The Geographical Dimension of Terrorism.* New York and London: Routledge, pp. 53–8.

Forsberg, T. (ed.) 1995a. *Contested Territory: Border Disputes at the Edge of the Former Soviet Empire.* Aldershot: Edward Elgar.

1995b. 'Karelia', in Forsberg (ed.), pp. 202–23.

1996. 'Explaining Territorial Disputes: From Power Politics to Normative Reasons', *Journal of Peace Research* 33 (4): 433–49.

Foucault, M. 1970. *The Order of Things: An Archaeology of the Human Sciences.* New York: Pantheon Books.

1990. *The History of Sexuality,* vol. 1: *An Introduction.* New York: Vintage.

Freedman, R. 2002. 'The Bush Administration, the European Union, and the Arab Israeli Conflict: Is a Euro-Atlantic Partnership Possible?', in Hanelt *et al.* (eds.), pp. 161–88.

Fulton, J. 2002. 'Religion and Enmity in Northern Ireland: Institutions and Relational Beliefs', *Social Compass* 49 (2): 189–202.

Galnoor, I. 1994. *Territorial Partition – Decision Crossroads in the Zionist Movement.* Beer-Sheva and Jerusalem: Ben Gurion University Press and the Magnes Press (Hebrew).

Galtung, J. 1969. *Peace by Peaceful Means: Peace and Conflict, Development and Civilization.* London: Sage.

1975. 'Peace Thinking', in Galtung, Johan, *Essays in Peace Research,* vol. 1: *Peace: Research, Education, Action.* Copenhagen: Christian Ejlers, pp. 76–108.

Garton Ash, T. 2006. 'We Must Not Kowtow to these Undemocratic Giants', *The Guardian,* 5 January: 27.

Gaudissart, M. A. 1996. 'Cyprus and the European Union: The Long Road to Accession', *The Cyprus Review* 8 (1): 7–38.

Gazioğlu, A. C. 1998. *Enosise Karşi Taksim ve Eşit Egemenlik [Partition and Equal Sovereignty against Enosis].* Ankara: Cyrep Yayınları.

Geddes, A. 1999. *Immigration and European Integration: Towards Fortress Europe?* Manchester University Press.

Gehring, T. 2002. *Die Europäische Union als komplexe internationale Organisation. Wie durch Kommunikation und Entscheidung soziale Ordnung entsteht*. Baden-Baden: Nomos.

Gellner, E. 1983. *Nations and Nationalism*. Ithaca: Cornell University Press.

Gibbons, H. S. 1997. *The Genocide Files*. London: Charles Bravos.

Giegel, H.-J. 1998. *Konflikt in modernen Gesellschaften*. Frankfurt am Main: Suhrkamp.

Ginsberg, R. H. 2001. *The European Union in International Politics: Baptism by Fire*. New York: Rowman and Littlefield.

Good Friday Agreement 1998. *The Agreement Reached in the Multi-Party Negotiations*, Belfast, 10 April, www.nio.gov.uk/issues/agreement.htm.

Goodman, J. 2000. *Single Europe, Single Ireland? Uneven Development in Process*. Dublin: Irish Academic Press.

Gowan, D. 2000. *How the EU Can Help Russia*. London: Centre for European Reform.

Grabbe, H. 2000. 'The Sharp Edges of Europe: Extending Schengen Eastwards', *International Affairs* 76 (2): 519–36.

  2006. *The EU's Transformative Power: Europeanization through Conditionality in Central and Eastern Europe*. Basingstoke: Palgrave Macmillan.

Greilsammer, I. and Weiler, J. 1987. *Europe's Middle East Dilemma: The Quest for a Unified Stance*. Boulder, CO: Westview.

  (eds.) 1988. *Europe and Israel: Troubled Neighbours*. Berlin: de Gruyter.

Guelke, A. 2001. 'International Dimensions of the Belfast Agreement', in Wilford, R. (ed.), *Aspects of the Belfast Agreement*. Oxford University Press, pp. 245–63.

Gundogdu, A. 2001. 'Identities in Question: Greek–Turkish Relations in a Period of Transformation?', *Middle East Review of International Affairs* 5 (1): 106–17.

Gunduz, A. 2001. 'Greek–Turkish Disputes: How to Resolve Them?', in Keridis and Triantaphyllou (eds.), pp. 81–101.

Guvenc, S. 1998/9. 'Turkey's Changing Perception of Greece's Membership in the European Union: 1981–1998', *Turkish Review of Balkan Studies* 4 (1): 103–30.

Haagerup, N. J. 1984. 'Report Drawn Up on Behalf of the Political Affairs Committee on the Situation in Northern Ireland', *European Parliament Working Document* 1-1526/83, 9 March.

Haas, E. B. 1968. *The Uniting of Europe: Political, Social, and Economic Forces 1950–57*. Second edition. Stanford University Press.

  2001. 'Does Constructivism Subsume Neofunctionalism?', in Christiansen, T., Jorgensen, K. E. and Wiener, A. (eds.), *The Social Construction of Europe*. London: Sage, pp. 22–31.

Hanelt, C. P., Neugart, F. and Peitz, M. (eds.) 2002. *Europe's Emerging Foreign Policy and the Middle Eastern Challenge*. Gütersloh: Bertelsmann Foundation Publishers.

Hannay, D. 2005. *Cyprus: The Search for a Solution*. London: I. B. Tauris.

Harris, R. 1986 [1972]. *Prejudice and Tolerance in Ulster: A Study of Neighbours and Strangers in a Border Community*. Manchester University Press.

Haukkala, H. 2003. 'Clash of the Boundaries? The European Union and Russia in the Northern Dimension', in Lehti, M. and Smith, D. J. (eds.), *Post-Cold*

248   References

War Identity Politics: Northern and Baltic Experiences. London: Frank Cass, pp. 275–98.

Hayes, B. and McAllister, I. 1999. 'Ethnonationalism, Public Opinion and the Good Friday Agreement', in Ruane and Todd (eds.), pp. 30–48.

Hayward, K. 2004. 'From Barriers to Bridges: The Europeanisation of Ireland's Borders', *Centre for International Borders Research Working Papers in Border Studies* CIBR/WP04–1, Queen's University Belfast, www.qub.ac.uk/cibr/WPpdffiles/CIBRwp2004_1.pdf.

Hederman O'Brien, M. 2000. 'The Way We Were', in O'Donnell, R. (ed.), *Europe: The Irish Experience.* Dublin: Irish European Association, pp. 6–17.

Hellenic Parliament 1997. *Minutes,* 6 November.

   1999a. *Minutes,* 29 January.

   1999b. *Minutes,* 15 December.

Heller, M. 2004. 'Israel–EU Relations: The Political Dimension'. *Israeli–European Policy Network Papers,* No. 1. Beer-Sheva: Ben Gurion University.

Heraclides, A. 2001. *Yunanistan ve 'Dogudan Gelen Tehlike' [Greece and 'the Threat from the East'].* Istanbul: Iletisim.

Hermann, T. and Yuchtman-Yaar, E. (eds.) 2002. *International Intervention in Protracted Conflicts: The Israeli–Palestinian Case.* Proceedings of a Symposium held 29 April 2002. Tel Aviv: The Tami Steinmetz Center for Peace Research, Tel Aviv University.

Herzfeld, M. 1987. *Anthropology Through the Looking Glass: Critical Ethnography in the Margins of Europe.* Cambridge University Press.

   1992. *The Social Production of Indifference: Exploring the Symbolic Roots of Western Bureaucracy.* Oxford: Berg.

Heslinga, M. W. 1971 [1962]. *The Irish Border as a Cultural Divide: A Contribution to the Study of Regionalism in the British Isles.* Assen: Royal Van Gorcum.

Higashino, A. 2004. 'For the Sake of "Peace and Security"? The Role of Security in the European Union Enlargement Eastwards', *Cooperation and Conflict* 39 (4): 347–68.

Hill, C. 2001. 'The EU's Capacity for Conflict Prevention', *European Foreign Affairs Review* 6 (3): 315–33.

Hobsbawm, E. 1991. *Nations and Nationalism since 1780: Programme, Myth, Reality.* Cambridge University Press.

Hollis, R. 1997. 'Europe and the Middle East: Power by Stealth?', *International Affairs* 73 (1): 15–29.

   2004. 'The Israeli–Palestinian Road Block: Can Europeans Make a Difference?', *International Affairs* 80 (2): 191–201.

Holtom, P. 2005. 'The Kaliningrad Test in Russian–EU Relations', *Perspectives on European Politics and Society* 6 (1): 31–53.

Hottinger, J. T. 2005. 'The Relationship Between Track One and Track Two Diplomacy', *Accord: An International Review of Peace Initiatives,* issue 16, www.c-r.org/our-work/accord/engaging-groups/trackone-tracktwo.php.

Houtum, H. v. and Naerssen, T. v. 2002. 'Bordering, Ordering and Othering', *Tijdschrift voor Economische en Sociale Geografie* 93: 125–36.

Hume, J. 1996. *Personal Views: Politics, Peace and Reconciliation in Ireland.* Dublin: Townhouse.

Indyk, M. 2003. 'A Trusteeship for Palestine?', *Foreign Affairs* 82 (3): 51–66.

International Crisis Group 2006. 'Enter Hamas: The Challenges of Political Integration'. *Middle East Report* No. 49, 18 January 2006. Brussels: International Crisis Group.

Ioakimidis, P. C. 1994. 'Contradictions Between Policy and Performance', in Featherstone and Ifantis (eds.), pp. 33–52.

    2000. 'The Europeanisation of Greece's Foreign Policy: Progress and Problems', in Mitsos, A. and Mossialos, E. (eds.), *Contemporary Greece and Europe*. Ashgate: Aldershot, pp. 359–72.

    2002. 'Turkey in a Europeanisation Crisis', *Ta Nea* (Athens), 16 August.

Jääts, I. 1995. 'East Narva and Petserimaa', in Forsberg (ed.), pp. 188–201.

Jachtenfuchs, M., Diez, T. and Jung, S. 1998. 'Which Europe? Conflicting Models of a Legitimate European Political Order', *European Journal of International Relations* 4 (4): 409–45.

Jæger, Ø. 1997. 'Securitising Russia: Discursive Practices of the Baltic States'. *COPRI Working Papers* 10. Copenhagen Peace Research Institute.

Jakobsson-Hatay, S. 2004. 'The Slippery Slope Towards Partiality: European Integration and Cyprus'. Paper presented at the ECPR Joint Sessions workshop, Uppsala, April.

Joenniemi, P. 1998. 'The Karelian Question: On the Transformation of a Border Dispute', *Cooperation and Conflict* 33 (2): 183–206.

    2003. 'Responding to Russia's Kaliningrad Offensive', in Birckenbach and Wellmann (eds.), pp. 49–60.

Joenniemi, P. and Makarychev, A. 2004. 'Processes of Border-Making and Border-Breaking: The Case of Kaliningrad'. *Working Paper Series in EU Border Conflicts Studies*, Working Paper No. 7. Birmingham: Department of Political Science and International Studies, University of Birmingham.

Joenniemi, P. and Sergounin, A. 2003. *Russia and the European Union's Northern Dimension: Encounter or Clash of Civilisations?* Nizhny Novgorod State Linguistic University Press.

Joseph, J. S. 1997. *Cyprus: Ethnic Conflict and International Concern*. New York: P. Lang.

Kagan, R. 2003. *Paradise and Power: America versus Europe in the Twenty-first Century*. New York: Knopf.

Kazakos, P. and Ioakimidis, P. C. (eds.) 1994. *Greece and EC Membership Evaluated*. London: Pinter.

Kearney, R. 1998. 'Towards a British–Irish Council', *Céide* 2: 11–13.

Kennedy, D. 1988. *The Widening Gulf: Northern Attitudes to the Independent Irish State, 1919–1949*. Belfast: Blackstaff Press.

Kennedy, M. 2000. *Division and Consensus: The Politics of Cross-Border Relations in Ireland, 1925–1968*. Dublin: Institute of Public Administration.

Kennedy, T. and Lynch, C. 2003. 'Towards an Island at Peace with itself: An NGO View of North–South Cooperation', in *CCBS, Year 5*. Armagh: Centre for Cross Border Studies, pp. 8–11.

Keridis, D. 2001. 'Domestic Developments and Foreign Policy', in Keridis and Triantaphyllou (eds.), pp. 2–18.

Keridis, D. and Triantaphyllou, D. (eds.) 2001. *Greek–Turkish Relations in the Era of Globalization*. Everett, MA: Brassey's.

Khristenko, V. 2001. 'Speech to the Northern Dimension Forum in Lappeenranta, Finland, 22 October', in *Results of the Northern Dimension Forum in Lappeenranta, 22–23.10.2001*. Helsinki: Prime Minister's Office Publications 2002/14, p. 2021.

Kirisci, K. and Carkoglu, A. 2003. 'Perceptions of Greeks and Greek–Turkish Rapprochement by the Turkish Public', in Rubin and Carkoglu (eds.), pp. 117–53.

Kislali, A. T. 1999. 'The Importance of Cyprus', *Cumhuriyet* (Istanbul), 14 July.

Kızılyürek, N. 2002. *Milliyetçilik Kıskancında Kıbrıs [Cyprus in the Claws of Nationalism]*. Istanbul: İletişim Yayınları.

KKTC 2004. *Kıbrıs Tarihi [Cyprus History]*. Nicosia: National Ministry of Education and Culture.

Kockel, U. 1991. 'Regions, Borders and European Integration: Ethnic Nationalism in Euskadi, Schleswig, and Ulster'. *Occasional Papers in Irish Studies* 4. Liverpool: Institute for Irish Studies, University of Liverpool.

Kohen, S. 2003. 'Greece, the EU's New Term President', *Milliyet* (Istanbul), 2 January.

Kolossov, V. 2005. 'Border Studies: Changing Perspectives and Theoretical Approaches', *Geopolitics* 10 (4): 606–32.

Koslowski, R. 2001. 'Inviting the Global Elite in and Keeping the World's Poor Out: International Migration and Border Control in the Information Age'. Paper given at the ISA congress, Chicago.

Kranidiotis, Y. 1999. *Η Ελληνική Εξωτερική Πολιτική: Σκέψεις και Προβληματισμοί στο Κατώφλι του 21ου Αιώνα [The Greek Foreign Policy: Thoughts and Quandaries on the Eve of the 21st Century]*. Athens: Sideris.

Krickus, R. J. 2002. *The Kaliningrad Question*. Boston: Rowman and Littlefield.

Krotz, U. 2004. 'Transnationalism, Europeanization, Denationalization? The Parapublic Underpinnings of Franco-German Relations as Construction of International Purpose'. Paper prepared for delivery at the Conference of Europeanists, Chicago, March, www.europanet.org/conference2004/papers/E8_Krotz.pdf.

Lachowski, Z. 1998. 'Kaliningrad as a Security Issue', in Joenniemi, P. and Prawitz, J. (eds.), *Kaliningrad: The European Amber Region*. Aldershot: Ashgate, pp. 130–48.

Laffan, B. and Payne, D. 2001. *Creating Living Institutions: EU Programmes after the Good Friday Agreement*. Armagh: Centre for Cross Border Studies.

Lavenex, S. and Schimmelfennig, F. 2006. 'Relations with the Wider Europe', *Journal of Common Market Studies* 44 (1): 137–54.

Lawrence, R. J. and Elliott, S. 1975. *The Northern Ireland Border Poll 1973: Presented to Parliament by the Secretary of State for Northern Ireland by Command of her Majesty*. London: HM Stationery Office.

Logue, P. (ed.) 1999. *The Border: Personal Reflections from Ireland, North and South*. Dublin: Oak Tree Press.

Loisel, S. 2004. 'The European Union and African Border Conflicts: Assessing the Impact of Development Cooperation'. *Working Paper Series in EU Border*

Conflicts Studies, Working Paper No. 8. Birmingham: Department of Political Science and International Studies, University of Birmingham.

Loizos, P. 1981. *The Heart Grown Bitter: A Chronicle of Cypriot War Refugees*. Cambridge University Press.

Lordos, C. 2004. *Economic Aspects of the Annan Plan and the Plan's Property Proposals*. Istanbul: TESEV.

Loughlin, J., Bullmann, U., Hendriks, F., Lidström, A. and Seiler, D. L. 1999. *Regional and Local Democracy in the European Union*. Report for the Committee of the Regions. Luxembourg EUR-OP GF-24-99-081-XX-C.

Luhmann, N. 1984. *Soziale Systeme. Grundriß einer allgemeinen Theorie*. Frankfurt am Main: Suhrkamp.

2000. *Die Politik der Gesellschaft*. Frankfurt am Main: Suhrkamp.

Lunden, T. 2002. *Över gränsen. Om Människan vid Territoriets Slut*. Lund: Studentlitteratur.

MacAskill, E. 2006. 'UK Accused of Complicity in Torture', *The Guardian*, 19 January: 17.

McCall, C. 1998. 'Postmodern Europe and the Resources of Communal Identities in Northern Ireland', *European Journal of Political Research* 33 (3): 389–441.

McCartney, C. 1986. 'Human Rights Education', in Standing Advisory Committee on Human Rights, *11th Annual Report*. London: HMSO.

McCracken, I. 2003. 'A Donegal Protestant's View of Cross-Border Co-operation', in *CCBS, Year 5*. Armagh: Centre for Cross Border Studies, pp. 22–4.

MacEvoy, B. P. 1988 [1987]. *Guide to Cross-Border Trade between Northern Ireland and the Republic of Ireland*. Belfast: Co-operation North.

Maginniss, A. 2001. 'Redefining Northern Nationalism: A Political Perspective'. *IBIS Working Paper* 3. Dublin: Institute for British–Irish Studies, University College Dublin.

Makarychev, A. 2000. 'Islands of Globalization: Regional Russia and the Outside World'. *Working Paper* 2. Zurich: Center for Security Studies and Conflict Research.

2005a. 'European and Russian Assessments of the "Kaliningrad Puzzle"', *The Annual of the Centre for Regional Security & Transboundary Studies* 2 (3): 44–60.

2005b. 'Pskov at the Intersection of Russian Relations with Latvia and Estonia', *Europe–Asia Studies* 57 (3): 481–500.

2005c. 'The Four Pathways in the EU–Russia Trans-Border Relations: Explanatory Possibilities and Agendas for Future Research'. Paper presented at the EUBorderConf project final conference, Brussels, 25 November.

Makovsky, D. 2004a. 'How to Build a Fence', *Foreign Affairs* 83 (2): 50–64.

2004b. *The Defensible Fence: Fighting Terror and Enabling a Two-State Solution*. Washington, DC: Washington Institute for Near East Policy.

2005a. 'Gaza: Moving Forward by Pulling Back', *Foreign Affairs* 84 (3): 52–62.

2005b. *Engagement Through Disengagement: Gaza and the Potential for Renewed Israeli–Palestinian Peacemaking*. Washington, DC: Washington Institute for Near East Policy.

Malki, R. 2006. 'The Palestinian Elections: Beyond Hamas and Fatah', *Journal of Democracy* 17 (3): 131–7.

Mälksoo, M. 2006. 'From Existential Politics Towards Normal Politics? The Baltic States in the Enlarged Europe', *Security Dialogue* 37 (3): 275–97.

Manners, I. 2002. 'Normative Power Europe: A Contradiction in Terms?', *Journal of Common Market Studies* 40 (2): 235–58.

2006. 'Normative Power Europe Reconsidered: Beyond the Crossroads', *Journal of European Public Policy* 13 (2): 182–99.

Manrod, F. M. 1974. *Cyprus: United Nations Efforts toward a Political Solution.* Maxwell Air Force Base, AL: US Air University, Air War College.

Marcussen, M., Risse, T., Engelmann-Martin, D., Knopf, H. J. and Roscher, K. 1999. 'Constructing Europe? The Evolution of French, British and German Nation-State Identities', *Journal of European Public Policy* 6 (6): 614–33.

Markides, A. 2002. Speech Presented at Panel on 'The Cyprus Question after Copenhagen', Association for Social Reform (OPEK), Nicosia, 16 December.

Mavratsas, C. V. 1998. 'Greek-Cypriot Political Culture and the Prospect of European Union Membership: A Worst-Case Scenario', *The Cyprus Review* 10: 67–76.

Meehan, E. 2000. '"Britain's Irish Question: Britain's European Question?": British–Irish Relations in the Context of the European Union and the Belfast Agreement', *Review of International Studies* 26 (1): 83–97.

Meinardus, R. 1991. 'Third Party Involvement in Greek–Turkish Disputes', in Constas (ed.), pp. 157–63.

Mendelson, M. H., QC. 2001. *Why Cyprus Entry into the European Union Would Be Illegal.* London: Embassy of the Republic of Turkey.

Messmer, H. 2003. *Der soziale Konflikt. Kommunikative Emergenz und systemische Reproduktion.* Stuttgart: Lucius & Lucius.

Miall, H., Ramsbotham, O. and Woodhouse, T. 1999. *Contemporary Conflict Resolution: The Prevention, Management and Transformation of Deadly Conflicts.* Cambridge: Polity Press.

Miard-Delacroix, H. and Hudemann, R. (eds.) 2005. *Wandel und Integration. Deutsch-französische Annäherungen der fünfziger Jahre.* Munich: Oldenbourg.

Mikenberg, E. 2005. 'Estonian–Russian Cross-Border Cooperation: The Warning Example of Tartu-Pskov', in Smith, D. J. (ed.), *The Baltic States and Their Region: New Europe or Old?* Amsterdam: Rodopi, pp. 313–22.

Mitchell, C. 2005. *The Politics of Religion in Northern Ireland: Boundaries of Belonging and Belief.* Aldershot: Ashgate.

Mitrany, D. 1965. 'The Prospect of Integration: Federal or Functional', *Journal of Common Market Studies* 4 (1): 119–49.

Moran, M. 1999. 'Why, So Far, the Cyprus Problem has Remained Unresolved'. *Washington Report on Middle East Affairs*, pp. 58–62.

Moravcsik, A. 2002. 'In Defence of the "Democratic Deficit": Reassessing Legitimacy in the European Union', *Journal of Common Market Studies* 40: 603–24.

Moreau, J. 1993. 'Nature et divergences des initiatives officielles et privées du rapprochement franco-allemand dans le domaine de la vie associative', in Jurt, Joseph and Frankreich-Zentrum der Universität Freiburg (eds.),

Von der Besatzungszeit zur deutsch-französischen Kooperation. Universität Freiburg, pp. 196–208.

Morgan, A. 2000. *The Belfast Agreement: A Practical Legal Analysis.* London: The Belfast Press.

Morozov, V. 2002. 'The Discourses of St. Petersburg and the Shaping of a Wider Europe: Territory, Space and Post-Sovereign Politics'. *COPRI Working Papers* 13. Copenhagen Peace Research Institute.

2004. 'Europe and the Boundaries of Russian Political Community'. Paper presented at the EUBorderConf Project Workshop in Copenhagen, 26 November.

Moshes, A. 1999. *Overcoming Unfriendly Stability: Russian–Latvian Relations at the End of the 1990s.* Helsinki: Ulkopoliittinen and Bonn: Institut für Europäische Politik.

Moustakis, F. 2003. *The Greek–Turkish Relationship and NATO.* London: Frank Cass.

Müller, K. 2004. 'Being "European" in Gibraltar', *Journal of European Integration* 26 (1): 41–60.

Nabulsi, K. 2006. *Palestinians Register: Laying Foundations and Setting Directions.* Report of the Civitas Project. Oxford: Nuffield College, University of Oxford.

Nan, S. Allen 2003. 'Track I Diplomacy'. Intractable Conflict Knowledge Base Project. Conflict Research Consortium, University of Colorado.

Nassehi, A. 2003. *Geschlossenheit und Offenheit. Studien zur Theorie der modernen Gesellschaft.* Frankfurt am Main: Suhrkamp.

Newman, D. 2000. 'Citizenship, Identity and Location: The Changing Discourse of Israeli Geopolitics', in Dodds, K. and Atkinson, D. (eds.), *Geopolitical Traditions: A Century of Geopolitical Thought.* London: Routledge, pp. 302–31.

2002. 'The Geopolitics of Peacemaking in Israel–Palestine', *Political Geography* 21 (5): 629–46.

2003. 'On Borders and Power: A Theoretical Framework', *Journal of Borderland Studies* 18 (1): 13–25.

2006. 'The Lines that Continue to Separate Us: Borders in our Borderless World', *Progress in Human Geography* 30 (2): 1–19.

Newman, D. and Peters, J. 2002. 'Kosovo as the West Bank: Macedonia as Israel', *Haaretz*, 30 October.

Newman, M. 1996. *Democracy, Sovereignty and the European Union.* London: Hurst.

Nic Craith, M. 2003. *Culture and Identity Politics in Northern Ireland.* Basingstoke: Palgrave.

Nicolaïdis, K. and Howse, R. 2002. '"This is my EUtopia ... "': Narrative as Power', *Journal of Common Market Studies* 40 (4): 767–92.

Noll, A. 2004. 'The Cross-Border Collaboration'. *Deutsche Welle*, 26 October, www.dw-world.de/dw/article/0,1564,1375959,00.html.

Noutcheva, G., Nathalie Tocci, N., Coppieters, B., Kovziridze, T., Emerson, M. and Huysseune, M. 2004. 'Europeanization and Secessionist Conflicts: Concepts and Theories', *Journal on Ethnopolitics and Minority Issues in Europe* 3 (1), www.ecmi.de/jemie/download/1-2004Chapter1.pdf.

O'Brien, J. 2000. *The Arms Trial.* Dublin: Gill and Macmillan.

O'Dowd, L., Corrigan, J. and Moore, T. 1995. 'Borders, National Sovereignty and European Integration: The British–Irish Case', *International Journal of Urban and Regional Research* 19 (3): 272–85.

O'Dowd, L. and Wilson, T. 1996. 'Frontiers of Sovereignty in the New Europe', in O'Dowd, T. and Wilson, T. (eds.), *Borders, Nations and States.* Aldershot: Ashgate, pp. 1–17.

O'Neill, J. 1998. *A Mapping Exercise of Cross-Border Links between Development Agencies in the North and South of Ireland.* Dublin: Irish Aid Advisory Committee.

Onis, Z. and Yilmaz, S. 2008. 'Greek–Turkish Rapprochement: Rhetoric or Reality?', *Political Science Quarterly* 123 (forthcoming).

Ozel, S. 2004. 'Turkish–Greek Dialogue of the Business Communities', in Belge, T. (ed.), pp. 163–8.

Paasi, A. 1999. 'Boundaries as Social Practice and Discourse: The Finnish–Russian Border', *Regional Studies* 33 (7): 669–80.

Pace, M. 2005. 'Report on EU Policy-Making Towards Border Conflicts'. Unpublished manuscript, Birmingham: Department of Political Science and International Studies, University of Birmingham.

2006. *The Politics of Regional Identity: Meddling with the Mediterranean.* London: Routledge.

Padgen, A. (ed.) 2002. *The Idea of Europe: From Antiquity to the European Union.* Cambridge University Press.

Papandreou, G. 2002. 'Why is the Old Enemy Greece Now Supporting Turkey?', *Wall Street Journal Europe*, 11 December.

2003. *Joint Press Conference of Greek and Turkish Foreign Ministers*, Athens, 21 October, www.papandreou.gr.

Papaneophytou, N. 1994. 'Cyprus: The Way to Full European Union Membership', *The Cyprus Review* 6: 83–96.

Pardo, S. 2004. 'A Fresh Breeze from Brussels', *The Jerusalem Post*, 25 August.

Parliament, Republic of Cyprus. 2002. *Transcripts of Proceedings.* Nicosia: House of Representatives.

2003. *Transcripts of Proceedings.* Nicosia: House of Representatives.

Pearson, F. S. 2001. 'Dimensions of Conflict Resolution in Ethnopolitical Disputes', *Journal of Peace Research* 38 (3): 275–87.

Pedersen, K. C. 1998. 'Kaliningrad: Armed Forces and Missions', in Joenniemi, P. (ed.), *Kaliningrad: The European Amber Region.* Aldershot: Ashgate, pp. 107–16.

Peristianis, N. 1998. 'A Federal Cyprus in a Federal Europe', *The Cyprus Review* 10: 33–43.

Perthes, V. 2004. 'America's "Greater Middle East" and Europe: Key Issues for Dialogue', *Middle East Policy* 11 (3): 85–97.

Peters, J. 1996a. *Pathways to Peace: The Multilateral Arab–Israeli Talks.* London: Royal Institute of International Affairs.

1996b. 'The Emergence of Regional Cooperation in the Middle East', in *The Middle East in the Post Peace Process: The Emerging Regional Order and its International Implications.* Tokyo: Institute of Developing Economies, pp. 75–117.

1999. 'Europe and the Middle East Peace Process: Emerging from the Sidelines', in Stavridis, S. *et al.* (eds.), *The Foreign Policies of the European Union's Mediterranean States and Applicant Countries in the 1990s.* Basingstoke: Macmillan, pp. 295–316.

Pettifer, J. 1994. 'Greek Political Culture and Foreign Policy', in Featherstone and Ifantis (eds.), pp. 17–23.

Phinnemore, D. 2003. 'The Draft Treaty Establishing a Constitution for Europe: The Implications for Northern Ireland'. Paper delivered to Conference on 'Northern Ireland and the European Constitution', Queen's University Belfast, September.

Piening, C. 1997. *Global Europe: The European Union in World Affairs.* Boulder, CO: Lynne Rienner.

Plate-forme Euromed 2007. 'Joint Statement of Palestinian Civil Society to the World Social Forum'. Nairobi: The Palestinian Delegation to the WSF, 18 January.

Platias, A. G. 2000. 'Greek Deterrence Strategy', in Chircop, A., Gerolymatos, A. and Iatrides, J. O. (eds.), *The Aegean Sea after the Cold War.* London: Macmillan, pp. 61–86.

Pletsch, A. 2003. 'Cross-border Activities between France and Germany'. Paper presented at the 3rd Annual Conference of the Viessmann Research Center on Modern Europe. Wilfrid Laurier University, Waterloo, Canada, 8–11 October.

Polat, N. 2002. 'Self-determination, Violence, Modernity: The Case of the Turkish Cypriots', in Diez (ed.), pp. 98–116.

Potemkina, O. 2003. 'Some Ramifications of Enlargement on the EU–Russian Relations and the Schengen Regime', *European Journal of Immigration Law* 5 (2): 229–47.

Pridham, G. 1991. 'Linkage Politics Theory and the Greek–Turkish Rapprochement', in Constas, D. (ed.), *The Greek–Turkish Conflict in the 1990s: Domestic and External Influences.* New York: St Martin's Press, pp. 73–88.

Probert, B. 1978. *Beyond Orange and Green: The Political Economy of the Northern Ireland Crisis.* London: Zed Press.

Prozorov, S. 2004a. *Political Pedagogy of Technical Assistance: A Study in Historical Ontology of Russian Postcommunism.* Tampere: Studia Politica Tamperensis.

    2004b. 'Border Regions and the Politics of EU–Russian Relations: The Role of the EU in Tempering and Producing Conflicts'. *Working Paper Series in EU Border Conflicts Studies*, Working Paper No. 3. Birmingham: Department of Political Science and International Studies, University of Birmingham.

    2004c. 'The Logic of Border Deproblematisation'. Paper presented at the 5th Pan-European IR Conference, the Hague, 9–11 September.

    2004d. 'The Russian Northwestern Federal District and the EU's Northern Dimension'. *DIIS Working Papers Series.* Copenhagen: Danish Institute for International Studies.

    2005a. 'The Structure of the EU–Russian Conflict Discourses: Issue and Identity Conflicts in the Narratives of Exclusion and Self-Exclusion'.

Working Paper Series in EU Border Conflicts Studies, Working Paper No. 13. Birmingham: Department of Political Science and International Studies, University of Birmingham.

2005b. 'EU–Russian Regional Cooperation: Logics of Regionalisation and the Challenge of the Exception', in Browning (ed.), pp. 123–42.

2005c. 'Russian Conservatism in the Putin Presidency: The Dispersion of the Hegemonic Discourse', *Journal of Political Ideologies* 10 (2): 121–43.

Quinlivan, E. 1999. *Forging Links: A Study of Cross-Border Community Co-operation in the Irish Border Region*. Monaghan: Co-operation Ireland Cross Border Community Development Project.

Republic of Karelia 2001. Программа Приграничного Сотрудничества Республики Карелии на 2001–2006 годы (Programme of Cross-Border Cooperation of the Republic of Karelia in 2001–2006), www.gov.karelia.ru/gov/Power/Ministry/Relations/Boundary/00.html (03.11.2003).

Reynolds, A. 2003. 'The Irish Government and the Peace Process, 1992–1994 – A Political Perspective'. *IBIS Working Paper* 5. Dublin: Institute for British–Irish Studies, University College Dublin.

Ribhegge, H. 1996. 'Euregion Pro Europa Viadrina', *WeltTrends* 13: 66–77.

Richmond, O. P. 1998. 'Devious Objectives and the Disputants' View of International Mediation: A Theoretical Framework', *Journal of Peace Research* 35 (6): 707–22.

2001a. 'A Perilous Catalyst? EU Accession and the Cyprus Problem', *The Cyprus Review* 13: 123–32.

2001b. 'A Genealogy of Peacemaking: The Creation and Re-Creation of Order', *Alternatives* 26 (3): 317–48.

2005. *The Transformation of Peace*. Basingstoke: Palgrave.

Ringmar, E. 2002. 'The Recognition Game: Soviet Russia against the West', *Cooperation and Conflict* 37 (2): 115–36.

Risse, T., Ropp, S. C. and Sikkink, K. (eds.) 1999. *The Power of Human Rights: International Norms and Domestic Change*. Cambridge University Press.

Rothman, J. 1991. 'Conflict Research and Resolution: Cyprus', *Annals of the American Academy of Political and Social Science* 518: 95–108.

Ruane, J. and Todd, J. 1996. *The Dynamics of Conflict in Northern Ireland: Power, Conflict and Emancipation*. Cambridge University Press.

(eds.) 1999. *After the Good Friday Agreement: Analysing Political Change in Northern Ireland*. University College Dublin Press.

Rubin, B. and Carkoglu, A. (eds.) 2003. *Greek–Turkish Relations in an Era of Détente*. London: Frank Cass.

Ruggie, J. G. 1993. 'Territoriality and Beyond: Problematizing Modernity in International Relations', *International Organization* 47 (1): 139–74.

Rumelili, B. 2003a. 'Liminality and Perpetuation of Conflicts: Turkish–Greek Relations in the Context of Community-Building by the EU', *European Journal of International Relations* 9 (2): 213–48.

2003b. 'A Crisis Still-Born', *EUBorderConf Newsletter* 2. Birmingham: Department of Political Science and International Studies, University of Birmingham.

2003c. 'Turkish–Greek Relations: Enabling EU Impact'. Paper presented at the CEEISA/ISA International Conference, Budapest, Hungary, 26–28 June.

2004a. 'The European Union's Impact on the Greek–Turkish Conflict: A Review of the Literature'. *Working Paper Series in EU Border Conflicts Studies*, Working Paper No. 6. Birmingham: Department of Political Science and International Studies, University of Birmingham.

2004b. 'Constructing Identity and Relating to Difference: Understanding EU's Mode of Differentiation', *Review of International Studies* 30 (1): 27–47.

2004c. 'The Micro-processes of Hegemonic Influence: The Case of EU and Greece/Turkey.' Conference Paper, presented at the International Studies Association Annual Convention, Montreal, Canada, 17–21 March.

2005a. 'Civil Society and the Europeanization of Greek–Turkish Cooperation', *South European Society and Politics* 10 (1): 43–54.

2005b. 'The European Union and Cultural Change in Greek–Turkish Relations'. *Working Paper Series in EU Border Conflicts Studies*, Working Paper No. 17. Birmingham: Department of Political Science and International Studies, University of Birmingham.

2007. 'Transforming Conflicts on EU Borders: The Case of Greek–Turkish Relations', *Journal of Common Market Studies* 45 (1): 105–26.

Rupnik, J. 1994. 'Europe's New Frontiers: Remapping Europe', *Daedalus* 123 (3): 91–114.

Sachar, H. 1999. *Israel and Europe: An Appraisal in History*. New York: Alfred Knopf.

Said, E. W. 1993. *Culture and Imperialism*. London: Vintage.

Scheipers, S. and Sicurelli, D. 2007. 'Normative Power Europe: A Credible Utopia?', *Journal of Common Market Studies* 45 (2): 435–57.

Schimmelfennig, F. 2001. 'The Community Trap: Liberal Norms, Rhetorical Action and the Eastern Enlargement of the European Union', *International Organization* 55 (1): 47–80.

Schimmelfennig, F., Engert, S. and Knobel, H. 2006. *International Socialization in Europe: European Organizations, Political Conditionality and Democratic Change*. Basingstoke: Palgrave.

Schimmelfennig, F. and Sedelmeier, U. 2004. 'Governance by Conditionality: EU Rule Transfer to the Candidate Countries of Central and Eastern Europe', *Journal of European Public Policy* 11 (6): 661–79.

Schmidt, V. 2004. 'The European Union: Democratic Legitimacy in a Regional State?', *Journal of Common Market Studies* 42 (5): 975–97.

Schulze, H. 1991. *The Course of German Nationalism from Frederick the Great to Bismarck 1763–1867*. Cambridge University Press.

Schwarz, H.-P. 1986. *Adenauer. Der Aufstieg: 1876–1952*. Stuttgart: Deutsche Verlags-Anstalt.

Serter, V. Z. 1970. *Kıbrıs Tarihi [Cyprus History]*. Lefkoşa: Kema Offset.

Shikaki, K. 2006. 'The Palestinian Elections: Sweeping Victory, Uncertain Mandate', *Journal of Democracy* 17 (3): 116–30.

Shirlow, P. 2002. *Sectarian Division in Northern Ireland According to the 2001 Census Results*. London: Royal Geographical Society.

Shlyamin, V. 2002. 'Prigranichny Rossiysky Region na Severe Evropy', *Chelovek i Karjera* 139 (4): 3.

Simonian, H. 1985. *The Privileged Partnership: Franco-German Relations in the European Community, 1969–1984*. Oxford: Clarendon Press.

Smith, D. J. and Chambers, G. 1991. *Inequality in Northern Ireland*. Oxford: Clarendon Press.

Smith, K. 1998. 'The Instruments of European Union Foreign Policy', in Zielonka, J. (ed.), *Paradoxes of European Foreign Policy*. The Hague: Kluwer Law International, pp. 67–85.

Smith, K. E. 2005. 'Beyond the Civilian Power EU Debate', *Politique européenne* 17: 63–82.

Smooha, S. and Hanf, T. 1992. 'The Diverse Modes of Conflict-Regulation in Deeply Divided Societies', *International Journal of Comparative Sociology* 33 (1): 26–47.

Sözen, A. and Çarkoğlu, A. 2004. 'The Turkish Cypriot General Elections of December 2003: Setting the Stage for Resolving the Cyprus Conflict?', *South European Society and Politics* 9 (2): 122–36.

Stålvant, C. E. 2005. 'Transnational Forces, States and International Institutions: Three Perspectives on Change in the Baltic Sea Affairs', in Browning (ed.), pp. 161–80.

Stavrinides, Z. 1999 [1976]. *The Cyprus Conflict: National Identity and Statehood*. Nicosia: CYREP.

Steinberg, G. M. 2004. 'Learning the Lessons of the European Union's Failed Middle East Policies', *Jerusalem Viewpoints* 510 (7) 5764/1.

Stephanou, C. and Tsardanides, C. 1991. 'The EC Factor in the Greece–Turkey–Cyprus Triangle', in Constas (ed.), pp. 207–30.

Stephens, B. 2004. 'Europe and Israel: What Went Wrong?', *The Jerusalem Post*, 2 January.

Stetter, S. 2003. 'Democratization without Democracy? The Assistance of the European Union for Democratization Processes in Palestine', *Mediterranean Politics* 8 (2–3): 153–73.

    2005. 'Theorising the European Neighbourhood Policy: Debordering and Rebordering in the Mediterranean'. *EUI Working Papers* RSCAS No. 2005/34. Florence: European University Institute: Robert Schuman Centre for Advanced Studies Mediterranean Programme Series.

    2007. *EU Foreign and Interior Policies: Cross-Pillar Politics and the Social Construction of Sovereignty*. London: Routledge.

Sutton, M. 1994. *Bear in Mind these Dead . . . An Index of Deaths from the Conflict in Ireland 1969–1993*. Belfast: Beyond the Pale Publications.

Tannam, E. 1996. 'The European Union and Business Cross-Border Co-Operation: The Case of Northern Ireland and the Republic of Ireland', *Irish Political Studies* 11 (2): 103–29.

Tarikahya, N. 2004. 'Turkish Greek Culture and Art Festivals for Promoting Dialogue', in Belge, T. (ed.), pp. 155–62.

Tavares, R. 2004. 'Contributions of Macro-Regions to the Construction of Peace: A Framework for Analysis', *Journal of International Relations and Development* 7 (1): 24–47.

Teague, P. 1996. 'The EU and the Irish Peace Process', *Journal of Common Market Studies* 34 (5): 549–70.

Thiel, A. 2003. *Soziale Konflikte*. Bielefeld: Transcript.

Tocci, N. 2005a. 'Conflict Resolution in the Neighbourhood: Comparing EU Involvement in the Turkish–Kurdish and Israeli–Palestinian Conflicts', *Mediterranean Politics* 10 (2): 125–46.

2005b. *EU Accession Dynamics and Conflict Resolution: Catalysing Peace or Consolidating Partition in Cyprus?* London: Ashgate.

2005c. 'The Widening Gap Between Rhetoric and Reality in EU Policy Towards the Israeli–Palestinian Conflict', *CEPS Working Document* 217. Brussels: Centre for European Policy Studies.

Todd, J. 2001. 'Redefining Northern Nationalism: An Academic Perspective'. *IBIS Working Paper* 3. Dublin: Institute for British–Irish Studies, University College Dublin.

Tovias, A. 2003. 'Israeli Policy Perspectives on the Euro-Mediterranean Partnership in the Context of EU Enlargement', *Mediterranean Politics* 8 (2–3): 214–32.

Treacher, A. 2002. 'Franco-German Relations and European Integration: Peeling Off the Labels', *British Journal of Politics and International Relations* 4 (3): 510–18.

Trenin, D. 2002. *The End of Eurasia: Russia at the Border Between Geopolitics and Globalization*. Washington, DC, and Moscow: Carnegie Endowment for International Peace.

Triantaphyllou, D. 2001. 'Further Turmoil Ahead?', in Keridis and Triantaphyllou (eds.), pp. 56–79.

Tsakaloyannis, P. 1980. 'European Community and Greek–Turkish Dispute', *Journal of Common Market Studies* 29 (1): 35–54.

Tsakonas, P. and Tournikiotis, A. 2003. 'Greece's Elusive Quest for Security Providers', *Security Dialogue* 34 (3): 301–14.

Turenc, T. 1999. 'Northern Cyprus Will Stay Where it is', *Hurriyet* (Istanbul), 15 December.

Turkish Grand National Assembly (TGNA) 1996a. *Minutes of 20th Period, 1st Legislative Session, 41st Meeting*, 20 April, www.tbmm.gov.tr.

1996b. *Minutes of 20th Period, 2nd Legislative Session, 1st Meeting*, 1 October, www.tbmm.gov.tr.

1998. *Minutes of 20th Period, 3rd Legislative Session, 38th Meeting*, 6 January, www.tbmm.gov.tr.

Ugur, M. 1999. *The European Union and Turkey: An Anchor/Credibility Dilemma*. Aldershot: Ashgate.

Urquhart, C. and MacAskill, E. 2007. 'Tehran Largest Donor in £500 M Muslim Pledges to Palestinians', *The Guardian*, 17 January: 15.

Valinakis, Y. G. 1994. 'Security Policy', in Kazakos and Ioakimidis (eds.), pp. 199–214.

Vassiliadou, M. 2002. 'Questioning Nationalism: The Patriarchal and National Struggles of Cypriot Women within a European Union Context', *European Journal of Women's Studies* 9 (4): 459–82.

Vassiliou, G. 2003. *The Economics of a Solution Based on the Annan Plan*, www. kema.com.cy/Annan%20Plan%20En.pdf.

Väyrynen, R. 1985. 'Is There a Role for the United Nations in Conflict Resolution?', *Journal of Peace Research* 22 (2): 189–96.

Veit, W. 2003. *A European Perspective for Israel: A Key to Solving Middle East Conflict*. Tel Aviv: Friedrich Ebert Stiftung.

Veremis, T. 2001. 'The Protracted Crisis', in Keridis and Triantaphyllou (eds.), pp. 42–51.

Viktorova, J. 2001. *Building a Common Security Space? The Case of the Russian–Estonian Border Area*, www.ut.ee/ABVKeskus.

Wæver, O. 1995. 'Securitization and Desecuritization', in Lipschutz, Ronnie D. (ed.), *On Security*. New York: Columbia University Press, pp. 46–86.

  1996. 'European Security Identities', *Journal of Common Market Studies* 34 (1): 103–32.

  1998a. 'Explaining Europe by Decoding Discourses', in Wivel, Anders (ed.), *Explaining European Integration*. Copenhagen Political Studies Press, pp. 100–46.

  1998b. 'Insecurity, Security, and Asecurity in the West European Non-war Community', in Adler and Barnett (eds.), pp. 69–118.

  2003. 'Securitisation: Taking Stock of a Research Program in Security Studies'. Draft Paper to be discussed at the PIPES seminar at the University of Chicago, 24 February.

Walker, R. B. J. 1993. *Inside/Outside: International Relations as Political Theory*. Cambridge University Press.

Wallace, W. 1999. 'The Sharing of Sovereignty: The European Paradox', *Political Studies* 47 (4): 503–21.

  2003. 'Looking after the Neighbourhood: Responsibilities for the EU-25'. *Policy Papers* No. 4. Paris: Notre Europe, Groupement d'études et de recherches.

Wallensteen, P. 2002. *Understanding Conflict Resolution: War, Peace and the Global System*. London: Sage.

Walters, W. 2002. 'Mapping Schengenland: Denaturalizing the Border', *Environment and Planning D: Society and Space* 20 (5): 561–80.

Weber, M. 1988. *Gesammelte politische Schriften*. Fifth edition. Tübingen: Mohr.

Welch, D. 1999. *Modern European History 1871–2000: A Documentary Reader*. London: Routledge.

Wellmann, C. 2003. 'Recognising Borders: Coping with Historically Contested Territory', in Birckenbach and Wellmann (eds.), pp. 273–9.

Wendt, A. 1992. 'Anarchy is What States Make of it: The Social Construction of Power Politics', *International Organization* 46 (2): 391–425.

Wilde, J. de 1991. *Saved from Oblivion: Interdependence Theory in the First Half of the 20th Century: A Study on the Causality Between War and Complex Interdependence*. Aldershot: Dartmouth.

Wilmer, F. 2002. *The Social Construction of Man, the State, and War: Identity, Conflict, and Violence in the Former Yugoslavia*. London: Routledge.

Wilson, T. M. and Donnan, H. (eds.) 1998. *Border Identities: Nation and State at International Frontiers*. Cambridge University Press.

Yacobi, H. and Newman, D. 2004a. 'The EU and the Israel/Palestine Conflict: An Ambivalent Relationship'. *Working Paper Series in EU Border Conflicts Studies*, Working Paper No. 4. Birmingham: Department of Political Science and International Studies, University of Birmingham.

  2004b. 'The Role of the EU in the Israel/Palestine Conflict'. *Working Paper Series in EU Border Conflicts Studies*, Working Paper No. 12. Birmingham: Department of Political Science and International Studies, University of Birmingham.

Yannas, P. 1994. 'The Greek Factor in EC–Turkey Relations', in Kazakos and Ioakimidis (eds.), pp. 215–21.

Yee, A. S. 1996. 'The Causal Effect of Ideas on Policies', *International Organization* 50 (1): 66–108.

Zoulas, S. 2003. 'Two Turkeys', *Kathimerini* (Athens, English edn), 28 May.

Index